# ASHES TO ASHES

# ANDREW FLINTOFF

### with Myles Hodgson

HODDER

First published in Great Britain in 2009 by Hodder & Stoughton
An Hachette UK company

First published in paperback in 2010

1

Copyright © Andrew Flintoff 2009

The right of Andrew Flintoff to be identified as the Author
of the Work has been asserted by him in accordance with
the Copyright, Designs and Patents Act 1988.

A CIP catalogue record for this title is available from the British Library

ISBN 978 0 340 95157 6

Typeset in Stone Serif by Hewer Text UK Ltd, Edinburgh
Printed and bound by Clays Ltd, St Ives, plc

Hodder & Stoughton policy is to use papers that are natural, renewable
and recyclable products and made from wood grown in sustainable
forests. The logging and manufacturing processes are expected to
conform to the environmental regulations of the country of origin.

Hodder & Stoughton Ltd
338 Euston Road
London NW1 3BH

www.hodder.co.uk

*For Rachael, Holly, Corey and Rocky*

# CONTENTS

# ACKNOWLEDGEMENTS

There are many people I wish to thank, both for encouraging me in one way or another during my career and for helping to put this book together. First and foremost is my wife Rachael. She has been wonderfully supportive, especially in the bad moments, and is an inspiration at all times.

Holly, Corey and Rocky, our lovely kids, make life even better. Thanks are due, too, to my mum and dad. They got me started in life and set me out on a career that has proved just right for me – and they always look out for me, through thick and thin.

Special thanks must go to David 'Rooster' Roberts for the major part he has played in my rehabilitation from so many injuries. He has been superb in his dedication to getting me right. Sometimes the future has seemed so bleak but with his great knowledge and skill, Rooster has determinedly pushed me through the pain barriers and I am eternally grateful to him.

Neil Fairbrother, my trusted friend, has always given me wise advice, and it was Neil who introduced me to Andrew 'Chubby' Chandler, who has also helped me to keep my feet on the ground. Both have done all they can to keep me focussed.

I must also single out Lancashire County Cricket Club for all their help and support throughout my career. It is a club I have supported since I was a boy and I am still very proud to be a Lancashire player.

My good friend and co-author Myles Hodgson has again reflected my 'voice' in the book. He helps me set down my recollections in such a calm but persistent way – displaying a degree of patience that is nothing short of miraculous. It is always a pleasure to work with him.

Finally, I would like to thank the team at Hodder & Stoughton – my publisher Roddy Bloomfield, who continues to show his inimitable enthusiasm at all times, and without whom all our efforts would have come to nothing, and Sarah Hammond for all her professional editorial work and photographic research. I'm especially grateful to Roddy for stage managing the production of my book so that it could be launched so soon after the great moment when England regained the Ashes!

# PHOTOGRAPHIC ACKNOWLEDGEMENTS

The author and publisher would like to thank the following for permission to reproduce photographs:

Action Images/Carl Recine, Philip Brown, Winston Bynorth, Gareth Copley/PA, Sean Dempsey/PA, Anthony Devlin/PA, Matt Dunham/AP/PA, Reuters/Mike Finn-Kelcey, Getty Images, Rob Griffith/AP/PA, Reuters/Stephen Hird, Reuters/Zahid Hussein, Altaf Qadri/AP/PA, Rick Rycroft/AP/PA, Kirsty Wigglesworth/AP/PA, Reuters/Tim Wimborne.

It is not the critic who counts, nor the man who points out how the strong man stumbles, or where the doer of deeds could have done them better. The credit belongs to the man who is actually in the arena, whose face is marred by dust, and sweat and blood, who strives valiantly; who errs and comes short again and again; because there is no effort without error and shortcomings; but who does actually strive to do the deed; who knows the great enthusiasm, the great devotion, who spends himself in a worthy cause, who at the best knows in the end the triumph of high achievement and who at the worst, if he fails, at least he fails while daring greatly. So that his place shall never be with those cold and timid souls who know neither victory nor defeat.

Theodore Roosevelt
With thanks to Jeffrey Archer

# PREFACE

25 August 2009

Today I start a new chapter in my life as a retired Test cricketer. My final Test was perfect in so many ways, with England winning the Ashes for a second time, four years after we enjoyed similar success at The Oval. In those four years, I've learnt a lot about myself as a person and a cricketer. I've dealt with self-doubt, injury and certain lifestyle problems, and I feel stronger mentally as a result – and I hope I've become a better person. I've done all the hard yards in the gym and the low points have made the good moments so much sweeter. The importance of playing for your country can never be overestimated, nor the responsibility that comes with it. It's not something you can take for granted. You need to keep working and cherish the moment. In all my eleven years of playing for England, the excitement I felt every time I walked on to that field wearing the three lions never wavered. It's difficult to put into words.

I'm very sad to have finished playing Test cricket, but the injuries I have suffered over the last few years gave me little option. My biggest regret is that I think I could still contribute to the Test team if injuries allowed it. In the circumstances, though, I'm happy with my decision, and it will allow me to concentrate on playing one-day and Twenty20 international cricket in the future and, who knows, it might even help to prolong my career. The first challenge I have is to get fit again after a second operation on my right knee, which entails being on crutches for six weeks.

I am more determined than ever to come back and play international cricket, and I hope to put the spare time I will have from not playing Test cricket to good use. The future is exciting because I don't really know what form it will take. What I'd like is to become the best one-day player in the world. I also want to spend more time helping the AF Foundation to raise funds for children's charities, and I cherish the chance to be more of a family man. For years, Rachael and the kids have had to put up with me going away on tour for weeks and months at a time, and while I will still be going on cricket tours, I should not be away as much. I am looking forward to being a more at home Dad than before, helping the kids with their homework and playing with them on a more regular basis.

Of course, I'll miss the excitement of playing Test cricket for England, and the adrenalin buzz of running in to bowl in an Ashes series. I'll have my memories, though, and maybe one day I'll even be persuaded to watch the best moments of my career on DVD.

# 1
# AFTERMATH OF THE ASHES

If you speak to English cricket fans, most of them can tell you where they were when we won the Ashes on that September evening in 2005. I know that last day at The Oval was a sell-out, but if you believe everyone who says they were in the crowd that day, there must have been coming on for 100,000 in the ground to celebrate with us, which isn't bad for a ground that holds nearer 23,000.

It took several days for the magnitude of what we'd achieved to sink in but we all knew how much it meant to the people in the ground that day. As soon as the match was declared a draw to secure our 2–1 series win, the whole place turned into one big party, on and off the pitch. I'm not sure who was enjoying the moment more – the players or the crowds.

The party went on all night, continued the next day with a bus tour through London and a visit to Downing Street – by which time some of us were in a fairly dishevelled state – and it was only then that the real impact of being an Ashes winner began to hit home. Even so, we thought we'd be flavour of the month for a week or two before someone else took their turn in the limelight, but we were totally wrong about that. We were transformed from a group of people who were possibly familiar to cricket fans into household names – we were even being called celebrities at one point. In every paper you picked up there would be a picture of one of us at some event or other and we became a lot more recognisable to the general public, which of course had an effect on our home life. My wife Rachael and daughter Holly were followed down the street by photographers in Knutsford, near where we live.

People still go on about 2005, but after everything that has happened since then, it's very much at the back of my mind. Sometimes you almost want people to drop it. You'd think it was the only time I'd ever played well for England. I remember playing well against South Africa in 2003 for instance, but no matter what I do, everyone always seems to compare it with 2005 and tell me my form isn't a patch on that summer.

To be honest, I've never sat down and watched the DVD of the series, although I've seen footage when it's been on the TV in the background somewhere. I'm not one of those people who dines out on things that have happened to me, but for all that, it has improved my family's lifestyle. Everyone who took part in that series is better off financially, although being in the public eye can have its good and bad sides. Nobody wants to be photographed at the shops or leaving a restaurant, but at the same time that success has opened a lot of doors for us.

We have been invited to show-business parties, and a particular highlight for me was being invited to Buckingham Palace to meet the Queen after the whole squad appeared on the 2006 New Year's Honours List. That was when this whole experience became completely surreal. When you start playing cricket as a kid in the back garden, the last thing you expect is to be awarded an MBE and have a reception in your honour at Buckingham Palace. I even got a few moments on my own with the Queen during the reception.

During my benefit year, 2006, I got to know *Shameless* actor David Threlfall, and performing with Elton John in Battersea Park was one of the most terrifying moments of my life. Elton was playing at a benefit dinner for me, and after a couple of songs I joined him on stage to sing 'Rocket Man'. I stood there, propping up the piano, loosened my tie and my top button as singers do, and tried a bit of crooning. I made sure I sang very low so you could hardly hear me under Elton's voice, which was so strong. He did look after me when I was on stage because he sang a bit louder to try to drown me out a little. It was a nerve-racking experience, but an amazing thing to do.

Rachael and I were also invited to a party in London hosted by David and Victoria Beckham shortly before the 2006 World Cup in Germany. The invitation was sent care of International Sports Management, who handle all my affairs, and at first I thought it was some sort of wind-up. Once we realised it was a proper invitation, I didn't know quite what to expect, but it was great. All the England football squad were there, most of whom I'd never met before, but they were very friendly. I knew Manchester United's Gary Neville slightly, from playing cricket with his brother Phil, but I hadn't seen him in years. We had a great night. David and Victoria made us feel really welcome and were excellent hosts. Robbie Williams and James Brown provided the entertainment – how good is that?

Thinking back, it all seems unreal for a big lad from Preston. When you're starting out in cricket, nothing can prepare you for things like that. Like any other young player, I was sent on courses on how to handle the media, which were supposed to help prepare you for life in the public eye, but generally they were a waste of time. You just don't know what it's like to be at the centre of a big story until it happens. They can give you as many briefings as you like and warn you about the questions you're going to be asked, but in my experience the best way forward is to be as honest as possible. I don't mind people writing about a bad shot or a poor spell of bowling, but some journalists write things that are based purely on their own assumptions. They write about your state of mind, or your motives for taking certain actions, when most of them don't know you at all, and it can get quite personal.

Becoming better known was one of the reasons given for England failing to build on that 2005 triumph. The media would have you believe we started to take ourselves too seriously and let outside influences affect our cricket, but I've never thought that was the case. We were unlucky with injuries so the Ashes-winning line-up was broken up virtually straightaway. Michael Vaughan, our captain, did not play as much cricket as he'd have liked after a succession of knee injuries, Ashley Giles played only a few times after that and Simon Jones has never played for England again. We also lost Marcus Trescothick, who played only a handful of Tests after

2005 having succumbed to a stress disorder which forced his premature retirement from international cricket.

That bad luck with injuries was underlined with our first series after the Ashes, when we lost in Pakistan, which was a big wake-up call to us all. Everyone said we lost because of some sort of Ashes hangover, but Pakistan is a very difficult place to play cricket because the conditions on and off the pitch are culturally different to what we're used to, and I'm sure injuries to Vaughan and Simon Jones played a big part. Fatigue and tiredness probably had a lot to do with it as well. It had been a long year with our tour to South Africa and then the summer series against Bangladesh and Australia, and those of us who played for the Rest of the World in Australia in October 2005, shortly after the Ashes, had an even bigger workload.

I regarded being selected for the Rest of the World side as a major honour and was keen to play simply because it meant preparing alongside – and in the same dressing room as – Sachin Tendulkar. I have admired him for a long time and was delighted to have a chance to play in the same side as him, even for just a couple of weeks. It was just my luck that Sachin had to withdraw and didn't make it, but I still found the time I spent in Australia valuable. I wanted to see how players from other countries approached the game, although in hindsight it might have been better had I stayed at home and rested after a long Ashes summer. My ankle was playing up again towards the end of that trip, and my body was tired. I know I felt a lot fresher and full of energy after having had the benefit of six or seven weeks off before I went to India at the start of the following year.

We were soundly beaten by Australia in the Test and the one-dayers, which just underlines that no matter how good a collection of individuals you have, they are unlikely to beat a team who have been together over a long period of time. If you look at all the successful sides, they don't come together in a matter of months, they take years to build. The Australian team were together for the best part of a decade, give or take a few players, and our Ashes-winning line-up of 2005 was at least a couple of years in the making.

I set off for Australia not long after I got back from London once the Ashes celebrations had died down, determined to make the most of the opportunity to get to know, if not Tendulkar, then Mark Boucher, Graeme Smith and Jacques Kallis. I ended up hanging around with the South African contingent quite a lot. They are an aggressive side and really tough opponents who are not shy of giving you their point of view. I'd had my run-ins with them in the past, particularly in 2003 when they seemed to be trying to wind me up, but I got to know them a lot better in Australia and saw a different side to them. One thing I missed, though, was the intensity of playing cricket that really matters. When you play for England there is real passion because it matters so much to you and everyone in the country. Being part of a Rest of the World team just wasn't as special. Whether I got Ricky Ponting out or he hit me for six didn't matter so much in that series.

Steve Harmison and Kevin Pietersen were also playing for the Rest of the World in Australia, and the three of us were allowed to arrive in Pakistan a few days after the rest of the team for our first series as holders of the Ashes. As a team, we were ill-prepared for the tour. We hadn't done the work in preparation – and we weren't made to do it. Everything seemed to have gone out of the window in the build-up to the series. We had the open-topped bus rides, players – including me – were going to various social events, and we turned up in Pakistan in no shape to beat them on their home grounds. Playing in Pakistan is one of the toughest tours of all and if you're not on your game both on and off the field you get found out – and we got found out.

The cricket is hard because you play in hot and dusty conditions, often on flat pitches against a team who excel in that environment and usually have at least two spinners who can turn the game. Off the field, it's a completely different culture that takes a bit of getting used to. I'm not putting the place down at all because, by and large, I've enjoyed my tours there. It's just that some of the comforts we're used to at home aren't always there, even in modern Pakistan, and it does take a period of adjustment. After all the attention we'd received following the Ashes, I think some of us were wondering what we were doing there, and that is not an attitude to have if you're going to win in Pakistan. We had perhaps celebrated too much and lost sight of what it is we do.

The tour did not begin well with Michael Vaughan, our captain, and Simon Jones breaking down with knee injuries, but despite those setbacks we should probably have won the First Test in Multan. Marcus Trescothick led the team in Vaughan's absence and got a big first-innings century to guide us to a competitive 418 and put us in control of the match by securing a 144-run lead. We bowled them out again fairly cheaply, leaving us to chase a winning target of just 198, which we should have reached, but somehow we lost the game. The wicket wasn't doing very much, although there was a bit of reverse swing. I remember being caught on the boundary trying to sweep. I got a top edge as I played the shot but the ball just seemed to carry for miles. Our failure to win in Multan made the task of winning the series all the more difficult. In that part of the world it's very hard to come back after going behind because they make it so very difficult for you by batting so patiently, and that was evident in the next Test at Faisalabad.

Vaughan returned to the side after his knee problems and we battled back from conceding 462 in the first innings to score 446 ourselves with both Ian Bell and Kevin Pietersen making determined centuries, but the match ended in a draw. During our second innings we were shocked by an explosion in the ground and immediately feared the worst. Rightly or wrongly, we all jumped to conclusions and thought it might have been some sort of terrorist attack. Mentally, half of us were already packing our bags to go home. It turned out that a gas canister attached to the drinks trolley had exploded and it was nothing more than a freak accident. I remember a bloke dressed in army uniform coming on to the pitch and assuring us that everything was all right, but I think a few of us needed a bit of convincing.

## PAKISTAN v ENGLAND
## (2nd Test)  at Faisalabad 20–24 November 2005

### Pakistan

| | | | | |
|---|---|---|---|---|
| Shoaib Malik c Flintoff b Hoggard | 27 | – | c Bell b Flintoff | 26 |
| Salman Butt c Jones b Harmison | 26 | – | lbw b Udal | 50 |
| Younis Khan c Pietersen b Flintoff | 7 | – | lbw b Hoggard | 27 |
| Mohammad Yousuf c & b Bell | 78 | – | b Flintoff | 20 |
| *Inzamam-ul-Haq run out | | | | |
| (Harmison) | 109 | – | not out | 100 |
| Shahid Afridi c Trescothick | | | | |
| b Hoggard | 92 | – | b Flintoff | 0 |
| +Kamran Akmal c Jones b Giles | 41 | – | c Jones b Harmison | 9 |
| Naved-ul-Hasan b Harmison | 25 | – | c Jones b Harmison | 1 |
| Mohammad Sami c & b Giles | 18 | | (10) lbw b Hoggard | 5 |
| Shoaib Akhtar c Flintoff | | | | |
| b Harmison | 12 | | (9) c Jones b Hoggard | 14 |
| Danish Kaneria not out | 4 | – | not out | 2 |
| B 5, l-b 3, n-b 15 | 23 | | B4, l-b 5, w 2, n-b 3 | 14 |

1/53 2/63 3/73 4/201 5/346  462   1/54 2/104 3/108 4/164  268
6/369 7/403 8/431 9/446 10/462     (for 9 wkts dec)
                             5/164 6/183 7/187 8/234 9/244

Bowling: *First innings* - Hoggard 22-0-115-2; Flintoff 29-2-76-1; Giles 20-1-85-2; Harmison 24.4-5-85-3; Udal 13-1-60-0; Bell 7-1-33-1. *Second innings* – Hoggard 16-1-50-3; Flintoff 27.1-2-66-3; Harmison 19-2-61-2; Giles 17-3-51-0; Udal 14-2-31-1.

### England

| | | | | |
|---|---|---|---|---|
| M.E.Trescothick c Kamran Akmal | | | | |
| b Mohammad Sami | 48 | – | b Shoaib Akhtar | 0 |
| A.J.Strauss b Naved-ul-Hasan | 12 | – | b Naved-ul-Hasan | 0 |
| *M.P.Vaughan b Naved-ul-Hasan | 2 | – | lbw b Naved-ul-Hasan | 9 |
| I.R.Bell c Kamran Akmal | | | | |
| b Shahid Afridi | 115 | – | c Kamran Akmal b Shoaib Akhtar | 0 |
| K.P.Pietersen c Mohammad | | | c sub (Asim Kamal) | |
| Yousuf b Shoaib Akhtar | 100 | – | b Naved-ul-Hasan | 42 |
| A.Flintoff b Shoaib Akhtar | 1 | – | c sub (Hasan Raza) | |
| | | | b Shoaib Akhtar | 56 |
| +G.O.Jones lbw b Shahid Afridi | 55 | – | not out | 30 |
| A.F.Giles b Shahid Afridi | 26 | – | not out | 13 |
| S.D.Udal not out | 33 | | | |
| M.J.Hoggard b Shahid Afridi | 2 | | | |
| S.J.Harmison run out (Naved-ul- | | | | |
| Hasan/Shahid Afridi) | 16 | | | |
| B 1, l-b 12, w 1, n-b 22 | 36 | | B 4, l-b 8, n-b 2 | 14 |

1/33 2/39 3/107 4/261 5/272  446   1/1 2/5 3/10 4/20 5/100  164
6/327 7/378 8/395 9/399 10/446     6/138 (for 6 wkts)

Bowling: *First innings* – Shoaib Akhtar 27-4-93-2; Naved-ul-Hasan 20-2-63-2; Mohammad Sami 19-4-51-1; Shahid Afridi 30.3-3-95-4; Danish Kaneria 32-3-102-0; Shoaib Malik 4-0-29-0. *Second innings* – Shoaib Akhtar 11-2-61-3; Naved-ul-Hasan 12-3-30-3; Mohammad Sami 6-1-18-0; Danish Kaneria 12-4-27-0; Shahid Afridi 7-2-16-0.

Umpires: D.B.Hair and S.J.A.Taufel
Match drawn

While all this was going on, we discovered that Shahid Afridi had done a bit of a dance on the pitch to scuff it up right on a length and help their bowlers. Shahid and I go back all the way to Under-19s cricket when we used to play against each other, and he's a good lad, if a bit excitable. He did some sort of pirouette with his spikes on the pitch, thinking he might get away with it and no one would see what he'd done. It was probably the most unsubtle thing I've ever seen – Darren Gough would have been proud of it on *Strictly Come Dancing*! I don't think it had occurred to him about all the television cameras there, and of course they picked it up. In our dressing room his name was mud, but I get on very well with him and couldn't get too angry because he's such a likeable bloke. I asked him about it the following day and he just stood there with this daft grin on his face, which was half embarrassment and half being pleased with himself for what he'd done. He paid the penalty in the end because he was banned for the final Test.

The absence of Afridi did not seem to weaken Pakistan's resources and we got hammered in the final Test in Lahore. We were bowled out for just 288 in the first innings and they piled on the runs when it came to their turn. Mohammad Yousuf scored a double century and Kamran Akmal, their wicketkeeper, also got a hundred. We were always up against it in our second innings and Shoaib Malik claimed five wickets to wrap up an innings win and a 2–0 Test series defeat – it was not what we had hoped for after winning the Ashes just a few months earlier.

As soon as the Test finished, all the lads who had played in the Ashes were asked to go for a meeting in the team room where we were addressed by the British High Commissioner. Clearly something out of the ordinary was happening because bottles of champagne had been placed around the room, which is virtually unheard of in a Muslim country. Then it was announced that we were to be awarded MBEs in the New Year's Honours List in recognition of our achievement, and the High Commissioner went around the room asking each player if they would formally accept their award. It was a strange situation because at that point I didn't feel I deserved anything just a few hours after being absolutely hammered in the Test. It certainly didn't feel appropriate to celebrate after losing the current series.

The one person I was really happy for was Phil Neale, who has organised everything on tour for as long as I can remember. Phil was awarded an OBE alongside Vaughan, Duncan and David Graveney, the chairman of selectors. I have known Phil ever since he was involved in the Under-19s and our relationship has gone through various stages of ups and downs, the downs being mainly due to me. When I was Under-19s captain I was a little boisterous, but Phil kept us all on the right track, and if any of us deserved recognition in that year's Honours list, it was him.

We stayed in Lahore to begin the one-day series against Pakistan and were again led by Marcus after Vaughan returned home to England for an operation. The series began well with Andrew Strauss getting runs while I played my best innings of the tour, hitting 72 off 65 balls, to help us score 327 for 4. We won the match quite convincingly after bowling them out for 285, although it would have been a far more comprehensive win but for Abdul Razzaq, who kept hitting me to the boundary. He was largely responsible for my unflattering figures of 3 for 73 from just 8.5 overs.

The second match of the series was also staged at Lahore's Gaddafi Stadium, but before then there was the BBC *Sports Personality of the Year* awards programme. I had been told I was going to win the main award, the first cricketer to do so since Sir Ian Botham in 1981, and there was even talk of me flying home to attend the evening and missing matches during the one-day series. I rejected that idea because I was playing for England and I didn't think I should miss matches for that reason, so a compromise was struck. I would be interviewed live instead. The only problem with that was that because of the time difference I was up until around 4.30 in the morning and then played in the second one-day game starting at 9.00. It obviously affected my performance because I was out for a duck and we lost by seven wickets. Geoffrey Boycott wrote a column afterwards, criticising me for taking part in the programme and not getting any sleep, and in retrospect he was right – it was no way to prepare for an international match.

Kamran Akmal had scored a century to help Pakistan win in Lahore and followed that up with another hundred in the next match in Karachi. This time Pakistan got a huge total, piling up 353 for 6, and we never even looked like threatening it before losing by 165 runs. We lost the next match in Rawalpindi by just 13 runs, and by now my ankle was starting to get sore again so I didn't bowl in the final match.

By the end of that tour we had adopted a team song, written by assistant coach Matthew Maynard. I can't remember all the words but one line ran 'beating teams out of sight' – and this was after we'd won just two games out of five!

We were all disappointed to have lost both the Test and one-day series, but Pakistan are a formidable side on their own soil and can be a match for anyone. We were also a very tired team. We had been through an amazing year, winning in South Africa before putting all that effort into beating Australia. When I got home that Christmas, I saw it as a chance to draw a line under what had happened in 2005 and start again. I was looking forward to the months and years ahead to see what could be achieved with this England team, but even I could not have begun to imagine just how eventful the next few years would be.

# 2
# INDIA AND THE CAPTAINCY

Talk to any young lad, whether he's kicking a ball in the back garden or trying to bowl like Brett Lee or bat like Kevin Pietersen, and he'll tell you how he's dreaming of captaining his country. I was exactly the same as a kid, batting and bowling in the back garden with my brother Chris, pretending I was England captain and leading them to an Ashes victory. Of course, I never thought I'd actually get the job.

I had the honour of leading England Under-19s on a tour to Pakistan when I was younger, which was a very proud moment for me, and a surprise. I thoroughly enjoyed it once I got started. After that, I harboured ambitions about doing it again one day for the senior England side, but with Vaughan fulfilling the role so well it was an opportunity I thought I'd never get. No matter what side I've played in, I've always offered my opinion and advice to the captain. They didn't always take it and that was up to them. At least I felt I was contributing all I could. That was as far as my input went until we arrived in India for the start of the tour in February 2006. Vaughan had been forced to return home from Pakistan before

Christmas because he was having problems with his knee, but he'd had an operation to sort it out and was back to lead us on one of the toughest tours in Test cricket.

What we didn't know then was that this was the start of several years of knee problems for Vaughan, which possibly contributed towards England failing to build on the 2005 Ashes win. Vaughan was clearly feeling his injury during the early stages of that India tour, and I was first approached by Duncan Fletcher, England's coach, about the possibility of taking on the captaincy during the warm-up game in Baroda. It was our last game before the First Test at Nagpur and Duncan talked to me about it just as were starting our second innings. By this stage we knew that Michael's knee wasn't standing up to it. He had already been left out of that game and was having a scan and an injection on his knee. Duncan told me that, since Marcus Trescothick was on the verge of going home for personal reasons, there was a chance I would be captain the following week for the Test, depending how Michael got on. With neither Michael nor Marcus available, I suppose I was the next alternative as the most experienced player left, so it wasn't that much of a surprise or a shock when Duncan approached me, despite the pair of us never having the closest relationship in the dressing room.

In Pakistan before Christmas, I'd been told that I was in the shake-up to captain the side for the First Test in Multan when Marcus got the nod and led us very well. It was flattering to be thought of then and I was delighted to be in the frame again in India, but I tried not to think about it too much at that stage because it was yet to be confirmed. It was only when it became clear that Vaughan wasn't going to be fit and I got the official nod from Duncan that I allowed myself to get excited and look forward to leading my country.

Before I accepted the job I had to have a long chat with Rachael about what it involved, because she was expecting our son Corey, who was born several weeks later. Rachael and I talked it through and I think we both realised that this was an opportunity I could not turn down, even though it would mean that leaving the tour was not an option. The plan had been for me to come home after the Second Test in Mohali, when the baby was due, but we thought he would probably arrive early, and that's how it turned out. At the time, I thought I made the decision to stay in India for the right reasons, but looking back, I must admit I got it wrong. I should have come home, and if I had my time again, I would have done – then again, there are a lot of things I would do differently second time around.

An extraordinary fuss was made about my decision to remain in India rather than attend the birth. There were phone-ins, discussion programmes and all sorts about it, as though I was the first cricketer ever to stay on tour in those circumstances. Rachael was very good about it and just shrugged it all off. She said to me that I'll miss the birth but when I explained it to Corey in years to come he would understand what an honour it was to captain England. Since then, several players, including Andrew Strauss and Matt Prior, have left tours to attend the birth of their child, and I should have done the same, but after accepting the captaincy, I didn't think I was in a position to do so. At the time we thought we'd made the right decision as a family and it was a mistake. For the life of me, though, even now I don't understand why it caused so much comment and debate.

Like any new father, I was delighted to hear I had a healthy son but it wasn't easy being thousands of miles away. Of course, I had pictures emailed to me, but it's not the same as being there. It sounds a terrible thing to say, but I almost didn't want to know about my new son when friends texted me after seeing Corey for the first time. I was missing Rachael and I wasn't able to meet Corey, and I found that so hard. I finally got to see the new Flintoff just after the final Test in Mumbai, when I was able to nip back for a few days before the start of the one-day series.

The ironic thing was the first member of the squad to find out I'd had a son was Duncan, who happened to be sitting next to me in a cab when the news came through. We were both going to a shop to look for some cheap suits and he asked me what the call was all about so I told him. He congratulated me but there weren't any big hugs and I don't remember being given a cigar, which is the traditional way new fathers celebrate the birth of a child. I don't think Duncan is an expressive kind of bloke so it was left to the rest of the lads to come to my room and celebrate with me.

On the positive side, there's no doubt it was an exciting time, with a new baby and the England captaincy. I just wasn't able to share the excitement with my family because they were at home and I was in India. I didn't even ring my dad to tell him about the captaincy until it was officially announced because I didn't want to raise his hopes if it didn't happen. When I'm away, I don't speak to many people at home much anyway. I tend to concentrate on things that are happening around me. I know he was absolutely delighted about it all, and I'm sure it was almost as exciting a time for him as it was for me in having a new grandchild and one of his sons appointed England captain.

Although my family were delighted by the captaincy, everyone else seemed very concerned about the effect it might have on me and how it might affect other parts of my game. I was looking at it quite positively but the rest of the world didn't see it in the same way, and the consensus seemed to be that it was bound to be too much of a strain. I, on the other hand, couldn't wait to start. As an all-rounder, I was used to being in the game all the time, batting and bowling and standing at slip, so I didn't think captaincy would hinder me – I was hoping it might bring out the best in me. I think the added responsibility did help me initially, and certainly took my thinking processes to the next level, but in hindsight it probably was too much.

During the early stages of my captaincy, I relied on the experienced Steve Harmison and Matthew Hoggard to tell me if I was taking on too much. I was particularly concerned about the bowlers because of the heat and how hard it is to bowl in India. I tried to keep every bowler down to four or five-over spells, because that was normally enough for any of us. The only time I really felt the extra responsibility was when I batted. I hadn't played that well in Pakistan, but in India I was batting well again. I wasn't trying to belt the ball and hit boundaries all the time. I felt more comfortable playing that way in India. I tried to concentrate on playing as I would like rather than focusing on what it meant to the side for their captain to get runs.

It helped that the team were a really good bunch of lads. Ashley Giles and Simon Jones had succumbed to injuries and losing them as well as Vaughan and Trescothick at the start of the tour pulled us together and we rallied around as a group. Everyone else may have been saying we had no chance, but we saw it as an opportunity. Alastair Cook, Monty Panesar and Ian Blackwell all made their debuts in the First Test. Cook took his chance and scored a hundred while Monty claimed Tendulkar as his first Test wicket, and also got Rahul Dravid out in the Second Test.

Even though everything was stacked against us and we'd been written off because of our inexperience, in some ways that allowed us just to go out and play. I never had any doubts that the lads would play for me and for each other. Here was a new-look side being given the chance to compete against India, and that's exactly what we did. We believed that we could give a good account of ourselves and that belief carried us through to a fantastic result. I thought we were magnificent throughout the series and to draw 1-1 in India, one of the strongest sides in the world, on their home soil, was a remarkable result given the injuries and setbacks we suffered on the tour.

What with all the disruption in the build-up to the First Test, and everyone seemingly worrying about everyone else, I just wanted the game to get under way, and once we started playing, it was a totally different atmosphere. I enjoyed it. The best thing about it was leading a young team, and what they achieved was just amazing. It was great to see lads such as Alastair Cook, then aged just 21, around the dressing room, wanting to play and to learn, and his enthusiasm was more than matched by Monty.

I remember our first session in the field at Nagpur. I was everywhere, all over the place – talking to the bowlers, bowling my overs a little quicker than normal. Steve Harmison took me to one side and told me to calm down and slow down, otherwise I was going to be knackered for the rest of the day. I had Steve, Hoggard and Paul Collingwood in my ear, and Andrew Strauss giving his two penn'orth, so I had plenty of good advice. It was a real team effort. Everyone pitched in. Monty, for instance, had a very good idea of what he wanted, and had all his field placings worked out in his head for his debut. I knew Monty from the Academy a few years back, and all he ever wanted to do was talk about cricket. He'd talk about the Indian team, Sachin Tendulkar, Ricky Ponting – he'd talk about anything to do with cricket. He just loved it and spent his whole time picking everyone's brains about this and that. He wanted to listen and learn and he's not changed all that much. Even now, all he does is talk about cricket.

Two days before the First Test, he came to my room and, using the notepad by the phone, went through what field he wanted to set for each batsman in the India team, in case he was selected. He also told me what to look out for when he was bowling, what the signs would be if he was getting tired and things like that. I thought that was absolutely fantastic for someone about to make his debut – it made my job as captain a hell of a lot easier. The evening before the game, when it was confirmed that he would be playing, he was wandering around with a big grin on his face, genuinely excited about playing against India the following day. There weren't any nerves or anxiety or anything like that. He just couldn't wait to get out there, and it was the same with Cook. They weren't hiding or worried about playing. They regarded it as their opportunity to give it a go at Test level.

There wasn't a great deal for me to do as captain, to be honest – I moved a fielder from here to there every so often, gave a team-talk and that's about it. I suppose it helped that I'm a bowler, and so perhaps understood more than most how the bowlers felt when runs were scored off them. The opposition is always going to score runs. Bowlers are going to get hit for the odd four or six, however hard they try to beat the bat. Sometimes it just works out like that. In the Second Test at Mohali, I remember bowling for a four-over spell when I didn't do particularly well, but it wasn't through lack of trying, so I can understand a bowler when he doesn't get it quite right.

Leading out the side for the first time was special and I probably stuck my chest out a little bit more than usual when we walked out on to the field at Nagpur. I'd had a little think about what I wanted to say to the team that first morning, but most of it was instinctive. Whether I'm batting, bowling, fielding or captaining the side, most of the things I do are by gut instinct. Before the first meeting, I'd written down a few things to say to the team, but once I started I just binned it and carried on talking. If I'd stood up and read from pieces of paper, I'm sure all the lads would have looked at me as if I had two heads.

I also hadn't given much thought to what sort of captain I wanted to be. There wasn't much time between Duncan telling me I'd got the job and the start of the First Test, so I had little choice but to get on with it. As far as I was concerned, I was a fill-in captain for Vaughan and I tried to operate as he would have done, and, certainly in India, that approach seemed to pay off. I didn't try to be clever by thinking about it too much. I just cracked on and did the job the way I thought best and the side responded to that. I still regarded myself as one of the lads and I didn't want that to change, because I like that side of being a cricketer, having a good crack. I still enjoy it. I think it helps me, and plenty of times it helps the side. I was the same throughout the tour. I still sat at the back of the bus and I still had my adjoining room with Harmy.

Having said all that, the Indian tour did make me realise how difficult the job of captain is. I don't think you appreciate what's involved until you actually do it, and have to handle such matters as selection and dealing with the press on a regular basis. I didn't have to do all those things full-time in India, but I really felt it when I was appointed for the Ashes tour.

## INDIA v ENGLAND
## (1st Test) at Nagpur 1–5 March 2006

### England

| | | | | |
|---|---|---|---|---|
| A.J.Strauss c Laxman b Sreesanth | 28 | – | c Dhoni b Pathan | 46 |
| A.N.Cook b Pathan | 60 | – | not out | 104 |
| I.R.Bell c Dravid b Harbhajan Singh | 9 | – | c Dhoni b Pathan | 1 |
| K.P.Pietersen b Sreesanth | 15 | – | c Dravid b Kumble | 87 |
| P.D.Collingwood not out | 134 | – | not out | 36 |
| *A.Flintoff lbw b Kumble | 43 | | | |
| +G.O.Jones lbw b Pathan | 14 | | | |
| I.D.Blackwell b Pathan | 4 | | | |
| M.J.Hoggard c Dhoni b Sreesanth | 11 | | | |
| S.J.Harmison st Dhoni b Harbhajan Singh | 39 | | | |
| M.S.Panesar lbw b Sreesanth | 9 | | | |
| B 7, l-b 7, w 1, n-b 12 | 27 | | B 12, l-b 7, w 2, n-b 2 | 23 |

1/56 2/81 3/110 4/136      **393**    1/95 2/97 3/221  (for 3 wkts dec) 297
5/203 6/225 7/244 8/267 9/327 10/393

Bowling: *First innings* – Pathan 23-5-92-3; Sreesanth 28.5-6-95-4; Harbhajan Singh 34-5-93-2; Kumble 40-13-88-1; Tendulkar 2-0-11-0. *Second innings* – Pathan 14-2-48-2; Sreesanth 10-2-36-0; Kumble 32-8-101-1; Harbhajan Singh 30-6-79-0; Sehwag 1-0-14-0.

### India

| | | | | |
|---|---|---|---|---|
| W.Jaffer c Flintoff b Hoggard | 81 | – | c Strauss b Flintoff | 100 |
| V.Sehwag c Pietersen b Hoggard | 2 | – | b Hoggard | 0 |
| *R.S.Dravid lbw b Hoggard | 40 | – | b Panesar | 71 |
| S.R.Tendulkar lbw b Panesar | 16 | (6) | not out | 28 |
| V.V.S.Laxman lbw b Hoggard | 0 | (8) | not out | 0 |
| M Kaif b Panesar | 91 | | | |
| +M.S.Dhoni c Jones b Flintoff | 5 | (5) | c Strauss b Harmison | 16 |
| I.K.Pathan c Flintoff b Hoggard | 2 | (4) | c Strauss b Flintoff | 35 |
| A.Kumble c Cook b Harmison | 58 | | | |
| Harbhajan Singh not out | 0 | (7) | b Harmison | 7 |
| S.Sreesanth lbw b Hoggard | 1 | | | |
| B 17, l-b 3, w 5, n-b 2 | 27 | | l-b 3 | 3 |

1/11 2/140 3/149 4/149      **323**    1/1 2/168 3/198  (for 6 wkts) 260
5/176 6/183 7/190 8/318 9/322 10/323    4/215 5/252 6/260

Bowling: *First innings* – Hoggard 30.5-13-57-6; Harmison 27-5-75-1; Flintoff 29-10-68-1; Panesar 42-19-73-2; Blackwell 7-0-28-0; Bell 1-0-2-0. *Second innings* – Hoggard 16-7-29-1; Harmison 17.2-4-48-2; Flintoff 17-2-79-2; Panesar 16-2-58-1; Blackwell 12-2-43-0.

Umpires: Aleem Dar and I.L.Howell
Match drawn

However, being occupied with the captaincy did help me cope with missing my family. It was great to fly back after our victory in the Third Test at Mumbai to see them again, even if it was for just three days. Holly had grown so much while I'd been away and Corey was nearly three weeks old by the time I got to see him. Once again we had photographers outside the house, but I had a stroke of luck when I got back to London. I was booked on the shuttle from Heathrow to Manchester but Paul Beck, Lancashire's sponsor, arranged for his helicopter to pick me up instead. It landed at the back of the house and I went in the back way. All the photographers were either outside the front of the house or waiting at Manchester Airport, so for once I dodged them. While they were all waiting for me there, I was already settled in back home. Once they realised I was there, they just camped outside the house and followed us everywhere.

We asked a photographer we knew to take a picture of us as a family to distribute to everyone, hoping it would stop the pursuit and send all the other photographers away happy, but they always seem to want more. It's a strange situation, to feel you have to submit an official photograph just to get a bit of peace and quiet. As it was, it didn't work. They still followed us. When Rachael went to the town hall to register Corey's birth, someone popped out with a camera to take a picture of her when she arrived, so she got back in the car and went home, and had to make another appointment. The photographer had obviously been tipped off that she was going that day.

## INDIA v ENGLAND
## (3rd Test) at Mumbai 18–22 March 2006

### England

| | | | | |
|---|---|---|---|---|
| A.J.Strauss c Dhoni | | | | |
| b Harbhajan Singh | 128 | – | c Dhoni b Patel | 4 |
| I.R.Bell c Harbhajan Singh | | | | |
| b Sreesanth | 18 | – | c Dhoni b Sreesanth | 8 |
| O.A.Shah c Dravid b Harbhajan Singh | 88 | – | run out (Tendulkar) | 38 |
| K.P.Pietersen c Dhoni b Sreesanth | 39 | (5) | c & b Kumble | 7 |
| P.D.Collingwood c Dhoni b Sreesanth | 31 | (6) | c & b Harbhajan Singh | 32 |
| *A.Flintoff c Tendulkar b Kumble | 50 | (7) | st Dhoni b Kumble | 50 |
| +G.O.Jones c Kumble b Sreesanth | 1 | (8) | c Pathan b Harbhajan Singh | 3 |
| S.D.Udal lbw b Patel | 9 | (4) | c Jaffer b Pathan | 14 |
| M.J.Hoggard b Patel | 0 | – | lbw b Kumble | 6 |
| J.M.Anderson c Yuvraj Singh | | | | |
| b Harbhajan Singh | 15 | – | c Dravid b Kumble | 6 |
| M.S.Panesar not out | 3 | – | not out | 0 |
| B 5, l-b 7, w 3, n-b 3 | 18 | | B 1, l-b 8, w 4, n-b 10 | 23 |

1/52 2/230 3/242 4/326     400     1/9 2/21 3/61 4/73 5/85     191
5/328 6/333 7/356 8/356 9/385 10/400     6/151 7/157 8/183 9/188 10/191

Bowling: *First innings* – Pathan 17-4-64-0; Sreesanth 22-5-70-4; Patel 29-4-81-2; Kumble 39-7-84-1; Harbhajan Singh 26.4-4-89-3. *Second innings* – Pathan 13-2-24-1; Patel 13-2-39-1; Sreesanth 13-3-30-1; Kumble 30.4-13-49-4; Harbhajan Singh 23-9-40-2.

### India

| | | | | |
|---|---|---|---|---|
| W.Jaffer c Jones b Hoggard | 11 | – | lbw b Flintoff | 10 |
| V.Sehwag c Shah b Hoggard | 6 | (7) | lbw b Anderson | 0 |
| *R.S.Dravid c Jones b Anderson | 52 | (4) | c Jones b Flintoff | 9 |
| S.R.Tendulkar c Jones b Anderson | 1 | (5) | c Bell b Udal | 34 |
| Yuvraj Singh c Jones b Flintoff | 37 | (6) | c Collingwood b Flintoff | 12 |
| +M.S.Dhoni run out (Anderson) | 64 | (8) | c Panesar b Udal | 5 |
| I.K.Pathan c Hoggard b Udal | 26 | (2) | b Anderson | 6 |
| A.Kumble lbw b Panesar | 30 | (3) | lbw b Hoggard | 8 |
| Harbhajan Singh c Jones b Anderson | 2 | – | c Hoggard b Udal | 6 |
| S.Sreesanth not out | 29 | – | not out | 0 |
| M.M.Patel b Anderson | 7 | – | c Hoggard b Udal | 1 |
| B 4, l-b 7, n-b 3 | 14 | | B 1, l-b 4, w 1, n-b 3 | 9 |

1/9 2/24 3/28 4/94     279     1/6 2/21 3/33 4/75 5/76     100
5/142 6/186 7/212 8/217 9/272 10/279     6/77 7/92 8/99 9/99 10/100

Bowling: *First innings* – Hoggard 22-6-54-2; Flintoff 21-4-68-1; Anderson 19.1-8-40-4; Panesar 26-7-53-1; Udal 16-2-53-1. *Second innings* – Hoggard 12-6-13-1; Anderson 12-2-39-2; Panesar 4-1-15-0; Flintoff 11-4-14-3; Udal 9.2-3-14-4.

Umpires: D.B.Hair and S.J.A.Taufel
England won by 212 runs

Since this was such a flying visit – I had to go back on the Sunday – we set out really to enjoy the few days we had before I had to rejoin the tour. It was extremely hard saying goodbye to the family again after such a short time, and when I got back it was to face seven one-day internationals. That was really tough – five would have been a lot, but seven was just unfair. The playing side of it was hard enough, but the travelling didn't make sense, either. It wasn't as if we were making a nice pattern around India – we were zig-zagging all the way through.

The ongoing routine of playing, going back to the hotel in the evening and then setting off for the next venue the following morning was difficult for everyone.

Our first match of the one-day international series was in Delhi and we should have built on our Test victory there by winning the one-day game, too. We limited them to 203 and Kevin and I were doing well at one point but, both of us having been dismissed in quick succession, we just collapsed to 164 all out. As a captain I rarely lost it with the team, but this time I was really mad and shouted in the dressing room afterwards. We were rubbish and I let the team know it.

The schedule took us to Faridabad next and again we lost a game we should have won. We were bowled out for 226, despite Straussy and Kevin both getting half-centuries, and they ended up winning with six balls to spare, but it wasn't as close as it sounded. We were never really in the game.

Next it was on to Goa where we played in unbelieveably hot conditions. I had been stumped facing Ramesh Powar, India's off-spinner, in the previous match and I told Kev I was going after him this time. I'd decided to have a go and, sure enough, got caught on the boundary. Yuvraj Singh had made a century in their innings, MS Dhoni was scoring runs towards the end of it, and we never really came close to their total of 294 for 6. Our losing sequence continued in the next match at Kochi. Yuvraj's run of good form against us showed no signs of abating. He got both runs and wickets to win the game for them again and secure the series for India. It was a huge ground and I got cramp when I was bowling, partly because it was so hot and I was sweating so much and also because it was such a big ground.

During that series it was like men against boys – they were far better than we were. The same thing happened in 2008 in India. They were better than us at one-day cricket then and they just seem to keep improving! They play so much of it, far more than we do, and they also get encouraged to play naturally. We talk about plans and hitting this many runs off the first few overs and set ourselves targets all the way through the innings, but when I played under Dhoni in the IPL for Chennai, he made it very simple. He just encouraged us to enjoy it, never mind the plans, and it seems to work for them. They know their game, they know each other, they are particularly good in their own conditions and they just back themselves to win if they play well.

I was down to play in the fifth match in Guwahati – a dead game in terms of the series, but the occasion proved to be more eventful than we imagined it would be. We were staying in a very basic hotel, which was probably a bit like the old days of touring India. The only part of the hotel that was under cover housed the actual rooms. The rest of it had no roof, so when it rained the whole hotel got drenched. When we arrived at the ground, it was pretty obvious that the weather was not going to allow us to play, but once the crowd realised that was the case, the people became very angry. At first, they started throwing things but then it got a bit nastier. They took all the television cameras out, fires started, and before we knew it there was a full-scale riot. We were taken away from it fairly quickly but I think the trouble rumbled on for some time after we'd been driven away. No one could do anything about the rain, but try telling that to all those people who had turned up to watch the cricket!

There had been a lot of talk around the squad and in the press about the possibility of resting players. We'd already lost the one-day series, so this was a good opportunity to have a week off, and also to have a look at a few other players. The World Cup was coming up just a year later, and up-and-coming players needed the experience.

Having said that, I was a little fed up having to travel around India for the last week when I could have been resting at home. It didn't make any sense to me whatsoever to travel from Guwahati to Jamshedpur and then to Indore for the final matches of the series when I could have got much better rest at home. I didn't want to ask to go home because it would have looked like I wasn't committed to playing for England, but I'd have far rather played in those last two matches than sit around doing nothing for the last week. The irony was that I was asked to play in the only match we won in Jamshedpur, but I had a bad hamstring strain and my ankle was playing up a bit.

# 3
# **TRIALS AND TRIBULATIONS**

Media attention had become part of my life ever since the Ashes victory, but I did notice a change in emphasis at the start of the 2006 summer. I had received plenty of plaudits for the way I captained the side in India and the way the side came back to level the Test series by winning in Mumbai. When it became clear the following summer that Vaughan would not be fit to lead the side again because of his knee problems, I was re-appointed captain by the selectors for the three-Test series against Sri Lanka.

Straightaway plenty of criticism was voiced about the decision. Needless to say, I didn't agree with it. At that stage I could handle being the team's all-rounder and captain – it wasn't until much later that it all became too much for me.

The First Test at Lord's ended in a draw despite our domination of the match. We just couldn't force the victory on the final day. I bowled more than 70 overs in all, which I lived to regret later that summer, but I thought that was the best choice at the time, given the context of the game. A few of my decisions were criticised. For instance, some people said that I didn't bowl the spinner as much as I should have done. The reason was that the conditions were perfect for seam bowling. Durham seamer Liam Plunkett beat the bat about thirty times. Batsmen were playing and missing and while the seamers were doing so well, I wanted to keep them going. Unfortunately we dropped 10 catches. We still took 19 wickets in the game and at the end of it my captaincy came into question! If we'd held our catches, we could have won halfway through Saturday, but instead we were still trying to bowl them out on Monday evening. One thing that perhaps gave a false impression of the wicket was Sajid Mahmood taking three quick wickets in the first innings with fast in-swinging yorkers. That enabled us to enforce the follow-on, but it wasn't that bad a wicket and they battled hard to survive.

After the experience of Lord's we moved on to Edgbaston for the Second Test, which was where I began to realise that luck plays a big part in whether you're regarded as a good or bad captain. I took myself off after two overs of the first innings, brought on Plunkett and he took two wickets in his first over. I moved a fielder from midwicket to fourth slip and the next ball was edged straight there. Everything seemed to go right but I could just as easily have been made to look a fool – it's a fine line between success and failure. You can't control how a bowler bowls or a batter bats. All you can do is try to make bowling changes at the right times and put the fielders where you think they should go. At least this time we came away with a win and the possibility of completing a series victory at Trent Bridge.

# ENGLAND v SRI LANKA
## (2nd Test) at Edgbaston 25-28 May 2006

### Sri Lanka

| | | | | |
|---|---|---|---|---|
| M.G.Vandort c Collingwood b Plunkett | 9 | – | c Jones b Plunkett | 105 |
| W.U.Tharanga b Hoggard | 0 | – | c Jones b Hoggard | 0 |
| +K.C.Sangakkara c Jones b Plunkett | 25 | – | c Collingwood b Panesar | 18 |
| *D.P.M.D.Jayawardene c Jones b Plunkett | 0 | – | lbw b Hoggard | 5 |
| T.T.Samaraweera c Collingwood b Hoggard | 3 | – | st Jones b Panesar | 8 |
| T.M.Dilshan c Trescothick b Flintoff | 27 | – | lbw b Hoggard | 59 |
| M.F.Maharoof c Jones b Mahmood | 5 | – | c & b Flintoff | 13 |
| W.P.U.J.C.Vaas not out | 30 | – | c Collingwood b Plunkett | 1 |
| K.M.D.N.Kulasekara c Trescothick b Mahmood | 3 | – | c Collingwood b Plunkett | 0 |
| S.L.Malinga lbw b Panesar | 26 | – | c Strauss b Flintoff | 2 |
| M.Muralitharan c Plunkett b Flintoff | 1 | – | not out | 0 |
| l-b 6, n-b 6 | 12 | | l-b 8, w 1, n-b 11 | 20 |

1/3 2/16 3/16 4/25 5/46   141    1/2 2/38 3/43 4/56 5/181   231
6/65 7/79 8/82 9/132 10/141     6/219 7/223 8/223 9/231 10/231

Bowling: *First innings* – Hoggard 15-4-32-2; Flintoff 13.2-4-28-2; Plunkett 12-1-43-3; Mahmood 9-1-25-2; Panesar 2-0-7-1. *Second innings* – Hoggard 22-8-64-3; Flintoff 19-3-50-2; Plunkett 13.2-6-17-3; Panesar 28-6-73-2; Mahmood 9-2-19-0; Collingwood 2-2-0-0.

### England

| | | | | |
|---|---|---|---|---|
| M.E.Trescothick c Sangakkara b Muralitharan | 27 | – | lbw b Muralitharan | 0 |
| A.J.Strauss run out (Samaraweera) | 30 | – | c Jayawardene b Muralitharan | 16 |
| A.N.Cook lbw b Muralitharan | 23 | – | not out | 34 |
| K.P.Pietersen lbw b Muralitharan | 142 | – | lbw b Muralitharan | 13 |
| M.J.Hoggard b Vaas | 3 | | | |
| P.D.Collingwood c Tharanga b Muralitharan | 19 | (5) | c Sangakkara b Muralitharan | 3 |
| *A.Flintoff b Malinga | 9 | (6) | not out | 4 |
| +G.O.Jones c Samaraweera b Muralitharan | 4 | | | |
| L.E.Plunkett c Vandort b Muralitharan | 0 | | | |
| S.I.Mahmood not out | 0 | | | |
| M.S.Panesar lbw b Malinga | 0 | | | |
| B 6, l-b 13, n-b 14, pens 5 | 38 | | B 2, n-b 9 | 11 |

1/56 2/69 3/125 4/169 5/238   295    1/9 2/35 3/63 4/73   (for 4 wkts) 81
6/290 7/290 8/293 9/294 10/295

Bowling: *First innings* – Vaas 16-6-30-1; Malinga 13.3-2-68-2; Maharoof 11-3-42-0; Muralitharan 25-2-86-6; Kulasekara 13-2-45-0. *Second innings* – Vaas 7-2-12-0; Malinga 7-1-29-0; Muralitharan 12.2-3-29-4; Dilshan 1-0-9-0.

Umpires: Aleem Dar and D.B.Hair
England won by 6 wickets

To say I was disappointed with the wicket at Nottingham would be an understatement. We were playing in England, the home of seam and swing bowling, and when I walked out to look at the wicket for the first time, I found something that would not have been out of place in India, Pakistan or Sri Lanka. It looked like the traditional sub-continent dust bowl, ideal for spinners – just what you need when Muttiah Muralitharan is in the opposition! If you're taking on Sri Lanka and Murali, you want to face them on a fast and bouncy wicket that's going to allow the ball to fly through, or failing that, on a green-top that's going to nibble around. It was pretty clear that on this wicket, bowlers who bang it in, such as myself, were going to be pretty ineffective.

Monty Panesar, England's only spinner, bowled well and got five wickets, but with all respect to Monty, he's not Murali. So when their lads really struggled against Monty, we knew it was going to be a tough task when we faced Murali. Having said that, we probably lost the Test when we failed to take a first-innings lead. We were able to take the momentum from Edgbaston into this Test and had Sri Lanka reeling on 169 for 9 until Murali came out smiling, and proceeded to swing his bat at everything. You try to put fielders in the right places but you just can't budget for it. He's my big mate and I'm as desperate to get him out as anyone, but he doesn't half frustrate you. I even tried bouncing him, but he was able to score 33 runs, which proved crucial to the balance of the Test.

That was my first defeat in charge of the side, and it taught me a lot about how the media treat you as an England captain.

When you win, all the interviewers from Sky, BBC and Channel Five are patting you on the back and everyone wants to be your friend, but it was totally different when we lost – no eye-to-eye contact in the press conference, just the questions. Normally, I'll have a bit of chitchat with various members of the press, but there was none of that this time. It was a lot less amiable than usual and, although I didn't expect it to be a happy affair, the difference was very noticeable.

A few more questions than usual about my activities away from the pitch cropped up. Everyone seemed to be worried about me burning myself out except me! I had not changed my lifestyle at all since being made captain, but now there was a lot more interest in what I did. Questions were raised before the Second Test about how much I was doing off the pitch, particularly with it being my benefit year. The crux of it was that I went over to Belfast on the Saturday night before the Test to watch Amir Khan's latest fight, returned by helicopter the following morning, because I was due to start the Great Manchester 10K run, and then went to the Beckhams' party in the evening. I could just as easily have gone out socialising around home and no one would have known anything about it, and I travelled by helicopter because I had to be back in Manchester by 10.00 a.m. to start the race. I didn't see that I had anything to apologise for in my behaviour. I was still practising and training as hard as I always did.

As far as I was concerned, the real cost of drawing that Test series against Sri Lanka was to my body. Throughout the game at

Trent Bridge, I was feeling my left ankle again. I'd felt a niggle at Edgbaston, but it got worse, continuing a pattern that has gone on throughout my career. I seem to have a period of rest, play for a while and then I get a sore ankle again. Scans and X-rays showed up inflammation around the ankle from the operation I'd had on it at the start of 2005, after the South African tour. That operation was a success but now three tiny bone fragments were identified as possibly causing the current problem. Eight times my body-weight of 16 stone was landing on my front foot when I bowled, so to put my ankle problems down to three minute fragments took some believing, but that was the start of the injury problems that would last for a couple of years.

Talk of an operation to remove the fragments came to nothing. Two specialists couldn't absolutely guarantee they were causing the problem, and for everyone involved, that wasn't good enough to go ahead. So it was decided that if I rested for five or six weeks, I might have a chance of playing in the Test series against Pakistan later that summer. I was criticised for not having the surgery straightaway, but I don't think any of those critics would have considered an operation as their first option if they'd been in my shoes.

During that time out, I spent six or seven hours a day with Dave Roberts, Lancashire's physiotherapist – 'Rooster', as he is universally known – and did a lot of work to strengthen my ankle with different exercises, as well as having specialist treatment. There was a lot of talk about how important it was that I was fit for the Ashes that winter, but I was looking beyond that. I was thinking about the rest of my career. The Ashes and the World

Cup were at the forefront of most people's minds but I wanted my career to continue way beyond that five-month period. I use Rooster for all my rehabilitation and he has become a close confidant of mine. We talk about everything from money to cars – everything – and he has kept me going during my long periods out of the game injured. People may find it strange that I use Rooster rather than go to the Loughborough, where the England and Wales Cricket Board's National Performance Centre is based, for treatment. The simple answer is that he is so well respected in the game that England are very happy for me to use him. He was an England physio during the time that Sri Ian Botham played and has a strong background in that and every step we take in my rehabilitation programmes is done in consultation with England. His methods are tried and tested and both myself and England trust him as the best man to handle my comeback programmes.

My first match back was for Lancashire. I played two Twenty20 Cup matches and then a championship match against Kent at Canterbury. That was to be the final hurdle I had to clear to prove my fitness before I made myself available for England again. I bowled a few overs and got my old mate Rob Key out first ball, which pleased me a lot, but during the game the pain in my ankle just got worse and worse. I had to keep going because if there was a slim chance that the pain might go away and I would be all right, I had to take it. On the flipside, if my ankle wasn't all right, I was heading for an operation anyway. Either way, I had to test it out properly.

After the game, a friend gave Rooster, Jimmy Anderson and me a lift back home. I was in a fairly despondent mood because, by then, I knew that another operation was the only option. We stopped to buy a few cans and drank them on the way, had a curry in Nuneaton and got back pretty late. The prospect of an operation was especially frustrating because I'd just spent all those weeks getting fit and losing weight.

The surgery itself turned out to be exploratory in some ways – one of the tendons that connects the big toe to the cartilage had moved a hell of a lot and dragged a muscle out of position. They cleaned it all up.

After every operation, the tough part is always the rehabilitation, and drumming up the motivation to put yourself through it all again, but I was determined to get fit for the winter. So it was back to spending five or six hours a day with Rooster, and training hard. Originally, I had been hoping to play in the Second Test against Pakistan at Old Trafford at the end of July, but I had the operation on the first morning of the game. I wanted to spectate, at least, but was put under house arrest by Rooster. Nevertheless, on the Friday, I sneaked out to Old Trafford for twenty minutes, just to see my former Lancashire team-mate Paddy McKeown, who had a box. While I was there my phone went and it was Rooster. He asked me what I was doing and I told him I was sat down with my foot up, but he knew where I was.

The one thing I was encouraged to do almost as soon as I got home after the operation was to keep the foot mobile. I was given exercises that would keep the tendon moving and avoid scar tissue causing a problem. When I got back in the gym, I started out with rowing and weights, and built up gradually until I was ready to run again. I often get very frustrated during rehab, and have to be reminded to be patient. While I was trying not to rush it, I managed to get myself into trouble again. I had been invited to watch England's opening match of the football World Cup against Paraguay in Frankfurt as a guest of the BBC. It had been announced that I would be taking a break to recuperate from ankle surgery, and since the rehab regime had not yet started, I didn't see anything wrong in accepting. I went with Harmy and Neil Fairbrother, my former Lancashire team-mate who now handles all my affairs. I'd been to a fortieth birthday party for Paul Beck's wife the previous evening, and once we got to Germany I had a couple of glasses of wine with lunch, which must have topped up what I'd drunk the night before. I thought I was all right, as you often do in that situation, so when the BBC asked me for an interview I agreed. I thought I'd done a great interview about how much I wanted England to do well and all that, and then the phone started to ring and I had various text messages from people who obviously thought otherwise.

All the lads in the dressing room were laughing about it and I got a lot of support from football fans, who all thought it was fantastic, but it wasn't that great from my point of view. It was an afternoon programme, probably seen by a lot of kids, and I know that I'm a bit of a role model. I shouldn't have done it and obviously I didn't come across very well.

I'm sure that incident didn't help when it came to the end of the summer and the selectors were sitting down to discuss who should be captain for that winter's Ashes series. Vaughan was still not fit after his knee operation, and Andrew Strauss had done well leading England to a Test series victory over Pakistan and drawing the one-day series against them.

My position was the same as it had always been – if the selectors asked me to do it, I would accept – but at the time all I was concentrating on was getting fit. I was very flattered to be linked with the captaincy again, but my main focus was just getting on the plane. If the selectors had picked Strauss, it wouldn't have been a problem for me. All I wanted was to be fit enough to go on the tour.

I spoke to David Graveney, the chairman of selectors, while I was in Portugal for warm weather training, but that was really to determine how fit I was going to be. When I got back, I went for a medical at Loughborough – all the players have one before every tour. It was a funny day, though. Since I was also going to a charity event in London that day, I was given a lift by helicopter to Loughborough and then on to London, where I was taken by speedboat to Canary Wharf. I was at the charity event for two hours and then it was back on the speedboat and a helicopter back to Loughborough for the other part of my fitness test. I felt like James Bond – it was brilliant.

Later that day I was asked, by phone, to captain the side in Australia and to go back down to London the following day for the press conference. It was a very exciting time for me. Ever since I was a child I had dreamed about playing in the

Ashes, so to captain the side as well was quite unbelievable. It was only when I started doing the job that my dreams were shattered. To start with, I still didn't fully realise all the implications, despite the Indian experience, but before we left I chatted with Michael Vaughan about it, at Geraint Jones's wedding, and with Neil Fairbrother but I was quite single-minded about it. By the day of departure, I'd worked out how I was going to approach it.

I don't think the delay in naming the captain did any of us any good. It took so long for a decision to be made that when it came it was almost a vote of no confidence, and the squad had, more or less, already been picked. The Australians do it this way round all the time, and have a well-oiled system in place. We don't, so when later criticism was being voiced about the composition of the tour party, I was in the firing line, despite having inherited the squad. In fact, the selectors and coach didn't seem to want anything to do with it. If I'd been appointed before the squad had been picked, I'd have wanted more input into the selection. I'd have definitely wanted one or two different personnel out there alongside me, and I'd have wanted a lot more say in what was going on. That proved to be the first setback of many in my brief stint as captain.

# 4

# BUILD-UP TO
# THE ASHES

You could not move in 2006, in England or Australia, without seeing or reading something about the Ashes. The hype was relentless – everyone had been looking forward to the re-match from the minute we won at The Oval. There was barely time to enjoy the moment – although some managed that better than others – before people were talking and writing about how we would fare in Australia. When I was there playing for the Rest of the World in the Super Series, shortly after we won, people would stop me in the street to say how much they had enjoyed the contest and how much they were looking forward to seeing the repeat series when we got to Australia at the end of 2006. All sorts of promotional events had been going on, with 500-day countdowns and such like.

Before the Ashes, though, we had the Champions Trophy tournament in India. There was a lot of talk as a squad about whether we should go straight from there to Australia and begin our preparations a few days early, or try to get a few days at home with our families. We decided that if we didn't get to the semi-finals, we would go home. Otherwise, we would go straight to Australia.

I would have preferred to go straight to Australia anyway. I didn't want to start the cricket any sooner, but I thought the wrench of having to say goodbye to the family again after just a few days at home would be very hard. In the end, we were knocked out early from the Champions Trophy and the flights were flexible enough for most of us to have a week at home before we set out for Australia, so we made the right decision.

We started our Champions Trophy campaign in Jaipur against the hosts and continued our losing form against them. My ankle was still not fully recovered so although I was leading the side I was just playing as a batsman. We did not start well and I was out for a duck attempting to flick Irfan Pathan to the leg side and fell lbw. We were dismissed for 125 which was never going to be enough against a side as good as India and they won very comfortably once again.

We stayed in Jaipur for our next match against Australia, which was built up as being a warm-up for the Ashes. We never really looked at it like that because we had a completely different team over there for that tournament than the squad we would have in Australia for the Ashes. There were players like Michael Yardy, James Dalrymple and Kabir Ali involved in that event who weren't involved in the Ashes. Having said all that, it would have been nice to have beaten them, but once again we under-performed. Ian Bell and Andrew Strauss gave us a solid start but after that we struggled. I failed to make a major score again and was caught at square leg trying to hit Shane Watson and we were bowled out for 169, which again was not competitive enough against opposition of that quality.

Our final game was against West Indies, which was the first match I had bowled in since suffering my injury earlier that year and we broke our losing duck in the tournament, even though it was not enough to secure our qualification for the last four. When you come back from injury you can be clinically fit and all the medical staff can give you a clean bill of health, but mentally it can take some time to get over an injury like that. Many times when I've come back from injuries, there is a point you will reach when you are completely happy again and can trust your body to do what you want it to do but that takes time. In my case there was a fear that my ankle would go and during those first few matches I was apprehensive about slamming my foot down every time I ran into bowl. We were chasing a tough target after Chris Gayle and Dwayne Bravo both scored centuries to guide them to 272 for 4, but we performed well as a batting unit and chased down their total with over an over to spare to set us up for our trip to Australia.

None of us really knew what to expect when we arrived in Australia. The whole series had been built up to such an extent we weren't even sure what would happen when we ventured out of the hotel. Would people be following us everywhere and abusing us? As it turned out, our arrival in Sydney was low key with nothing like the fuss we'd been warned about and had been fearing. We sneaked out of the airport to face just a few photographers and members of the press. Fortunately, Kylie Minogue had got off a plane not long before us and for some reason the snappers were more interested in pictures of her.

We didn't have any trouble out and about in Australia, either, despite a consistent campaign to run us down. You couldn't avoid the 'Tonk a Pom' adverts – images of Matthew Hayden walloping the ball and putting his hand to his forehead to see just how far it had gone, accompanied by the slogan: 'Tonk a Pom'. They were an indication of how big this Ashes series was and how badly the Australians wanted to win it. The Aussies tried to get at us from the day we arrived. They call it mental disintegration, which is normally concentrated on systematic sledging on the field, but this time they set about it before a ball had been bowled. The newspapers published a picture of some of the lads eating sushi when the press thought they should have been practising, some of their players made remarks about the series that were disparaging to us, and it all started gathering momentum.

For the first couple of days we took it easy in order to acclimatise. We didn't want to go at it too hard straightaway. It was going to be a long tour so we warmed up by exercising in the gym before getting down to our first net. Pretty soon after that, on 10 November, we had our first match, a one-day game against a Prime Minister's XI in Canberra, which didn't start us off as well as we'd hoped. We had enjoyed a really good net the day before the game, although the size of the Manuka Oval was a surprise. I mentioned it and Kevin Pietersen picked up on it as well. We said that we were unlikely to hit too many sixes there. It didn't seem to affect the Prime Minister's XI, though, who proceeded to smash the ball all around the park after I won the toss and decided to bowl first. I fancied chasing, rather than setting, a target and it started off well when they scored about 15 runs off the first six overs. Everything was hunky-dory up until the moment Phil Jacques came in and started hitting out. I've never seen a cricket ball hit as far and as often as he did that day. Then everyone else in their line-up followed suit – they hit eight sixes in all during the innings and this was on a very, very big ground. I don't think any of us bowled particularly badly but Sajid Mahmood bore the brunt of it, being hammered for nearly a hundred in his 10 overs. That was a tough introduction to the Ashes tour.

Afterwards, the feeling in our camp was one of apprehension. I told the lads it was a one-day game and they were fielding specialists while we had our Test squad playing, but there was no disguising the fact that they took the mickey out of us the way they played. It was bad enough being slammed all over the park but when we batted Shaun Tait came running in and bowled with real pace. In our dressing room, you could almost hear the players thinking, 'If this is only the Prime Minister's XI, what's going to happen when we play the Australian side?'

While our team was certainly inexperienced – in the First Test, none of our first six had previously played a Test match in Australia – I did feel that the Aussies had learned from their mistakes in 2005. We'd been prevaricating about who was going to be captain while they'd been preparing hard for the 2006 series, and they had really done their homework. We'd been worrying about how we were going to announce the squad and those sorts of things, while they'd been working on strategies to beat us, and they put them into effect brilliantly from the minute we stepped off the plane.

That first game was followed a few days later by a three-day warm-up match against a strong New South Wales team in Sydney. Michael Clarke, Nathan Bracken, Brett Lee, Stuart Clark, Stuart MacGill and Glenn McGrath were in the side, so they clearly weren't messing around. Once again we came up against Phil Jacques, and he scored another century against us, playing exceptionally well. Each side was allowed 13 players, which gave everyone match practice and enabled us to have a think about our team for the final warm-up match, against South Australia in Adelaide the following week.

After the game in Sydney, Geraint Jones got the nod as wicket-keeper for the start of the Test series. Chris Read had come into the Test side during the second half of the English summer, after Geraint had struggled to get runs, and did all right against Pakistan. Geraint had gone back to county cricket to try to get some runs and boost his confidence. He hadn't got as many as he would have liked, but we felt he was the right man for the First Test. I thought his wicket-keeping was under-rated. Geraint and I had enjoyed several good partnerships over the years, and we also bat well together. We seem to complement each other because we hit the ball in different areas. For instance, I have always been strong hitting straight down the ground, whereas Geraint was stronger square of the wicket. That caused problems for the opposition to try and set fields. Duncan and I had a long chat about it and decided to go with Geraint.

That decision was hard enough to make, but the squad as a whole was rocked when it became clear that Marcus was going to be flying home. Marcus had been an outstanding player for England ever since he forced his way into the team back in 2000, and I would have turned to him regularly for advice had he stayed. He had been struggling with a stress-related illness for the previous year or so, a type of homesickness and depression that totally took him over. It had ruled him out of the Champions Trophy in India, but he was passed fit for the Ashes. Of course, I knew he was struggling a little but I didn't know to what extent it was affecting him until Duncan spoke to me about it during the match in Sydney. I don't pretend to understand because it's not something I've been through myself, but my heart went out to him. Everyone liked Marcus a lot, but we all knew there was no room for sentiment, particularly against the Aussies. We also knew that Marcus would have wanted us to get on with things without him and that's exactly what we did. You can't afford to dwell on things like that, however much we felt for Marcus, because we had a Test match to prepare for in the next couple of weeks.

The game in Sydney was a great exercise for us. New South Wales batted so well, it gave all of our bowlers – including me – a decent workout, and we all performed creditably. We wanted an even spread among the bowlers, so rather than push for victory, it was important to give the spinners a run out and allow the seamers to get some overs in their legs. I bowled 15 overs in the first innings and was pleased enough with my progress to cut that down to four when they batted again. I knew I was going to have to bowl in the next game in Adelaide. You would have to play pretty badly to lose a three-day game and, equally, they are very difficult to win, but we got what we could out of it. Despite that, I noticed a feeling in the camp that we were struggling to gain any momentum before the First Test.

The key to our victory in 2005 had been the way we'd built up momentum with a run of successes achieved by a settled side. That never happened in Australia. We needed all our key players to perform for us, but we just never got going. Marcus had to go home, I was just coming back from an ankle operation and wasn't in peak form, Ashley Giles was also just coming back from injury and Simon Jones was still missing through injury. Four players who'd played a big part in winning the Ashes in 2005 were struggling to make an impact just over a year later, making our challenge that winter an even greater one. This new young team hadn't had the chance to build up a feeling of invincibility, as the 2005 team had done.

We were also saddled with unrealistic expectations from back home. A lot of people thought we would go to Australia and perform as we had in 2005 all over again, but it was never going to be that easy. We were expected to beat the best team in the world at a time when they were playing much better than we were.

The day after the Sydney game, we moved on to Adelaide for our final warm-up match against South Australia. Once again, I was pleased with the way it went, both for myself and for the team. As a bowler, I always have half an eye on the number of overs I'm bowling because I believe I've got a limited number left in my body and I want to save them for when I'm really going to need them. I could have bowled more than 18 overs in Adelaide, but I was satisfied with that. As a batsman, I'd been working hard in the nets, including with Duncan while we were in Sydney. At the start of my innings in Adelaide my feet felt like they were stuck in glue or something. They certainly weren't moving. I ground it out for a while and made a decision to bat for as long as I could because I knew time in the middle would be invaluable. Eventually, the situation improved. I ended up with 47 and had to be pleased with that.

As soon as the game was over we flew straight to Brisbane for the First Test, which was due to start on 23 November. The whole squad now seemed very calm and relaxed. Other people kept going on about the fact that we hadn't had that much preparation for the series and we'd struggle because of it, but I think most of us felt better after the South Australia game, and were happy with our form and practice thus far. In fact, we had practised very hard.

Until we arrived in Brisbane, the build-up had seemed similar to most tours, playing warm-up matches and getting ourselves right for the series ahead, but as soon as our plane touched down it became clear we were about to be part of something special. You could feel the atmosphere around the hotel and the city. A lot of English fans were in town, and for all of us, the sense of anticipation was huge. An air of excitement hung around the camp. The change in the players' mood was noticeable. The start of the Ashes was just days away, and for some members of the tour party, this would be the biggest moment of their cricketing lives so far. I remember our first practice at the Gabba. Everyone seemed suddenly to realise that this was what we were here for. This was going to be Test cricket at its toughest. Personally, the idea of leading the side out for an Ashes Test in Australia was phenomenal, but I wouldn't say I was more nervous than usual, and I was sleeping well.

We were in the fortunate position of having plenty of competition for places. Usually, when teams go on a tour, the selectors have a fair idea of their first Test line-up, but in this case we'd had a few important decisions to make during the build-up. We had already decided to go with Geraint as wicket-keeper, but we still had to decide which of the two spinners to choose for such an important game. Ashley Giles got the vote ahead of Monty Panesar for that First Test, but it was such a hard choice to make. Monty had done brilliantly the previous winter in India and throughout the summer against Sri Lanka and Pakistan, and had become a big favourite with the crowd. He had taken the wickets of some good players and was very disappointed when we decided to go with Ashley, but he hadn't been bowling well in the build-up to the Test. We were well aware that Ashley hadn't played much cricket because of the hip injury that had kept him out for most of the year, but I've always believed he was a vastly under-rated cricketer. He had done a great job for us over a number of years and was a crucial part of the 2005 Ashes line-up. Another factor was that crucial No. 8 position in the batting line-up. Ashley was a better bet there than Monty, and gave us far greater depth for the Test. We didn't think the wicket at the Gabba would offer a great deal for a spinner, and in the event Ashley was hit for around three an over, which I thought was a fantastic effort in the circumstances. He also scored over 50 runs, so I thought our selection was justified, no matter how harsh it was on Monty.

Duncan explained the reasons for our decision to Monty before the Test, and despite his disappointment, he understood completely. In fact, Monty being Monty, he worked harder and harder in the nets to try to prove us wrong, until he forced his way back into the side. It was a great attitude to see. He was always asking questions of Duncan and me to find out what he had to do to get back into the side. He worked unbelievably hard on his batting and fielding, which were obviously the weaker parts of his game, and his fielding did improve noticeably during the tour.

Once we had settled on the team, the build-up flew by until it was time to board the coach for the Gabba on the morning of the match. I still think walking out for my first Test at Lord's as captain the previous summer against Sri Lanka was one of the most special moments of my career, but I will always remember walking out with Ricky Ponting for the toss at Brisbane, albeit for different reasons. The ground wasn't full by any means, and as we approached the middle quite a few people were still coming in. I was aware of what had happened the last time England had played there, when Nasser Hussain won the toss, decided to bowl first which allowed Australia to get loads of runs on the first day. I was determined not to make the same mistake if I won the toss. The problem was they had minted a special coin to commemorate the Ashes series. One side, heads, represented the badge of England and the other, tails, represented the badge of Australia. I always call tails when I go out for the toss, but I couldn't possibly call against the badge of England could I? I had no option but to go against my usual instincts and go for heads, and what happened? It came down tails of course and I was absolutely kicking myself because I was convinced that winning the toss was going to be crucial. On a superb batting wicket, we would have to bowl extremely well to limit Australia to a decent total. As it was, the wicket remained pretty good throughout the match, but we batted poorly.

Before the start of the Test they have a tradition in Australia for both teams to line up and stand there while their respective anthems were played. I'm not anti-tradition or anything like that, but it was not what I really wanted just moments before I was due to lead the side out for the start of the Test. I'm sure it's done for the right reasons but all I wanted to do was get the team together and get out on the field and get started.

The big talking point on the first day was the first ball. We'd stressed beforehand the need to start well in order to put Australia under as much pressure as we could, because we knew it was going to be a hard first day with them batting on such a good wicket. The press had made a big thing of how important the first ball was going to be, which it is, but at the same time a poor first delivery isn't the end of the world. I've played in many matches when the first ball hasn't been great but we've gone on to get the opposition out for a low score. You can be hit for 20 in the first over, but you can still get a couple of wickets in the next over and you've got the advantage.

I'd been asked before the game who would take the first over. Matthew Hoggard had been doing it, and doing it well, but I just thought that Steve Harmison had set the tone with his first over in 2005 at Lord's when he bowled really rapidly, and I wanted him to do it again.

They tell you as a kid that if you're standing at first slip, you should watch the ball, and if you're standing at second slip, you should watch the bat. Fortunately, I've always ignored that advice and watched the ball wherever I've fielded, and it's probably just as well – otherwise I'd have been the first England captain to be carried off after the first ball of a Test! I don't know whether Steve was unusually nervous or not but the ball slipped out of his hands and instead of causing Justin Langer a problem, it flew straight to me at second slip. It's your dream for the ball to come to you at second slip on the first ball of an Ashes Test, but ideally you want it come off the edge first! I saw it come out of his hand and head straight to me, but there was no point making a fuss about it because I know Steve didn't do it on purpose. I just threw the ball on to one of the other lads as if it was completely normal. I didn't want to make a big thing of it.

I don't think Steve was the only one to be affected by nerves that first morning. Quite a few of the lads hadn't played in an Ashes series before and we had the look of a nervous team during the first hour or so in the field. I'd have been upset if they hadn't been nervous, because an Ashes series means a hell of a lot. I thought Langer and Matthew Hayden, who have played God knows how many Tests, looked nervous, too, and there were a lot more edges flying around than you would have expected in the first few overs on a good batting wicket. I'm not saying we could have had them 50 for 5 or anything like that, but it could have been slightly different if one of those edges had gone to slip instead of just wide or over, or gone to gully instead of flying past for four.

As it was, they got off to a good start. I was pleased to get Hayden's wicket, both to stop their run flow, and also because I hadn't bowled in a Test match for some time and it's always good to come back with a wicket. We bowled well in patches. One thing we'd been successful at over a period of time was bowling as a unit and I don't think we did that very well at the Gabba. We kept trying to search for wickets instead of applying pressure by keeping to the same areas. Too many of us were guilty of trying too many things instead of sticking to a plan, and that helped them to get a massive first-innings total. In hindsight, I probably waited too long before I came on to bowl. I always found it hard as captain to work out when was the best time for me to bowl, and I used to give the other lads a chance before bringing myself on. In any event, you know for a fact that whatever you do, someone else is going to have a different opinion about it, and not be shy about telling you what you should have done.

On the second day, they declared on 602 for 9, knowing we were going out to bat at the end of two long days in the field, and with the light fading. Having said that, Glenn McGrath came in with some superb bowling. He'd had a bit of stick in the press before the Test series, with comments about him being too old or over the hill. All I can say is that anyone who thought that should have tried facing him! The critics must have been people who weren't playing against him any more. We weren't under any illusions. He put the ball in an area where it was extremely hard for both left and right-handers, and he got his rewards with two wickets, leaving us struggling on 53 for 3 by the close. Next day, we were all out for 157 and he'd notched six wickets.

Australia would have been perfectly within their rights to enforce the follow-on, since the deficit was 445, but I always suspected they would bat again. Various cracks were appearing in the wicket, resulting in the odd variable bounce, and it was only going to get worse. They also had to think about McGrath, who had already bowled 23.1 overs to claim his 6 for 50. I remember when we enforced the follow-on at Trent Bridge against Australia in 2005 it very nearly cost us because the bowlers were so knackered. Michael Vaughan asked the bowlers about it at the time, but sometimes you get caught up in the moment and we all said we were eager to bowl again. It's only when you're back out there and 10 overs in that it suddenly becomes very hard indeed. It makes a massive difference if you can go back to the hotel, shake off the tiredness with a good night's sleep and go at it again the next day, so I wasn't surprised that Ponting decided to bat.

Once again, Ponting got runs, Langer got a hundred and there was a lot of talk about how Australia wanted to grind us into the dust after what happened to them in 2005. When they finally declared, we were 647 runs behind and needed to bat for the final two days to save the game, which was always going to be a big ask. The cracks in the wicket had become quite wide, but when the ball hit them, it would divert so much, the delivery didn't normally get you out. A couple disappeared down the legside, but I don't think a crack cost us a single wicket in our second innings. It was more the thought of the cracks that defeated us. I know it shouldn't be the case, but when you're going out to bat and you see these large cracks, you're always suspicious of them and are not likely to play as freely as you would on a good batting wicket on the first day of a match.

We lost three early wickets, again, but an important partnership developed between Collingwood and Pietersen. We took comfort from that, believing it would be crucial for the remainder of the series. Had we gone down without a fight it would have been a lot more difficult to recover, but those two gave us all hope with a superb stand of 148. I can't say their efforts put Australia under pressure, because they were so far in front, but to see two of our lads score runs and win a mini-battle for themselves lifted the whole dressing room and gave us all cause for optimism.

# 5

# AGONY IN ADELAIDE

My biggest concern after losing the First Test by 277 runs was our attitude out in the field – we were a little star-struck. Instead of seeing the Aussies as good players, just as capable of getting out as anyone else, some of us seemed to be regarding them as invincible. When I pointed this out to the team, the response was quite defensive, but I trusted the players' ability to bounce back in the next Test. We'd started slowly before, and did seem to have a knack for coming back hard after a heavy defeat.

Steve Bull, the team psychologist who helps us out from time to time with our mental approach and preparation, joined the tour party and we all had a chat with him about how to approach the next Test. After that, the lads requested a team meeting and it was a really honest affair. Everyone stood up and talked about their experiences in the First Test and how they felt about their own performance and that of the team. Plenty of advice was passed on and a few admissions came out, where people had struggled. It was important for players not to blame everyone else without looking at themselves, and nearly every player talked about what he'd done well and what he hadn't done so well, and where he perhaps needed help and where he could help someone else. Everyone came out of the meeting feeling as if we'd achieved something as a squad, and the especially good thing about it was that it wasn't prompted by Duncan or anyone else from the management team – it came from the lads. They realised they had not performed as well as they should have done and set about trying to do something about it. The management were at the meeting, but it was taken over by the players.

The immediate result was one of our most intense practice sessions of the tour. After his net, Kev said it was like playing in a Test match. I faced Plunkett and Harmy, who were both charging in and trying to knock my head off. All the bowlers gave the batsmen the sort of going over they were likely to receive in the middle. It was so satisfying and back at the hotel everyone involved was absolutely buzzing.

After losing the toss in Brisbane, I was very tempted to change my call in Adelaide, which is notoriously a batter's paradise and then traditionally helps out spinners on the final day. We obviously didn't want to be facing Shane Warne on a turning pitch, and I was still in two minds about what to do as I walked out for the call. On the way through the seated area, I spied someone I knew among the spectators – David, a huge Lancashire fan, who stays with his niece in Adelaide every year.

'What do you think I should call, David?' I asked him.

'Heads,' he replied, which made up my mind.

I kept thinking to myself that I couldn't walk back into the dressing room having called tails if it comes down heads. So I called heads, heads it was and I was very relieved. The Barmy Army gave huge cheers as soon as it was announced, and celebrated like we'd already won the Test – but we knew we still had to go out there and bat well.

We made a solid start. Ian Bell continued the good form he'd shown from the beginning of the tour with a solid 60, but the reason we were able to post a big total was due to Paul Collingwood at No. 4. In county cricket, when Paul gets a good score, he tends to go on and make it into a really big innings. He had already got a couple of 90s in his Test career, and this time he kept going to score a superb double hundred, England's first for a couple of years. It came at such a good time for us after what had happened in Brisbane. I was delighted for Colly, because he'd worked so hard and waited a long time to get his Test spot. He'd battled to make that No. 4 slot his own, working out how best to score runs in that position and tailoring his game for it. He's very good at adapting. This was his reward for all that.

Kevin also produced a stunning innings, turning in a wonderful 158. What I most liked about it was his determination. After he got to a hundred, he just wasn't prepared to stop. I think he took between half an hour and forty-five minutes to get from 100 to 110. That's what singles out the great players from the good ones. Mohammad Yousuf, Brian Lara, Ricky Ponting, Shivnarine Chanderpaul and Inzamam-ul-Haq, for instance, keep going and produce big innings, and Kevin is capable of doing that as well. When he's on good form, whipping the ball through the legside, he makes it look easy. His natural talent is obvious to everyone who watches him, but he also has a strong work ethic. When he played for Natal as an off-spinner and batted down the order, he had to figure out a technique for himself. That's the basis of his style, which is unique!

Those two innings gave the team belief. We were starting to think, 'Maybe we can do something here.' Plenty of people were expecting us to be beaten but we put ourselves into a competitive position.

We were criticised for scoring slowly but it was important to concentrate on running up a decent total. When to declare became an issue, and while I was batting Monty kept coming on and off with drinks, new gloves and messages from the dressing room. Our initial plan was to declare at around 570, but I thought our eventual score of 551 for 6 was worth more than it looked because of the wicket.

I took the new ball at the end of that second day instead of giving it to Harmy, because I thought I should do for those few overs. It wasn't meant as any sort of slight. Our efforts to take a quick wicket were rewarded when Langer flashed at one of my deliveries and edged to gully. Another wicket before the close would have been great, but we were happy with our position overnight.

That evening, when I did a question and answer session with David Lloyd, the former Lancashire and England coach, I was asked how I thought the Test was going to go. I replied immediately that if we were going to win, it would have to be in the last session of the last day. In other words, it was going to be hard-fought. I knew it wasn't going to be the sort of game where you bowl the opposition out for 220, then bowl them out again when they follow on and win on the fourth day. We were going to have to sit in, set fields that were slightly different from what might have been expected, and try to make the batsmen think.

I tried putting fielders on the drive and setting a slip cordon wide and scattered, and I thought we did well. Matthew Hoggard was quite outstanding in their first innings. Unless you were there, it's impossible to realise just how fierce the wind was. He bowled nearly all of his 42 overs into it and still came away with seven wickets. I couldn't praise him enough for the way he bowled in that Test. Their innings was very similar to our innings. We took three early wickets and then a big fifth-wicket partnership developed between Ponting and Mike Hussey. The big moment that everyone remembers is Ponting being dropped on 35 off Hoggy. We had put Giles out there for the pull, because there was a theory that when Ponting plays that shot he always falls short of the boundary. This one was strange. When he hit it, the ball seemed to keep going and didn't look like it was going to drop. It flew straight to Ashley, who failed to take the chance, but it wasn't a regulation catch. It wasn't like an underarm throw that you would expect anyone to catch – it was a difficult one and Ashley was just the man to be underneath it because he has an incredibly good pair of hands. Things like that happen in cricket and as a team it's important to get over them and get on with the next ball. Unfortunately, the people you drop rarely get out next ball, and Ponting went on to make 142.

Even so, we still felt we were in the game, once Hoggy came back with the new ball to get Ponting and Hussey and leave us bowling at Michael Clarke and Adam Gilchrist at the end of the day. In the morning session, Gilchrist hit a couple that bounced just short of fielders. I was bowling in areas that made it uncomfortable for him, but I could have done with a bit more bounce from the wicket. A couple fell short, but I was happy with the way I was bowling, and accepted that he was going to hit some great shots and blaze me through the covers every now and then. I just felt this was the way to get him out.

The big secret to Australia's success during that series was that there was always someone who could do what was necessary, and on this occasion it was Michael Clarke. His partnership with Warne took them to within reach of our total. We were criticised for sticking with the same team and putting Giles in at No. 8, but look how important Warne was to them batting at No. 8 and scoring 43. We were happy to get them out for 513 and claim a 38-run lead, but it was a tricky one because, in the time left, only two results were then possible – a draw or an Australian win. By the end of the fourth day, we had lost just one wicket and the result was by no means a foregone conclusion. However, to bat them out of the game, we could not give them more than a session to chase the runs, and we didn't do it well enough.

Our plan was to bat for as long as we could, and see where we were then. If we were in a position to declare and put Australia under pressure, so much the better. It was always going to be very difficult, but two outstanding spells of bowling that morning from Shane Warne and Brett Lee didn't help. Warne bowled superbly into the rough, and our scoring options were greatly reduced with him bowling like that at one end and Brett Lee tearing in at the other, reverse swinging it at 90mph on a last-day pitch. When the ball starts reverse swinging, it's great for the bowler because an incoming batsman has no chance to play himself in. The wicket at Adelaide was especially suited to reverse swinging and Brett got the best out of it, and, of course, Ponting set his field to cut off runs, unless you were prepared to take a risk. In that situation, the incoming batsman's plan has to be to get through the first few overs, assuming you don't receive a ball with your name on it, and hope the conditions and the bowling ease enough to let you score. By not scoring in those tough batting conditions, we played into their hands. We needed to be making progress but we went nowhere, and in many ways the tone was set. We scored at less than one run an over, which left Australia needing a couple of wickets to get back in the game, and that's what happened. We just couldn't get out of our negative mindset, and from being in a position of strength, with the dressing room buoyant after Collingwood's innings, the mood changed. All of a sudden, insecurities and doubts came rushing in, the dressing room was full of nervous people and we became fragile, so the inevitable happened. We were bowled out for 129 after starting the day on 59 for 1.

That left us up against it because all Australia needed was 168 in 36 overs. They would have to attack us to score those runs, though, and a few early wickets would put them under pressure. From the second ball, Justin Langer showed us what he was going to do by smashing Hoggy through midwicket for four. When the batsmen are setting out like that, it forces you to set your field back instead of putting pressure on them with closer infielding, but the way they were playing also kept us in the game, and we did manage to take a couple of early wickets to leave them on 33 for 2.

In that game, particularly in the second innings, the problems faced by the batsmen were almost the reverse of what was usual. Normally, you want to face the ball once it gets a bit older, but at Adelaide the best time to bat was against the new ball, so the first 20 overs of their innings became a case of damage limitation – try to restrict their scoring options and get a few wickets to put them under pressure for when it became harder to score. Unfortunately, by the time we got to that stage, the game had gone. Ponting and Hussey batted well together and when the ball became softer at around the 20-over mark, they had already progressed to 116 for 2. Hussey was punching the air every time he hit a boundary, which was starting to wind me up. One of the most frustrating things about Australia's victory chase was that the ball had just started to reverse swing as they won. If we'd been able to bowl with that ball from the first delivery, I'd have fancied our chances, but instead it was Australia who were dancing around the pitch, celebrating their victory.

I don't think I've ever felt as low about a defeat as I did that day. I've had various low points in my career, but that really hurt. We'd worked so hard and to lose like that was heartbreaking. The people who accused of us of not caring were not there in the dressing room to see just how much it hurt us all. We sat around, some stunned, others relieved the day was over. The beers came out in the end and a few of us went over and had a few drinks with the Aussies in their dressing room. We were criticised for staying there too long, but I don't think we overdid it. Even when we were socialising with them, though, I could see some of our players mentally comparing themselves to their opposite number in the Australian team and thinking, 'I'm not as good as this fella.' In my mind, we had just experienced the flipside of our great win at Edgbaston in the Second Test of the 2005 Ashes. If they'd got those few runs then to win the game rather than losing by two runs, I'm sure the momentum could have carried them to a 5–0 win.

Perhaps the hardest thing for me immediately after that defeat was to explain it all in a press conference. As captain, you always have to speak to the press after a match, win or lose. I'd experienced a losing press conference before, after we'd been beaten by Sri Lanka at Trent Bridge the previous summer, but this was different. I was totally shattered. I just tried to be honest, but it was a horrible time. There was a tear in my eye when I sat in the dressing room beforehand, and several people have told me since that they'd never seen me so upset, and they were probably right. There wasn't a lot I could say. We'd played well for four and a half days, and an hour and a half's play had cost us the Test.

While we were in total shock, the suddenness of our defeat seemed to send everyone else into some sort of frenzy. Press, fans, everyone was looking for someone to blame. We got a lot of stick, and some of it may have been deserved, but some of the things that were written were quite hard to take, especially the accusation of not caring. That's a terrible thing to say about an international sportsman. There wasn't a player in the dressing room who didn't give his all during that Test and to accuse us of not caring was very harsh. I took the loss personally, but I wasn't hurting any more than anybody else in the dressing room – it was a collective feeling of hurt and disappointment.

In the media, debate raged about selection and my relationship with Duncan. Everything was a talking point. There was even one story about Harmy and I falling out – we've never fallen out in our lives and I can't imagine we ever would. The way we talk to each other in public might sometimes be construed as arguing but that's just the way we are with each other. We have a lot of banter.

I was lucky to have Harmy on that tour because, as a senior player and a friend, he was one of the few people I could turn to for help and advice. After that defeat, the players tended to retreat into themselves, which is normal behaviour for most professional sportsmen in those circumstances, but I couldn't do that as captain and there was a little bit of whispering among the players.

# 6

# FEELING THE PAIN

It was my birthday the day after we'd lost in Adelaide. I tried at least to look excited about my cards and presents, but I just wasn't in the mood. Next day we flew to Perth, I had a nice birthday lunch with Rachael and tried, unsuccessfully, to forget about it all. In the evening, we had a date with Adam Hollioake. I got to know Adam through playing with his brother Ben as a youngster. Adam had settled in Perth after retiring from playing county cricket with Surrey. We were going to go out, but had a few drinks in the hotel bar instead – it was good to catch up with someone I hadn't seen for some time and take my mind off the last few days. The whole squad had taken a knock with the defeat in the Second Test and were a bit subdued in training over the next couple of days. I include myself in that because I know I wasn't at my best.

However, the way the itinerary worked gave some of us a chance to have a few days off. I spent a lot of the time with Rachael and some on my own, just thinking and beating myself up over the match in Adelaide. Truth to tell, I was in a bit of a muddle and didn't really know how to get out of it. I was questioning myself and my own ability, and I was questioning the team. I had a few drinks and then a few more, but I knew that wasn't a way out. It was a release, though. For a few hours, all the pressure was taken off. It didn't matter that we were 2–0 down going into the Third Test, it didn't matter that the team seemed to be breaking into factions, and it didn't matter that I was finding it hard to hold them together. Of course, when I woke up the following morning with a thick head, not only were all the problems still there, but they seemed ten times worse. The only way out of it that I could see was for one of us to do something really special in the next Test, but I didn't think anyone was playing well enough to be able to do that. On top of all that, my ankle was troubling me. In fact, I had several jabs for the pain during the trip.

I'm not very good at speaking up in situations where I need help, and that is probably a weakness of mine. I tend to go into my shell and try to deal with it all myself, which is probably the worst way of handling any situation, but on the other hand I do get on with it and have a go. Looking back, I'd love to say I'd handle it all differently now, but that's an easy thing to say. The only way I could have done anything differently would have been by not being captain. The most influential relationship in any team is the one between the coach and the captain, and we have seen what can happen when that doesn't work with Kev and Peter Moores. Nasser Hussain and Duncan aren't my favourite people in the world but they had a really good relationship and because of that the team worked. It was the same with Michael Vaughan and Duncan, who worked well together, but Duncan and I couldn't emulate that, although our relationship wasn't all bad. When I was playing well and taking wickets, it would be quite good, but when I was struggling, our relationship altered. This started well before I was appointed captain. Perhaps I thought it would change, but I've always said I don't get everything right – I would never profess to do that.

Several of the lads played for the Academy in a one-day game at Lilac Hill, near Perth. Adam Hollioake and Alec Stewart were also in the side. Then we had a two-day match against Western Australia at the WACA, which was useful because the lads were able to assess the conditions before the Third Test began on 14 December. As a team, we talked about the history we had created over the previous few years. We'd beaten the West Indies for the first time in years, won in South Africa, won the Ashes – they were all achievements to be proud of. We regarded Perth as an opportunity to add to that history, a Test in isolation rather than part of the series. If we could win this one, the rest could look after itself.

I was sent for a scan to make sure the discomfort I was feeling in my ankle was nothing serious. It was showing signs of troubling me in the way it had the previous summer, which of course led to another operation. I was feeling the same sort of discomfort in the same area, but not to the same degree. Previously, it had prevented me from bowling but this time I could still bowl, although not as quickly as I'd have liked. I didn't bowl much in the nets in the build-up to the Third Test, but that didn't worry me. I hadn't been happy with my performance with the bat and so I'd been working hard on that in the nets without improving as much as I wanted to, which was very frustrating. Everyone always says that the harder you work the better you'll get, so you work and work, but sometimes, no matter how hard you work, there's no real improvement. Some lads from the Academy came to bowl at us, which we appreciated because it's always good to have some fresh faces around. I'd scored a 30-odd in the previous two Tests but nothing more than that, so I went into the Third Test determined to be more aggressive to see what happened. In the first innings I nicked one, so in the second I decided just to have a go.

Monty played his first match of the series in Perth. There was a lot of talk about him back at home and why he hadn't been picked. We went with Ashley to begin with because he was a good, experienced player, but we thought Perth was a good time for a change, so Monty came in and Saj replaced Jimmy Anderson. We couldn't carry on as we had done in the previous two Tests. We had to try something different, and by mid-afternoon on the first day it seemed to have done the trick. To have bowled Australia out for 244 on the first day after they won the toss was an outstanding effort. Harmy bowled particularly well for his four wickets and I was really pleased for him after all the effort he had put in with coach Kevin Shine in the nets to get his rhythm and consistency right.

Of course, Monty came in and got a five-wicket haul straightaway. Having left him out of the first two Tests, I suppose it was inevitable he would do well. I always expected him to come in with a point to prove, but he exceeded everyone's expectations with his performance on that first day. We were all delighted for him – his enthusiasm is totally infectious. He was quite nervous to start with, but he was bowling into a stiff wind, which gave him the opportunity to flight the ball. He kept it tight initially, and probably didn't get his wickets with his best deliveries, but because he'd built up the pressure, he frustrated the batsmen. That contrasted with my performance. I wasn't happy at all with the way I bowled during that first innings. The ankle wasn't ideal, but I wasn't going to use that as an excuse. I didn't bowl as well as I can do.

We were aiming for a half-decent score of 350 or 400 in our first innings to put us in control, but we faced a dangerous 14 overs before the close. Periods like that are never easy to negotiate, so although we finished on 51 for 2, I thought we were doing all right. Next day, we didn't get off to the best of starts. Collingwood fell to the twentieth ball of the day when he pushed McGrath to gully, and Strauss got a bad decision – given out caught behind when it didn't look like he'd hit the ball.

After that, we started losing wickets and Australia were on a roll again. My dismissal was a classic example. I wasn't playing too badly against Brett Lee at one end, so Australia brought on Andrew Symonds to bowl seam up, and he started swinging it. I've played with Symo at Lancashire and I know he's not the worst bowler around by any means, but I must have relaxed a bit because I edged him to slip in one of his early overs –

fortunately, he's very good about things like that, and didn't mention it that often every time I saw him for the rest of the series! He got Geraint Jones in his next over and we were grateful for the way the tail batted to get us to within 29 runs of Australia's total.

Hoggy bowled Langer with the first ball of Australia's second innings and, as usual when things like that happen, we hoped we could get on a roll. Throughout the series, passages of play occurred that you knew would be crucial to the outcome of the match, and this was one of them. They had a slender first-innings lead and had lost their opener to the first ball of their second innings – we needed someone to pull something out of the bag. We were usually very good at that, but during this series, all too often Australia took the initiative. On this occasion, Ponting and Hayden combined in a superb partnership and took the game away from us.

Australia's batsmen were all in form and they really showed it in this innings. Gilchrist, for instance, arrived at the crease on a pair and we almost got him early in his innings when he edged just past Bell, and after that he just exploded. Some of his shots were unbelievable. For a couple of sixes that he hit off Monty he came down the wicket, didn't quite get there but the ball still flew into the stand somewhere. It helped that he came out to bat with Australia already on 365 for 5, but there was no bowling at him on that day. Everything he tried seemed to come off. Monty was bowling into the wind, so those shots may have been wind-assisted, but I've seen Gilchrist hit the ball a long way on days when there was no wind at all. It wasn't as if he hit all his runs from that end, either – he was hitting as well from both ends. We didn't know it at the time, but his century off 57 balls was the joint-fastest in Test history.

Part of the problem was that we didn't get the swing in Australia that we had been able to get in England during 2005. There probably isn't as much help in the wickets, either, so bowlers just try to bore you into making mistakes, continuously putting the ball in the same place to wear you down. McGrath has done that for years and Stuart Clark did a similar job throughout the series. It's a lot easier, of course, when you've got the world's greatest leg-spinner at the other end.

When a batsman is playing as Gilchrist was that day, you've just got to hope he misses one, or spoons one up in the air, sooner rather than later. His hitting helped Australia put on 162 in just 20 overs, and, as often happens when you get big stands like that, we lost an early wicket when they declared and gave us six overs to negotiate before the close.

Momentum plays a big part in cricket and the momentum was definitely with Australia. The crowd were behind them, and the people on their balcony were buoyant, having watched Gilchrist's innings. It gave their whole team a lift. When we came out to bat for those few overs before the close, we got just what we didn't need – a dodgy lbw decision. In the very first over, Strauss fell to Brett Lee, which summed up the luck he was having with decisions during that tour. We finished on 19 for 1 and needed a good partnership to give us any chance of saving the Test.

Bell and Cook answered that particular call, batting superbly to take us past lunch on the fourth day and build a 170-run partnership. That stand should have set the tone for our innings, but we were unable to continue their good work and, just before the close, McGrath put us in trouble again. He was given the second new ball and claimed two wickets in three balls – Cook caught behind and Hoggy, our nightwatchman, bowled two balls later. I had a feeling when Hoggy walked out to bat that I would be having a crack that night and so it proved. Once again, one of those crucial periods of play had been won by Australia. If we had finished that session two or three down with one day to go, I think we'd have fancied our chances of winning on the final day, but those two late wickets were a killer.

At the start of the innings we were chasing 557 to win, which would have been a world Test record had we achieved it. It may have sounded like mission impossible against Australia, playing as well as they were, but as soon as we went five down overnight, I knew our one chance of avoiding defeat was to go for it. The way I was playing I wasn't going to be able to bat all day to save the game, so the only other option was to go for a win. We started the final day needing 292 to win and the only way we were going to achieve that was for Kev and I to put together a big partnership. The pitch was still good, even if it was spinning a bit. I was a bit scratchy at first, but I felt better the longer I stayed at the crease, and I started to play a few shots just to get the adrenalin pumping. Kev looked pretty solid at the other end and if we could have stayed together a little longer, who knows what would have happened – the Australians may have got a little twitchy and nervous. I had been seeing the ball well during my previous innings in the series but I just hadn't been able to hit it. This time, I'd been connecting with a few, but Warne drifted one in shortly before lunch, it got underneath me and he bowled me with a yorker.

After that, the tail were blown away and we were nine down by lunch. I particularly felt for Geraint, who was run out by Ponting as he waited to discover the outcome of an lbw appeal from Warne. That dismissal completed Geraint's pair for the match and it was obvious how low he was about it. It was a bizarre dismissal and probably one that shouldn't happen at that level, but that's sport. He'd never had a duck for England before that Test and ended up with a pair of them. I went to speak to him on the balcony afterwards. Every one of us in that dressing room had been in a similar situation and it's a terrible feeling. You think that you've let the team down and start doubting your own ability. I tried to reassure him.

Shortly after lunch the match ended and we'd lost the Ashes it had taken us so long to regain – 16 years and 142 days I read later. It had taken Australia just 463 days to win them back. The real impact of the loss didn't start to sink in until the next day, and it wasn't a nice feeling. My disappointment was only partly lifted by the news that there was nothing seriously wrong with my ankle. I'd been for yet another scan, because I'd been getting quite worried about it and had bowled just 19 overs during Australia's second innings in Perth.

Having just lost the Ashes, the last thing I needed was the team turning against me, so I wasn't best pleased to hear that Sajid Mahmood, my Lancashire team-mate, had written a column in a newspaper saying I hadn't had enough faith in him. I get on very well with Saj and I think he's a fine bowler, but at that point I felt that his natural ability had been coached out of him. He was getting a bit of tap and he wasn't bowling very well, so I asked him what was happening. He told me he couldn't find his solid base, which is one of those coaching phrases that just confuses the hell out of me. It's something to do with your stance while bowling. I asked Saj if there was any chance of him locating it that day and he didn't know, so I took him off. After that, Saj did his piece in the paper and I think he was a bit embarrassed about it when it came out. I can't imagine it was written the way Saj meant it to be, but I didn't approach him about it and waited for him to come to me instead, which he did do eventually. He came over to me in the dressing room and said, 'About that thing in the paper, I didn't say that.' That was it, done and dusted as far as I was concerned. I like Saj too much to fall out with him over something like that, and besides, I had bigger worries.

Everyone always goes on about what good mates we all were in the 2005 team, but in reality we had our ups and downs as much as any other team. We would get up in the morning, go to the ground, play aggressive cricket together and then go home at night. Some members of that side were really good mates and others didn't get on as well. It was just the same as in any other work situation. If you ask people who work in an office about their colleagues, I'm sure they would say they get on with some people better than others. It was no different in the 2005 side. When you put a team together, the one thing those people have in common is playing cricket, and not necessarily much else. It's a lot easier for everyone to get on if you're successful because everyone is happy, but as soon as you start losing regularly, like we did on the 2006 Ashes tour, the cracks start appearing.

In Australia, it showed how fragile we were. Relationships were definitely becoming strained, which I suppose is only natural given the situation we were in, but the most upsetting thing for me was how few people offered to help. Over the years, I have tried to help everyone who has come into the side in any way I could – even if it was just trying to make them feel welcome – because I remember how tough it is to enter the dressing room for the first time. I needed their help more than ever at this time. It was obvious I was struggling and what my state of mind was. They could see how difficult I was finding leading England in an Ashes series in Australia and what it was doing to me on and off the field. I needed an arm around my shoulder or a few nice words from someone. Even someone standing up in a team meeting and giving me a bit of backing would have been a start. Harmy was great and I knew I could rely on him, but a bit of extra support would have been nice. I felt massively isolated. As a team, we needed a boost to get us through those final two Tests and I didn't seem able to provide it. My form still wasn't great, either, and that made me feel worse as we moved to Melbourne for the Fourth Test.

# 7

# DOOM AND GLOOM AT CHRISTMAS

In Melbourne, we had four or five days without any cricket, but still trained three or four times to keep in shape for the Boxing Day Test. After losing the Ashes, I don't think any of us were exactly full of the joys of the festive period, despite having time off to be with our families, who had come out to join us. Everywhere you went people were talking about the cricket, so it was impossible to escape the pressures. We were staying in some horrendous apartments that had been chosen especially to make the families feel more at home than they might have done in a hotel. The rooms were dark and dingy and although we tried to lighten the spirit by putting up Christmas decorations, it didn't really work. Normally, with Mum and Dad and my family around me I'm the life and soul of the party, but not this time. I tried to put a front on for the time we were together, but I don't suppose I fooled anyone.

Before Christmas, we had yet more team meetings and kept going through the analysis of their batters and bowlers to try to find a weakness. It was all very monotonous. There are only so many times you can talk about the need to bowl consistently on an off-stump line, trying to get their batsmen to nick off and not bowling short and wide. The meetings weren't doing anything to bring the team any closer.

I was thinking about it all the time, trying to come up with ways to stop Australia winning again and to make us more competitive, and I suppose it all came to a head at Christmas. We ate together as a squad with our families. The food was nice and some people were trying to get into the Christmas spirit, but there weren't any laughs and it was a bit of a false atmosphere. The whole day seemed very strange, and it didn't help that I was feeling depressed about the evening before. Mum and Dad, my brother Chris and I had toasted Christmas Eve, and I ended up getting a bit emotional and apologising to Mum and Dad for letting them down, which upset my dad particularly. I explained I was giving my all and doing my best, but it was a terrible moment both for me and my parents. That was one of the toughest moments of a very tough tour.

The build-up to the Boxing Day Test in Melbourne had been dominated by announcements from Warne and McGrath that they were retiring from Test cricket at the end of the Ashes series. For Warne in particular, the Melbourne Test was a special one on his home ground, and everyone was focusing on the retirements. Looking back now, I should have made an announcement of my own and stepped down as captain, because I wasn't happy and the team weren't happy. I'm most effective as a player when I'm enjoying my cricket, and in Melbourne I couldn't have been further from that. I may not have shown it out on the pitch – and I still kept running in and trying my best for England – but inside I was racked with self-doubt and my confidence was at an all-time low. No matter how big a personality or sportsman you are, I can guarantee there are times when you just don't know what to do or how to get out of your rut, and I was at that stage.

The Boxing Day Test has always been regarded as a big event in Australia, attracting enormous crowds to that huge stadium, and I was desperate for us to put on a show. England fans had spent a lot of money to come all that way to see us play and I didn't want to let them down. I'd read and heard a lot about playing at the MCG on Boxing Day and had high expectations of what it would be like, but it didn't really live up to them. The ground might even be too big. It was quite a strange atmosphere to play in, almost eerie. I'm a bit of a traditionalist when it comes to cricket grounds and I like a pavilion and a couple of stands, so the MCG was a disappointment in that respect. It just wasn't what I expected it to be.

Bearing in mind how I was feeling, it was quite ironic that I won the toss, because it was the one toss I really didn't want to win, and I wasn't sure what to do. The wicket held a little bit for the bowlers, but I thought that after the first couple of hours, it might well flatten out and enable us to post a competitive first-innings total. I knew it would be tough at the start of the game, but I thought that would even itself out by us not having to bat last on a wearing wicket. It was also a drop-in wicket – one that's put down shortly before the Test – so we weren't able to study how previous games had gone at the MCG on that wicket. I think we all expected it to behave like the one we'd batted on in Christchurch, New Zealand, a few years earlier, which did a lot early on and then flattened out and was good for batting. On that basis, I decided to bat first.

The wicket did a bit, then it rained and we played in constant drizzle for a while. Every time we thought it was going to flatten out, it rained again to liven up conditions, so in that respect we were unlucky. If I was presented with the same pitch again, I think I would still bat first, because even though we were bowled out for 159, we had them 84 for 5 in reply and were right back in the game. I knew it would be a difficult decision when I went out to look at the pitch before the start of play. Normally, quite a few of the people who congregate out in the middle, such as Geoff Boycott, Ian Botham and various other people, offer advice and suggest whether to bat or bowl, but it was noticeable on this occasion that nobody gave me any tips on what I should do. Of course, afterwards several popped up to say we should have bowled first, but I don't remember them saying that beforehand.

We lost a couple of early wickets but recovered to reach 101 for 2, and if we could have made 250 from there, it may well have made all the difference on that wicket. Shane Warne bowled superbly, probably as well as I've ever seen him bowl in my time of playing against him. He was spinning it out of the damp, really fizzing it and making it very difficult to bat against him. He gave the batsman virtually no options and just kept nagging away until you made a mistake. It was a brilliant exhibition of bowling from a brilliant bowler.

We had decided to make a change with Chris Read coming in for Geraint, who had clearly been struggling with the bat in the first three Tests, but it failed to stop our habit of collapsing. On this occasion, we lost eight wickets for 58 runs and when you do that against any opposition you are always going to be struggling, never mind against that Australia side. It was very hard to understand how and why this trend had started after several years when we showed great character by scoring useful lower-order runs. Of course, it's not easy coming out to bat against Australia. From the very first ball they come at you. Whether it's Warne or Brett Lee, it's very hard to get through that first half-hour to an hour. Once you're settled, it gets easier to find the gaps and score runs, but you have to get through the great pressure of those first few overs.

We had lost both Cook and Bell early and everyone was wondering who was going to be Shane Warne's 700th victim. Warne started the Test needing just one wicket to reach the milestone and no one wanted to be the one to help him, to avoid the inevitable press follow-up as much as anything. Strauss was the unlucky one, despite playing well. He had played and missed a few times but he told us later he didn't know how he'd missed the final one. That's often the way when you're facing Warney. All I know is that, as the next man in, I'd never had an ovation like that before, when going in to bat!

Things started to happen for us when we took the field, and we reduced them to 48 for 2 overnight, but we could have been in an even better situation. When you're in that position, chasing the game, you need everything to go right for you. Monty had a couple of close shaves with appeals and I had a good shout against Ponting, but they weren't given – these are the things you need to go for you and it just wasn't happening for us. The whole team were getting very frustrated by it. Normally, we're good at accepting decisions, but on that day I think we all felt enough was enough. As it was, we managed to keep our tempers intact, but I was told afterwards that the cameras had picked me up and kept focusing on me, but I wasn't bothered – I was that annoyed I didn't care.

By the end of the day, they could easily have been 48 for 4 or 5, but I was proud of the way we got ourselves back into it the following morning, reducing them to 84 for 5 before Symonds came in under a fair bit of pressure. He had been recalled to the side as a replacement for Damien Martyn, who retired in mid-series, and his plan seemed to be to go for it. The way we handled that attracted a fair amount of comment. People said I should have done this or that, but the longer I was captain the more I realised that I was going to be criticised no matter what I did. Symonds played a few shots that came off for him and he had a bit of luck with a couple of decisions. We didn't help ourselves by not taking our chances in the field, but by the time Symonds and Hayden had put on 279 we were staring down the barrel. The new ball was coming up, so we were trying to get through the overs as quickly as possible, and they were trying to delay it by the way they were playing. I tried Paul Collingwood, I tried Kevin Pietersen, I tried everything, but the Australian pair kept hitting their shots and we weren't able to finish them off until the following morning.

When we went out to bat in that second innings, we approached it by taking the scoreboard out of the equation completely. We decided to concentrate on batting as well as we could, and to ignore the fact we were a long way behind. It was better not to think about how many runs we needed to stay in the game or for how long we needed to bat, and we made a good start, just before lunch. However, yet another way in which the Australians differed from us in that series was that all their bowlers were on song at the same time, so they bowled well as a group. It was strange, almost like we were playing on two different wickets. Batting against Warne, Clark, McGrath and Lee was incredibly hard. Any side at the top of their game is a tough proposition, I tried everything, but Australia during that series were at a different level again. Ultimately, to win the series, we all had to play well at the same time and it just didn't happen.

It was during the Melbourne Test that our bowling plans for the Australian batsmen went missing. I wasn't angry because at that point it was probably the funniest thing I'd heard in six weeks. The way people were talking you'd have thought someone had come into the dressing room and nicked the crown jewels. I wouldn't have minded if our strategies had been brilliantly successful, but here we were playing in the Fourth Test, already 3–0 down, and people were worried it would wreck the rest of the series for us. I think Matthew Hayden probably already had a good idea we were trying to get him to nick off, or we might try to get him lbw with a ball that swung back into him, without seeing our plans. I'm sure Shane Warne was aware we were going to bowl a few bouncers at him and hit him on the hand – it wasn't rocket science!

Believe it or not, there was a whole inquest into how the plans had gone missing, and it was amazing to listen to people trying to assign blame. These things are pinned up all around the dressing room, and what with all the coming and going, it wouldn't have been difficult for anyone to get their hands on them. To be honest, if I'd been in the Australian dressing room, I wouldn't have admitted having them. I'd have probably laughed, or said something like, 'We've got your plans and they're not working, mate!' We've all heard stories about rugby and football teams spying on each other at World Cups, or photographing training sessions, but this wasn't in that league. Losing those plans was not the reason we lost the Ashes 5–0, and I felt we had far bigger worries to concentrate on.

We ended up losing inside three days at Melbourne. Some mates who were renting a house at Palm Beach, about an hour outside Sydney, had been going to come over to watch the match, but I told them not to bother. I told them that Melbourne's cold and it never stops raining – just like Birmingham! – and they'd be better off staying on the beach. It turned out I was right, because I'm sure none of the England fans in Melbourne enjoyed watching us lose in two and a half days.

We travelled to Sydney for the final Test and the media made a big issue about us not celebrating the New Year together as a team. Why would we want to do that? We'd hardly spent an evening together during the rest of the tour, so why would New Year's Eve be any different? I told the lads to do what they wanted. I'd flown out everyone who had worked on my benefit committee the previous year and we had a great night on a boat in Sydney harbour. Neil Fairbrother and his family were there, Paul Beck, Mike Summerbee and my brother Chris. It felt good to be among friends I hadn't seen for a while. When they arrived, there was an element of pussy-footing around until they saw where my head was, but they soon relaxed and it was back to normal again with the old banter. Harmy, Jimmy Anderson and Geraint Jones came, too, and I think everyone enjoyed it. We watched the fireworks and just for a few hours it felt like I wasn't on this tour from hell. I was fortunate that Rachael had been around for those first six weeks because God knows what would have happened if she hadn't been there. Anyone who criticises the WAGS being on tour and distracting the players doesn't know what it's like when times get tough. Speaking personally, Rachael kept me sane during that tour.

We had one last chance to redeem ourselves in front of all the England fans who were in Sydney for the New Year, and the team showed real determination to play well. We didn't want to be beaten 5–0. The build-up to the game was dominated by Warne's and McGrath's retirements and the news that Justin Langer, too, was retiring after this Test, which made us even more wary of them because we knew they'd all want to finish on a high.

It was a good wicket – seamed around a little with the new ball but nothing too difficult. To be bowled out for 291 was very disappointing because on that wicket we'd hoped to get 400 or more to put some pressure on Australia. I was batting all right, and stayed with the tail to some effect, but once Harmy went, I took it on a bit more. I think the first shot I played in anger was the one I got out to. They had the field spread and I came down the wicket to give myself a bit of room, and was unlucky. I got an edge, which most of the time would have gone over the slips for four, but I edged it finer than I'd hoped and it went behind instead. I went for 89. We knew we would have to bowl them out for somewhere near our score and try to catch up on a last-day pitch when we came to bowl at them again. Behind on the first innings by 102 runs, we slipped to 118 for 5 before the end of the third day, with McGrath claiming a couple of wickets, and were eventually bowled out for 147. That left them 46 to win, and they were never likely to mess that up.

We gave Justin a guard of honour as he walked out for his final Test innings. Hayden tried to gatecrash it, so we dispersed very quickly. It was amazing once they got out to the middle. There were these two Australian heroes, two big mates who had played all that cricket together, and Hayden's welling up and almost starting to cry. I was thinking, 'What's going on here?' A big soft lad starting to cry in the middle of a match because his mate was retiring? Can you imagine me running in to bowl with tears in my eyes when Harmy announces his retirement? I might shake his hand and say well done, but I think that would be about it. Justin thanked me for the guard of honour and asked if there was any chance of a few easy runs. Can't blame him for trying! 'No mate,' I said. 'We're going to bomb you.' And we did, for one last time. It didn't have much effect, though, because they reached their target inside 11 overs and began to celebrate their 5–0 victory, their first whitewash in an Ashes series since 1920–21.

Some people said they went over the top, but just as we had at The Oval in 2005, they had earned the right to celebrate. The after-match presentations seemed to go on forever. In Australia, you don't get interviewed as you do in England, you have to make a speech, which came as news to me. I just got up there and winged it because I didn't have anything prepared. I thanked the fans, I thanked the 20,000 Australians who'd been calling me something rotten for the past four days, and I thanked Ricky Ponting and his lads for pulling our pants down!

Then I had a couple of days off, staying with my mates at Palm Beach. My brother Chris came too, and I hired a limo to take us – didn't deserve to travel in such style, but I was past caring. It was nice to get away. We had a lovely barbecue and went down to nearby restaurants. I had a good, long chat with Chris and felt a tremendous release of pressure. Just as I did with Mum and Dad on Christmas Eve, I broke down in tears. I think it was a release of everything that happened. I was so relieved my spell as captain was over and I could return to the ranks. Vaughan was back fit again and ready to the lead the side. I could have happily stayed in Palm Beach for a few weeks

– it was such a release. The Aussies we bumped into while we were out and about seemed a lot friendlier towards me now the Ashes series was over. They were obviously happy to have stuffed the Poms, but I got some pats on the back and a few people wanted to shake my hand – maybe that speech I gave at Sydney helped. Everyone was complimenting me on it, but to this day I'm not sure quite what I said.

# 8

## AN OVERDUE SUCCESS

When I joined up with the rest of the squad in an awful hotel back in Sydney, I had a good chat with Vaughan. We reckoned that, since we were in Australia for another five weeks, we might as well enjoy the rest of the tour. If we were going to spend that time moping around, licking our wounds and feeling sorry for ourselves, we might as well go home. So the plan was to get on with the one-day series with as much enthusiasm as we could muster. I think by then I was virtually on auto-pilot anyway.

We started as we finished the Test series, by being heavily beaten in a Twenty20 International in Sydney, which was a bit of a farce because of the pitch. The wicket changed so much between their innings and ours. When we went in to bat, it was very dewy and wet and made us look stupid. They were hitting sixes and fours all over the place and we were struggling to get bat on ball because it was swinging and seaming around. We got turned over big time, and it was the same when we played the one-day internationals in Sydney – there was far too big an advantage in batting first, because under lights it's much more difficult to chase a total. Despite that, I did enjoy the Twenty20 match, simply because I wasn't worrying about who to bring on next at the other end. In some ways, I had forgotten what it was like just to play rather than to captain.

Around this time we had an influx of new players, including Ed Joyce, Jon Lewis and Ravi Bopara, and that helped lift morale and brought about fresh competition for places. It also helped that we were in contention again, playing in a separate competition that we could actually win, whereas for the last two Tests we had been attempting to avoid a whitewash. We also had a new team to play against in New Zealand, which was a novelty after months of playing against Australia.

We were all hoping that the start of the one-dayers would turn things around for us, but the day before the first match against Australia in Melbourne, I had the worst practice I think I've ever had. My head had gone, probably with what had happened in the Ashes, and I had a really bad net because of it. Normally, I don't react to a bad net and just try to get it right next time, but this time, with the frustration bubbling inside me, I exploded. My bat was leaning against the bench in the dressing room and I put my foot through it and broke it – not the most intelligent thing to do in the circumstances! I walked out but came back a few minutes later and tried to make light of it by asking, 'What's happened here?' I donated what was left of the bat to Jon Lewis's benefit in the end.

However, despite feeling so miserable about my practice, I decided that come what may I was going to enjoy the game.

I was playing in front of a full house at the MCG for England against Australia with a chance of setting the record straight in a one-day international. I think that was the view of most of the side, certainly those of us who had been involved in the Ashes whitewash. We started promisingly and Kev looked in good form until he was hit in the ribs attempting another of his outrageous shots against McGrath. It must have hurt him badly because, although he carried on, you could see him wincing with every shot, and he got out slogging for 82 and played no further part in the one-day series. I was pleased to contribute an unbeaten 47, particularly after a scratchy start, but we lost our way in the final overs and were restricted to 242 for 8.

Once again, Australia got off to a very good start and won with some overs to spare. Gilchrist was in one of those moods where you couldn't really bowl at him. Someone as talented as he is will play brilliantly from time to time and when he does, despite our best-laid plans, there's not much you can do.

We moved back to Sydney and on to Hobart and Ian Botham was given some stick for leading me astray the night before the game against New Zealand. We had a few drinks and I probably should not have stayed up as late as I did. Sometimes cricket is a strange game, though. It can give you little reward when you play really well and on other occasions things come off when they probably shouldn't have done and this was possibly one of those times. I had not prepared as I should have done but I responded with one of my best all-round performances of the series the following day. I think all the lads were looking forward to the game in Hobart because it was our first match against New Zealand – we were finally playing a different team. Our enthusiasm was reflected in our performance and we claimed our first victory of the tour – 72 days after landing in Sydney! We bowled well to restrict New Zealand to 205 for 9, but nearly messed it up with a sluggish start to our innings.

To me, this game illustrated how fine the margins are between success and failure in cricket. Just a few days after my dreadful net session in Melbourne and scratchy start at the MCG, when I got away with a slog sweep off Michael Clarke that could have gone anywhere, I arrived at the crease in Hobart and just felt right. From early in my innings, I felt better about the way I was playing, and I finished unbeaten on 72 to help win the game. For those of us who had gone through the Ashes, it was a big win. We were desperate for any kind of win, just to get us going again, and you could see some of the smiles returning in the dressing room.

Celebrations were put on hold virtually immediately, however, when we learned that Vaughan had damaged his hamstring and would be out for some time. It looked fairly innocuous when he did it, and I thought it was just a twinge, so I didn't think about the implications for the captaincy. When it became clear that Vaughan could well be out for the rest of the series, I had a few talks with Duncan about taking it on again, and we decided to give it another day while we travelled to Brisbane. The decision was going to be made the morning after we arrived there for the next match, to give me a night to think things over. It wasn't that I didn't want to captain the side, but the effort of doing it during the Ashes had absolutely drained me and I needed to think about it. When we arrived at the hotel, however, all the media were sat around waiting for the story. So instead of being able to think about it overnight, I was given an hour. I had a twenty-minute chat with Duncan and spoke to Neil Fairbrother and Rachael about it. Actually, I don't think I had any option but to take it. It would have been abdicating my responsibilities not to accept.

We drafted in Mal Loye, my Lancashire team-mate, as a replacement for Vaughan – I obviously had an input in that choice – and he played well in his first game, taking the Australians by surprise by slog-sweeping Brett Lee for six. I've seen quite a lot of that shot at Lancashire, and by playing it in Brisbane, he just changed the tempo. Even McGrath bowled a couple of bad balls. Unfortunately, we failed to build on Mal's innings and were dismissed for 155. We knew we'd have to bowl really well to have a chance, but it was under the lights at the Gabba and the pitch had juiced up. Jon Lewis gave us a good start by removing Gilchrist and Hayden early, and if Michael Hussey had been given out caught behind off Jimmy Anderson early in his innings, we might have stood a chance of winning the game.

From there, it was back to Adelaide. We all had bad memories of what happened in the Second Test when Australia won by six wickets, and I'll be quite happy if I never play another game of cricket there ever again. Back-to-back matches against New Zealand and Australia both ended badly. In the first game, against New Zealand, we were very much in it because they scored 210, which you would fancy chasing in most games of cricket. Then Daniel Vettori claimed four wickets, we never really got going and were bowled out for 120, which was a desperately disappointing result and performance. Having been hammered in that game, it got even worse in the next one. The match against Australia was a humiliation. We were bowled out for 110 and Australia won with over half the overs remaining. We were rubbish in both games and it was a terrible week to be an England cricketer. For one of the first times as captain, I got really wound up. I'd obviously been disappointed during the Ashes, but this just got to me. To add salt to our wounds, our defeat by Australia happened on Australia Day, so you can imagine what sort of a day that was for us all.

We had a lot of 'fine' meetings as a team, which were not my idea but designed to build team spirit. They go on during a lot of tours and consist of a judge and jury doling out fines for someone wearing a bad shirt on Wednesday, someone else turning up late for a team meeting the day after, and that sort of thing. These meetings would inevitably lead to a few drinks and we even adopted a team song. A few years earlier, Johnny Cash's 'Ring of Fire' had helped us win the Test in Mumbai, but this time it was more a case of gallows humour. We often had to play Australia on a Monday, so we adopted the Boomtown Rats' song 'I don't like Mondays'. We didn't like Mondays because we kept getting trounced by Australia.

After that defeat, I had quite a late night, and the following day in Perth, where we'd travelled for our next match, against

New Zealand, I didn't help things by having a couple of drinks on the plane. The upshot was I turned up for nets the next morning not in the best of shape, although I wouldn't say I was as bad as Duncan has since said I was. I'm not going to try to make excuses because I know I should not have arrived for training smelling of booze. It was unprofessional, but it was indicative of my state of mind at the time. Rachael had gone home and, I probably needed someone to get hold of me and tell me to cut it out. I wasn't the only one, I hasten to add, and it wasn't just the players – most of the support staff were at it more than we were. It was like being on a booze cruise. Duncan reacted to me turning up for nets in a dishevelled state by giving me a stern talking to, fining me and threatening to take the captaincy away, but nothing the management could have done could possibly have made me feel any worse. I was annoyed and disappointed in myself, and that was the biggest punishment of all.

We lost to New Zealand, but we did bat better and took some encouragement from that. We'd talked about the batting and what was going wrong and managed to improve. If we could get both disciplines, batting and bowling, functioning in the same match, we could still be competitive. We had to get better as a side because we couldn't get much worse.

We needed to win our last two matches if we were to reach the final of the tournament, which you would have got long odds on us achieving at that stage. I know results suggested otherwise but, even at our lowest point, I honestly thought we still had a chance. We'd played so badly for such a long time, I believed that surely we'd start playing well again soon. The law of averages suggested we had to do so at some stage. I knew the players in that squad and I knew they were capable of performing at much higher levels.

Then, despite all the drinking and going out, which I would never try to justify, from that low point we somehow did turn it around. We were so down as a squad, maybe everyone relaxed, because suddenly we started winning. The catalyst for the turnaround was Ed Joyce. Ed had hit 66 in the defeat by New Zealand and looked good while he was at the crease, but it was his performance in the next match, against Australia in Sydney, that really kick-started us.

In fact, the newer players got us through. Instead of the experienced players pushing the team on, the less experienced members of the squad played a leading role, and they gave the more experienced players a kick up the backside. Ed hadn't played a lot of international cricket, but his hundred at Sydney sent a message to more established members of the squad that it could be done. Luck plays a big part in sport and maybe the story of our one-day tournament would have been very different had he not been dropped early in his innings. Ed had come in when we moved Strauss down the order, and we were taking the mickey out of him initially because he arrived with this big new bat with a pink handle, but he shut us up with the way he played. Jimmy Anderson had been forced to go home with a back problem and Liam Plunkett stepped up as his replacement. Liam, with a delivery he will probably remember for the rest of his career, bowled Gilchrist in his first over with an in-swinging yorker. It was the perfect ball for Gilchrist and got us on a roll. We were helped by Symonds going off with an arm injury, but we deserved the victory. We'd not beaten Australia once before on the tour, and we all enjoyed that one.

One more win would get us into the final, and this time I chose a different style of celebration – I stayed in my room and watched *Rocky 2* on the movie channel with Mal Loye. Even though I was sensible, I still didn't get to sleep until nearly 6.00 a.m. just because of the adrenalin and the excitement about the prospect of reaching the final against all expectations.

Our progress was dependent on New Zealand losing to Australia in Melbourne and then us winning our last match against New Zealand in Brisbane, and I was totally wrapped up in it all. We flew to Brisbane in preparation for our final group game, but there was obviously a lot of interest in the other game and I was glued to the television watching every ball of it. Our security officer, Reg Dickason, comes from Brisbane and he arranged a barbecue for the team, but it was on the same day as the other game and I'm afraid I was a bit rude because I spent the whole evening watching Australia win instead of mingling.

Vaughan was now fit again after his hamstring strain, and I was more than happy to relinquish the captaincy. We approached the game against New Zealand as a semi-final but got off to a stinking start, losing three early wickets, and then Collingwood came in. He picked up from where Joyce left off in the previous game and hit a brilliant century to guide us to 277, which we knew was going to be competitive. New Zealand began positively with Lou Vincent and Stephen Fleming, but Monty broke their partnership, and although Fleming played well for his hundred, he got bogged down a little, fell behind the rate and we won. That put us in the final and extended our stay in Australia, which for some of us had lasted three and a half months already, with very little to show for our efforts. Earlier, when we were losing, there was a lot of talk about going home, and I don't think any of us would deny that we would have liked to have gone. I don't think we would have been human if we hadn't, but we all wanted to return having achieved something. We didn't want to come home having suffered an Ashes whitewash and an early exit from the one-dayers. Another four or five days wasn't going to kill us. Now we were in the final against Australia, we were determined to win.

The first game was in Melbourne and, once again, Australia began like a train, but they lost nine wickets for 82. At one stage it looked like we were going to be chasing about 320 but instead we were able to restrict them to 252. I was captain again because Vaughan had aggravated his hamstring in the previous match against New Zealand, and after we got Ponting out I brought all the team together and gave them a right roasting. We had been terrible up to that point. We had been ragged in the field and we were playing like a side who wanted to go home. It's very rare to get back into a game if you let Australia get off to a flier, but this time we managed it. They had been cruising at 170 for 2 but by fighting back we at least gave ourselves a chance.

Unfortunately, we suffered another disastrous start with the bat and slipped to 15 for 3, but Collingwood came in and played one of the best innings I've seen as an England player. He was playing against the best side in the world, everything was at stake and, until he scored a century in the previous game, he had been struggling for runs. Where those two centuries came from I don't know and I'm not sure he did, but it summed up the determination of the side as we won the game.

The second match was in Sydney, and the extra incentive to win that one was that it would spare us a deciding game – in Adelaide! We were all desperate to avoid a return visit there. However, we also knew the situation with day-night matches in Sydney. The statistics told us that sides who batted first scored a very high percentage of wins because of the dew factor under the lights. Another ground where this is happens is Newlands in Cape Town and I do think it's something that needs to be addressed by the authorities, but we weren't complaining when we won the toss.

We were quite pleased to score 246 for 8, although I thought we could have played the final overs better. Rain was threatening during Australia's reply but we got an early wicket before it came down. Then, with the first ball after the break, Plunkett came around the wicket and bowled Gilchrist. We needed to get to 20 overs to constitute a game and we came off after 17.5 overs, so we were getting a little nervous about it. I went and had a word with the groundsman because the ground staff had been as fast as you like when the Australians were out in the field to get the covers out. When we were in the field, it was very different and they were messing about with the fence, pretending they couldn't get through the gate. I was going mad about it and shouted at them to get a move on. In hindsight they were probably doing their best, but it didn't seem like it at the time, so I had a word.

When we got back out, we thought the weather wouldn't allow us much time, so I put Monty and Jamie Dalrymple on to bowl to get through the first two overs quickly before I brought the seamers back on. In situations like that, when you're on top but unable to influence the result, you can start feeling sorry for yourselves. We were all thinking that, after everything that had happened on that trip, it would be a fitting way to finish – to be denied victory by rain and have to go back to Adelaide. That would have just about finished us off. I had a table booked at home a few days after this match for St Valentine's Day, as did a few of the lads. None of us wanted to ring home and say we were going back to Adelaide instead.

When we did go back on, Brad Hodge and Shane Watson began to get a bit of a partnership going, but the game turned firmly in our favour with a brilliant diving catch by Dalrymple to remove Watson. The game had been reduced to 33 overs and it was a question of juggling who bowled when, but it was one of those days when bowling changes worked. Dalrymple removed Hodge, and then Collingwood returned to claim a couple of wickets at the end. It was a great feeling once we'd won. In an ideal world we would have had a proper game of cricket without any rain intervening, but by the time rain finally stopped play, we did have them nine down.

I'll always remember the after-match presentation because it took place in the pouring rain and everyone had gone home! It was a bit different from my speech in Sydney after the Ashes, when we'd just been beaten 5–0 and there were over 20,000 in the ground. Unfortunately, when we won, there was no one there. It was great to win a trophy, though, at the end of a long tour, and we were all delighted to have beaten Australia in their own backyard. Despite that, it could not make up for losing the Ashes. This competition was the first I had ever won as a one-day international cricketer, but it will never make up for the 5–0 whitewash.

# 9

# CAUSING A SPLASH AT THE WORLD CUP

None of the people I usually knocked around with on tours were in the squad for the World Cup in the Caribbean in spring 2007, so it was a question of getting to know everyone and fitting in just as a player again, although I had been appointed vice captain. Inevitably, I missed Harmy. When you spend as much time together as Steve and I do on tour, that was bound to happen. I found myself keeping company with the younger lads, such as Plunkett, Jimmy Anderson and Ravi Bopara, more than the older, more experienced members of the squad. It was very different from Australia for me, and quite a strange build-up to the competition. We had a slow first week in St Vincent with nothing to do but practise. That part of the trip seemed to drag. Not many of us left the confines of the hotel where we were staying, which made the week seem that much longer, but I enjoyed fading into the background and letting Vaughan take up the captaincy role again.

Although everyone was eager to do well, some of us felt a little jaded. In the nets, all I wanted to do was top up my bowling. I didn't want to do too much after nearly four months with hardly any break from cricket. The morale of the squad that had soared after our marvellous win in Australia was still excellent, and we had high expectations of qualifying for the next round, especially considering our group included Canada, Kenya and New Zealand. We were expected to beat the first two, and while New Zealand were a very good side, we had beaten them recently in Australia, so there was no reason to go into that match with an inferiority complex. The rules of the tournament stated that if you beat your fellow qualifier from the group, those points were taken forward to the Super Eights and gave you a better chance of qualification for the final stages.

Hopes of having a good tournament were boosted by our performance in our opening warm-up match against Bermuda, when we bowled them out for 45 after the batters got a decent work-out. Our second warm-up match was slightly different because it was against Australia, and we knew they would be keen to beat us after suffering the shock of losing to us so recently. There were mixed thoughts in the squad about how to approach the game. We wanted to get as much out of it as we could to improve our form before the tournament started, but as important as the match practice was, we were also keen to beat them again. When you're playing against Australia, whether it's 13-a-side or not, you want to win, and beating them three times in succession would have done wonders for our confidence. As it turned out, we had a collapse chasing their score and they won quite convincingly, but the beauty of it was we could pass it off as 'just a practice game'. If we'd won, though, I'm sure we'd have made something of beating the Aussies again.

Although it was a disappointment to lose, as a squad we didn't regard it as a disaster. We knew we hadn't played well but there were bigger things around the corner with the first game against New Zealand. We would have preferred to have played them in the last game, but instead we were scheduled to take on the next strongest team in the group first.

Before we could knuckle down and start the tournament, though, all the teams had to travel to Montego Bay, Jamaica, for the opening ceremony. We were told later that it looked quite impressive from the stand, but out on the pitch it was difficult to understand what was supposed to be happening. We had to wear our suits and sit where we were told, which was right in the sun, and we couldn't see or hear what was going on. From a player's perspective, it was probably as good an opening ceremony as the one at Lord's in 1999 when everything that could go wrong did go wrong! They had flares in the middle of Lord's for that one but because of the wind none of the spectators were able to see the rest of the ceremony because smoke filled the ground. Despite that, the trip to Montego Bay did us some good. After our week working in the nets and on fitness training, I know both Vaughan and Duncan thought we were a bit heavy-legged for the warm-up against Australia. The trip to Jamaica at least gave us a couple of days off and rested some tired people before the tournament started. It allowed us to arrive in St Lucia for our first game fresher than we might have been.

We were all relieved to be in St Lucia. Our time in St Vincent seemed to pass so slowly that we were just delighted the tournament was finally under way. Until then, it probably hadn't quite hit home that we were at the World Cup. There was a definite change in mood once we got there. The other thing that happened once we arrived was that individual players were encouraged to talk to the group about skills in an effort to concentrate our minds on the task ahead. At Lancashire, years ago, Bobby Simpson encouraged a similar thing when he was coach. I remember him asking Neil Fairbrother to give a talk to the Lancashire squad about building a one-day innings during a pre-season tour, and Peter Martin gave another talk about bowling. We'd never really done it with England before, but Duncan decided it was going to be a theme of the tournament and, from time to time, players would be asked to talk about a subject. Ian Bell and Liam Plunkett began with Ian talking about batting and Liam about slower balls. They both went down well but that was as far as it went – we never did it again for the whole tournament for some reason. Talks like that can easily be done tongue in cheek for easy laughs, but Ian and Liam took it seriously. Liam had spoken with Jon Lewis beforehand to prepare his talk and I for one learned something from what he was saying. Ian spoke about batting against spin and both got their message across really well. Any player will tell you that practice can get very monotonous if you do the same thing every day, but varying the session like that made everyone think a bit more about what they were doing. I'm also sure both Ian and Liam learned something new just by gathering the information together so they could give the talk. Liam will have learned from Jon Lewis, for instance, who is extremely knowledgeable when it comes to bowling. I used to talk to him about it during the tournament.

Unfortunately, during the build-up to the New Zealand game, Jimmy Anderson, who was one of our key bowlers, got a nasty bang on his finger. There was talk about him going home because it was such a bad break – New Zealand's Jacob Oram said he'd have his finger amputated to play in the World Cup! – but Jimmy just went quietly about his business, strapped up his finger, had a jab and got on with things. He's always had a high pain threshold. A couple of years ago he got back from the tour to India with a stress fracture of his back and all he'd complained about while we were there was a bit of stiffness! He's a tough character and I never had any doubt he would play.

We started off shakily, losing three early wickets, but Kevin Pietersen and Paul Collingwood put us back on course, and Paul Nixon and Plunkett got us to a respectable score of 209 for 7. We thought that it was under-par but we were in with a shout, until Scott Styris played a really good innings and guided them home.

Back at the hotel after the game, I checked my emails in the team room. I had no plans to go out that night, believe it or not, but in the end went to a local bar with Jeremy Snape, the team psychologist, to have a chat about thought processes over a couple of drinks. Some others from our camp were there, but no one had gone out with the intention of making a big night of it – certainly not as big as it turned out. Some of the lads went on to a nightclub up the road. By this time, I was chatting to a few journalists, and so I followed later. Not long after I arrived at the club, I realised I'd had enough to drink and slipped out intending to walk back to the hotel. Instead of walking down the road I decided it would be nicer down the beach and come into the hotel from the back. It was a decision which was to have huge repercussions for the rest of my World Cup. A row of kayaks caught my eye but none of them had any oars. Next to them were some pedalos, and I remember dragging one to the edge of the water, presumably because I fancied a ride, but for the life of me I couldn't work out how to get on it, or my legs into it, so I let go of it and it quickly drifted away from the shore. Had I been sober, I might have attempted to retrieve it, but I knew enough to know that I was in no fit state to go after it, so I let it go. I got myself to bed and, when I woke up in my room with sand between my toes I knew what had happened. If you've ever woken up after having had too much to drink, you'll know how quickly the memory dawns, as you come to, of how stupid you've been the night before. I just thought to myself, 'I didn't, did I?'

All sorts of reports followed in the newspapers. Some said I had to be rescued from the sea, but I can assure you that didn't happen. If I had managed to get on the pedalo, I would have been in trouble, because it drifted out to sea at some pace, but fortunately I wasn't able to do that. Any rescuer would have had to be walking past at that time in the morning – and be a very strong swimmer to drag me back in. I think I slipped and fell over in a few inches of water but nothing more than that. I'm not trying to diminish the incident, and obviously I was wrong to be out drinking that late after a game, but some of the reports were way off target.

It soon became clear that the previous night's events were no secret. The whole squad were summoned to a team meeting and we had to write what time we had arrived back at the hotel on a board at the front of the room. As soon as I got the call to go to the meeting I knew I was in trouble. I probably contributed to my fate because I had no idea what time I had come in but thought it might have been around 4.00 a.m. As it turned out, I'd left the club a couple of hours earlier, which still wasn't very professional, but saying four in the morning certainly didn't help my cause. The rest of the lads wrote their times on the board and it was decided that anyone out after midnight was going to be fined. We'd never had a curfew before, but I don't think any of us was in a position to complain. We knew we'd messed up, but I did speak up in defence of Ravi Bopara, who admitted going to bed at 12.30 a.m. I said I didn't think he should be disciplined because all he was doing was playing pool. He doesn't drink. He just got to bed a little late, and I think he was let off. Poor Kevin Shine, who was our bowling coach for the World Cup, had not been out all winter, including during the Ashes tour. His brother was in St Lucia and he agreed to meet him at the same nightclub as the players, but he put his hand up and accepted the fine. All the players who were out late at the nightclub – Jimmy Anderson, Jon Lewis, Ian Bell, Paul Nixon and Liam Plunkett – were fined alongside Kevin and Jeremy

Snape. I was fined £1500, and told to expect more sanctions because Duncan felt that a fine would not have a big enough impact on me. Next day I was stripped of the vice-captaincy and suspended for the next game. So that bit of stupidity on my part resulted in three hits. I held up my hand straightaway for what I'd done, but I did have to correct the management committee on a few things, because they seemed to regard the *News of the World* report as the gospel truth on the matter. It was an uncomfortable meeting for us all, especially for me, although I only had myself to blame.

Vaughan and Duncan told me not to come to the ground the following day for the game against Canada because of the press attention it would cause. Not being able to play for England was the hardest of the three punishments. I'll never try to say I was anything but stupid that night, but being denied the chance to play for my country really hurt. I went straight back to my room after the meeting, feeling pretty low. Reg Dickason, the security consultant with the team, came to see me a bit later to see how I was. I really appreciated that gesture because I was feeling a bit sorry for myself at the time.

Reg also came the following day when the lads were playing against Canada. While the game was going on, a few photographers turned up to try to get pictures of me sitting around the hotel, so I kept my head down, not stirring from my room. I couldn't stay there forever, though. The TV in my room didn't seem to be receiving any pictures of the cricket and I didn't know what the hell was going on in the game, although I was texting Phil Neale, the team manager, to find out the scores and he was keeping me up to date. Eventually, I cracked and ran down to the team room, and there I stayed for about seven hours, to avoid the photographers and TV cameras waiting outside. I drank bottles of water and then used them to pee into because I didn't want to risk getting caught on camera when I made a dash for the toilet. Even so, I didn't get to see England play because the TV in the team room was showing live coverage of the match between Australia and Holland, but I did see the closing overs of our victory.

I'd been hoping and praying England would win, because I would have felt responsible had Canada caused an upset, and I was just so relieved when it was over and the players came back to the hotel. I spoke to Rachael during the day and also to Neil Fairbrother, who flew out a couple of days later to try to talk some sense into me. It was good to have him around for a few days, and I spent quite a bit of time with him, trying to get my head straight and get back on track. Through all this, we were still in the World Cup. Vaughan encouraged me to get back into the team environment, which I wanted to do.

The incident reflected badly on everyone involved, but I felt sorry for Jon Lewis and the others, because of the attention they got in the newspapers, and the photographs that appeared of them with girls. People often want to have photographs taken with the players, but for those people to send the pictures to the newspapers and try to make out there was more to it was very distasteful.

The day after the Canada game, I was required to give a press conference in the Chinese restaurant in the lobby of our hotel to explain myself and my behaviour. I just tried to be honest, to put the record straight. Some fans who had managed to be in the vicinity were shouting encouragement and I didn't really know what to do. Duncan was sitting next to me, presumably to show we were united, but I imagine the body language would have shown we were anything but. I said how ashamed I was of my behaviour and how determined to redeem myself with the team and the fans. Perhaps the strangest part was when Duncan was asked by Mike Selvey of the *Guardian* whether I would have been suspended if we had been playing Australia or South Africa in the next match rather than Canada. I was expecting him to say the opposition was immaterial, but instead he made this strange statement about there being a lot of ifs and buts in life. I thought it was a really odd answer. The management committee obviously thought my offence was serious enough to ban me for a game, in which case it should not have mattered who we were playing.

My anger with myself came out in the following day's net session, which was our first practice since the night out, and I tore in when I was asked to bowl. Liam Plunkett and Jimmy Anderson weren't in the best of humours that morning, either. We were bowling at Vaughan, Ed Joyce, Strauss and Collingwood and all three of us let it rip, making it hell for them. It was a tricky net for all of us. You could say we were channelling our anger about the incident into our cricket, which I am sure was the response everyone wanted as we tried, as a squad, to put the incident behind us and somehow build some momentum in the World Cup.

# 10

# THE DEPARTURE OF DUNCAN

Our next game was against Kenya, and I wasn't too surprised to hear the crowd singing and taking the mickey, mostly in a fairly good-humoured way, including several renditions of 'What do you do with a drunken Freddie?' Such was my determination to do well and prove that I deserved my place in the team, I struggled a bit with no-balls because I was trying so hard, but I took a couple of wickets. A few edges went past the slips, but I was happy enough to be back out there, playing in a comfortable victory that put us through to the Super Eight stage, our minimum expectation at the start of the tournament. The big problem was we had no points to carry over, following our defeat by New Zealand, which meant we started the second stage at a disadvantage. We tried not to focus too much on that, because it was new territory for all of us, including me in my third World Cup. In fact, getting beyond the first stage was almost like winning it after the disappointment of the previous two. England had been knocked out at the first stage in both 1999 and 2003.

We moved on to Guyana for the next match, against

Ireland, who had surprised everyone by qualifying ahead of India in their group. I don't know what bug I'd contracted, but for the next fortnight of the tournament I felt very tired most of the time, had a sore throat and struggled to get through each day. I know people will think it was connected to the pedalo incident, but I can assure you it was nothing to do with that. I felt absolutely drained, and sometimes it was quite hard to deal with net sessions, which were very lively. We had some good net bowlers, including former West Indies fast bowler Reon King. In one session he hit me on the head off a good length and I threw my bat away, not just because I wasn't playing very well, but because I'd been hit on the head three times and I didn't seem to have the energy to take it in my stride.

Nevertheless, the match against Ireland was one of our better performances and I managed to contribute a decent 43 by grafting out in the middle. I hadn't scored runs for a while, and even though it wasn't the most testing of bowling attacks, it felt better just to have spent some time at the crease with a bat in my hand.

From there we travelled to Antigua, where we were joined by our families, but what should have been a good time for us all was spoilt by the substandard hotel. Several of the lads complained they had seen rats around the place and the hotel staff made it clear that any request made to them was a major chore. Two of the biggest matches of the tournament so far were coming up – against Sri Lanka and Australia – and we had quite a few days to kill between games, so the environment was important. Staying in that hotel wasn't the best preparation for those matches.

While things were not right off the pitch, we began brightly against Sri Lanka, who were rightly regarded as one of the favourites to win the tournament. They had an enviable batting line-up with Sanath Jayasuriya, Mahela Jayawardene and Kumar Sangakkara, and at one stage they looked like getting around 280, but we managed to peg them back to 235 on a slow wicket. Once the new ball was gone, it was difficult to put on runs and I was caught for a low score, this time at mid-on. Sometimes cricket can be a cruel game. Their seamer Dilhara Fernando sent down a slower ball, which I've picked in the past because you can see his fingers separate at the top of the ball. I thought a drive over the top was a good option, with mid-on and mid-off back, but it didn't bounce and I was out before I'd got in.

The one thing you need more than anything as a batsman is an element of luck. Even the best player in the world needs that and I wasn't getting any, although some critics would have argued that I didn't deserve any. For around three years, leading to and including the Ashes win in 2005, I had it all my own way and was scoring runs as well as taking wickets. Now I had begun to find it harder to play both disciplines well at the same time. Quotes along the lines of 'the harder I work, the luckier I get' are often bandied around, but I'm not having that – not after the way I worked during that tournament for so little reward. I was feeling so down about it that I struggled to get excited even when we went close to beating Sri Lanka.

We needed three off the final ball when Fernando bowled Ravi Bopara and prevented him pulling off one of the great comebacks. I was mostly disappointed for Ravi, who really showed what he is capable of. I've seen some people come in after an innings like that, when they've got runs, quite happy with what they've done, irrespective of the result, but Ravi was heartbroken. I thought he was going to cry. He got the man-of-the-match award but he just wasn't interested. He got us so far and played so well I think he deserved to win the game for us just for what he did.

We opted for a change of approach for the next game, against Australia, with Strauss dropping out and Ian Bell moving up to open with Michael Vaughan. It worked, because Bell hit a superb 77, which, for my money, was the best innings from an England player during that tournament. That may sound strange, since Kevin Pietersen scored a century in the same innings, but Bell's timing and the placing of his shots were absolutely superb. Those two contributions put us in a very strong position and we were 160-odd with 20 overs remaining, but once again we lost our way, which was a feature of our batting during that tournament. We still thought 247 was a competitive total, especially as the wicket was similar to the one we played on against Sri Lanka, when it became harder and harder to score as the game progressed.

Throughout that tournament, Australia were getting off to good starts and they did so again, Hayden and Gilchrist adding 50-odd in the first 11 overs to set up the run chase. They were extremely clinical and we were played off the park.

I did offer to bat at the top of the order. One theory was that facing the new ball would suit me better at the start of the innings, and I thought I could give us a bit of impetus while still allowing the others to bat through lower down the order. However, the feeling was that No. 6 was the best place for me, and I was happy to fit in with what was wanted. My confidence with the bat was still very low, even though I was trying not to show it. When you're not playing well, your confidence is bound to be dented. I don't think it's anything to do with mental fragility – it's just how the world works. I spoke to Duncan about my bottom hand choking the bat and restricting my shots, and worked on relaxing my grip a little at his suggestion. I'd have tried anything, to be honest. Once you start looking at your grip and your stance, though, all sorts of demons creep in. I hadn't struggled with poor form for some years, and it does eat away at you.

Despite losing those two matches, we still stood a chance of progressing to the semi-finals – it seemed harder to be knocked out than to progress! – and we travelled to Barbados to play Bangladesh. The wicket, fast and bouncy – quite the opposite of those we'd played on in Antigua – was perfect for that game. I came off at one point because I felt drained again, but managed to return. It was over as a contest after we bowled them out for 143, although our batting was again a concern.

The next match, against South Africa, was the big one because it would decide who went through to the semi-finals, and despite our inconsistent form, we fancied our chances. My preparation was disrupted when I had to go for blood tests after waking up with swollen glands. Taken together with the tiredness and constant sore throat, glandular fever was a possibility but, fortunately, it wasn't that bad. Some sort of bug was diagnosed and treated with antibiotics.

Events did not improve much on the pitch. We seemed to have saved one of our worst performances of the World Cup for the match that could have earned us a semi-final place. Once again our batting let us down. Andrew Hall claimed five wickets to bowl us out for 154 and, after that, the outcome was never in doubt. Both A.B. de Villiers and Graeme Smith gave chances, and both edged just over the slips, but you have to give them credit for the intent they displayed from the off. As a bowler, you feel hard done by when batsmen get lucky, but they played very well.

When we were knocked out in 2003, the Zimbabwe issue dominated proceedings, which wasn't our fault, so we felt angry. This time was different. We were all disappointed, of course, but we couldn't expect to go through after the way we'd played.

We still had one game to play, against West Indies, even though we'd both already been knocked out, and I think we were all anticipating a team inquest into what had gone wrong in the tournament. Duncan was never the sort of bloke to show his real emotions, and I was unaware of what was happening behind the scenes in the build-up to that final game in Barbados. He always kept his cards close to his chest, particularly with me, although we were aware there was a lot of talk in the media about him stepping down, and he did come in for a fair amount of flak about our World Cup exit. The first time we had a sense of something unusual happening was at nets the day before the match. Three-quarters of the way through practice, Duncan called us all around. That was unusual in itself, because if he did address us, he would normally wait until the end of a practice session, and I realised then what he was going to say. He told us he was resigning and he had enjoyed working with us all. He got quite emotional about it, which was surprising for someone who had always kept himself to himself, but it showed how much the job meant to him. Michael Vaughan thanked him for his efforts, and he got upset as well – it was quite an end to the net session!

Duncan had been with us for eight years, and my international career up until then, bar a couple of Tests, had been with him. He had helped almost everybody who came into the squad during that time.

Immediately, as players, we began wondering who was going to be the new coach. Peter Moores and Tom Moody seemed to be the most likely candidates. Tom had done a good job with Sri Lanka, guiding them to the World Cup final. I knew him socially because he was friends with Rooster, who had worked with him at Worcestershire a few years previously, but Peter Moores was appointed a few days later, and Tom ended up going home to coach Western Australia.

I was a little nervous about meeting Peter again because the only time I'd spoken to him we'd had a row. The incident occurred during a Lancashire v. Sussex match at Hove a few years earlier, when Peter was coach there. It was quite funny, looking back. Mushtaq Ahmed was coming off the field after bowling his allotted 10 overs. I get on very well with him and couldn't resist a bit of banter from the balcony about the fact he was coming off after finishing his bowling stint. He smiled and said something about he wasn't going to field, but Peter came rushing out of the Sussex dressing room to have a go at me. I told him to go away, using some fairly choice language, but fortunately he didn't hold it against me when he became England coach and we enjoyed a fantastic relationship. Before his appointment was announced, I asked around about him and everybody spoke highly of him. Rob Key and Owais Shah had spent that winter in Australia with the Academy, where Peter had been coach, and they both thought he was fantastic, and Harmy spoke well of him, too, from sessions he had done with Peter at Loughborough.

Duncan's last game in charge was special for a number of reasons. There was a full house at the Kensington Oval for Brian Lara's last match before he retired, and the team wanted to bow out on a high for Duncan. Neither side had done as well as they had hoped in the tournament, so although it was a dead game in terms of the World Cup, quite a lot of pride was riding on it. The game didn't start well for us because Chris Gayle had one of those days when there was virtually no bowling to him, and at one stage they looked as though they were going to score 380. I felt particularly sorry for Plunkett during that spell, because he'd come back into the side after not playing for a while and Gayle just kept hitting him into the stand. I was called upon quite early and wondered what he was going to do to me, but fortunately he just pushed the first ball from me on to the off-side for a single. I managed to get him caught at third man, which was a huge relief for us all, and that brought Lara out to bat. He had promoted himself to No. 3 for his final match. I thought I'd got him early when he smashed one through the air to gully, but it flew over the top of Ravi Bopara for four. They were playing quite loose throughout the innings, though, and we knew if we could take some wickets, we could get back into it.

The big wicket was Lara's, as usual. We gave him a guard of honour as he walked out to bat, to an amazing ovation, but we all wanted to be the last person in history to get him out. As it was, he was run out after a mix-up with Marlon Samuels – I still can't believe Marlon didn't sacrifice himself and let Lara bat on. I wouldn't have liked to be Marlon, walking back into the dressing room later on. In Lara's position, I think I'd have throttled him.

We started almost as well as they did and got over the line with a ball to spare after a brilliant century from Kevin Pietersen. Stuart Broad showed signs of composure with the bat, remaining remarkably calm in the final over, for such a young player, and hitting the winning runs. Everybody was pleased we'd won but very few of us were celebrating, because we'd gone out of the World Cup early again and weren't there for the business end of the tournament.

At the start of the World Cup I'd felt jaded but optimistic that we would do well. I felt worse as the tournament progressed, with the bug and my general restlessness, and by the end I was disappointed and knackered. My original idea had been to go on to America, hire a motorbike and ride up the East coast from Miami to New York, to get some bike-riding experience. When it came to it, though, at the end of a long winter I just wanted to spend some time with the family. So I postponed the biking trip to another time, and since we were all in Barbados anyway, we thought we might as well stay there. We'd had a house on the island for a couple of years that we rented out but had never seen, so we went to have a look at it, and stayed nearby.

The only thing I did all week, other than relax, was give a talk to a travel company's clients as part of an arrangement I have with them. On my way back from that, I dropped into a bar in Old Town for a few beers with Warren Hegg, my former Lancashire team-mate, Chubby Chandler, who owns the management company that handles my affairs, and Lee Westwood, the golfer. Rachael came to join us and we had a really good night – I even got in on the karaoke singing 'Copacabana', although not very well, with a lot of English fans egging me on. We were tipped off about a couple of photographers hanging around, but I didn't see anything untoward in having an evening out with my wife and some friends on my week off. I made sure to sign autographs and pose for pictures with other customers in the bar when they asked, because I felt we'd let them down on the field, but when I found myself all over the papers again a few days later, the stories didn't show me in a particularly good light. I wasn't acting any differently from the way I had done when everyone thought I was great, and my behaviour made me a normal person. The only difference was that then England were doing well and my form was good. I've never tried to be a celebrity, or claimed to be one, and being in the papers and having people follow us around had made me start to think about what I wanted for the future. After the World Cup, I had reached a point where I wasn't sure what I wanted to do with the rest of my life or my career.

# 11

# **TIME TO TAKE STOCK**

The World Cup was an important tournament, but I didn't particularly enjoy it. I had felt pretty much on my own throughout the time in the Caribbean. Everyone blamed the pedalo incident for spoiling our chances, but that wasn't it. The side had become fractured before then. Definite groups had sprung up within the team and the atmosphere wasn't great. Back in England, all I knew was that I had to get back to Lancashire and play some cricket. Fortunately, spending time in the Lancashire dressing room was just what I needed. Being with the Lancashire lads made me realise how much I still loved the game and I started to enjoy it again. I wasn't in great form, so I had to fight and battle for every run, which is rewarding in itself when it comes off. Everyone knew the winter hadn't been good for me, but Lancashire have always been supportive. In the face of all that criticism, the club were always behind me. I wanted to give them something back and the best way to do that was to play.

In the nets, I worked on my batting with Mike Watkinson, the Lancashire coach, and Neil Fairbrother, trying to get some rhythm going. Perhaps my form reflected my mood. I'm no good at pretending to be positive when I'm feeling down. I remember getting wickets at the World Cup and not even celebrating, which underlines how off the game I was at that point. It wasn't as if I wasn't trying. I was giving everything I had, but for some months after the Australian tour, I just took no pleasure from playing cricket.

The hard work in the nets at Old Trafford appeared to have paid off during a championship match at Hampshire in early May at the start of the 2007 season, against a team that included Shane Warne and Stuart Clark, which was just what I needed so soon after the Ashes. It rained overnight, we didn't play the first day and the wicket was still wet the following morning when the game started. Facing a seamer as good as Clark on a lively surface meant I had to get my head down and graft. The ball was nipping around all over the place and I concentrated on being disciplined, leaving it when necessary. My judgement can't have been too bad because my first error came when I got out to Warne for 60-odd. I had a bit of a heave at a full toss – my eyes lit up when I saw it, because I'd been grinding out the runs up until then. I also bowled for around nine overs until my ankle gave out, in a different place from before, and I came off straightaway.

The West Indies had arrived and, a couple of days later, I reported for England duty before the First Test at Lord's, with the help of an injection, but I had an idea that the problem was serious.

Michael Vaughan's team had been playing together for several years and winning the Ashes in 2005 was the highlight.

Meeting the Queen after receiving my MBE was an unforgettable experience. I was genuinely star-struck.

Michael Vaughan's long-running knee problems began in Pakistan, when he was forced to sit out the First Test.

Marcus Trescothick took over the captaincy from Vaughan in Pakistan. His premature retirement from Test cricket was a massive loss for England.

It had been a lifelong dream to captain England in an Ashes series. Here I am pictured with Ricky Ponting before the start of the disappointing 2006–07 series

Removing Matthew Hayden on the first day of the opening Ashes Test in Brisbane was a relief after a nervous start.

Some critics claimed Glenn McGrath (*below left*) was a fading force before the 2006–07 series but it didn't stop him making an impact. We had some stars of our own, though, including Kevin Pietersen (*below right*), who scored a century in Adelaide.

*Below left:* Steve Harmison gave us a great chance of bouncing back in Perth with four wickets to help dismiss Australia for 244.
*Below right:* Sometimes you have to take your hat off to great performances, and Adam Gilchrist's century in Perth was certainly one of those.

*Far left:* Brett Lee gave us no opportunity to score a big hit in our second innings in Adelaide.
*Left:* Ricky Ponting continued to lead from the front in Adelaide, and scored another century to put Australia on top.

*Right:* We were all desperate not to become Shane Warne's 700th Test wicket. That place in history fell to Andrew Strauss.
*Below:* My 89 in the final Test in Sydney could not lift our spirits, or prevent us suffering a 5–0 series whitewash.

Duncan Fletcher and I were different characters, but we both enjoyed our one-day series win in Australia, which came soon after defeat in the Ashes. It was especially gratifying for me as captain.

The 2007 World Cup began badly with defeat against New Zealand. It got much worse with the now infamous pedalo incident. I apologised for my behaviour at a press conference.

Returning to play for Lancashire at the start of the 2007 season rekindled my love of cricket.

I felt much better at the crease during my comeback Test against South Africa at Headingley.

Everyone described my battle with Jacques Kallis as crucial during the Edgbaston Test, but I was just delighted to get South Africa's best batsman out.

On the Monday, I bowled a couple of spells in the nets and had another injection. A few days later I bowled in the nets again. It wasn't feeling good but I very nearly declared myself fit because, rightly or wrongly, I thought I could contribute as a bastman. In the previous Test I had scored 89 against Australia in Sydney, and although I'd not had a great Ashes series, I wasn't the worst by any means. I made that point to Peter Moores, but it cut no ice. I had nothing against Owais Shah, who replaced me in the team, but I thought I could have played a part.

By the next day, it was almost irrelevant anyway, because my ankle was nearly hanging off, but I was so mad I just kept going in the nets. In hindsight, it wasn't the right thing to do. It was a kick in the teeth not to be selected, but Peter was right. From when he started as coach, I found Peter to be a breath of fresh air. I thought the atmosphere before that First Test was great – so different from the World Cup, almost as if some of the lads had a new lease of life.

After the previous two operations both surgeons assured me I was going to be fine, and the third surgeon, James Calder, was almost certain he had got to the bottom of it.

The exercises are always the same after an operation, but the rehabilitation after this one was the hardest of them all. For six weeks beforehand I'd followed a similar programme to try to avoid having surgery at all, so this was the fourth time I'd undertaken the same routine. Working with Rooster, otherwise known as Lanchashire physio Dave Robert, helped, but to go through it all again was awful. The programme doesn't just affect you, it affects the family as well, getting up at stupid o'clock to go training, and it does cross your mind that maybe all the hard work is not worth it.

Around this time, Michael Vaughan gave an interview in which he blamed the pedalo episode for ruining our World Cup. As I have said all along, I wasn't Robinson Crusoe. Other people were out later than I was that night, and I truly and honestly believe the morale of the squad had gone before then. Vaughan gave the interview just before the Third Test at Old Trafford, which I thought was bizarre timing. Even if I had been to blame for preventing us doing well at the World Cup, why bring it up then, when a new coach had taken charge and the tournament was behind us? A lot was made of it, and Jim Cumbes, Lancashire's chief executive, came out and defended me. I wasn't that fussed about it, but I met Michael at our Lancashire offices, had a short conversation with him and it was amicably settled. This was not a big issue as far as I was concerned and I know from experiences that sometimes you can get tied into knots by the press when they ask you questions.

When my ankle had mended again, my planned return was in a second-team game against Derbyshire at Blackpool towards the end of July, but it was rained off without a ball being bowled. I did get a game against Sri Lanka A at Liverpool and scratched around for 20-odd in a low-scoring match on a damp wicket. By the end of the day, the wicket had dried out considerably, so I went out and had a 45-minute knock, which was useful practice.

I finally came back against Sussex at Liverpool at the start of August, in a match that was a fantastic advert for the county game. The cricket played in those few days was just as entertaining as in any Test match. Its intensity and the skills involved were amazing. I was very nervous before going out to bat, so I sat on my own, trying to still the nightmares about my scratchy innings against Sri Lanka A. I left the first ball, and to the second, I played one of the best forward defensive strokes I've ever played. That gave me confidence and I got off the mark with a drive on the up through cover, and then I started playing my shots. Everything was falling back into place, it was the best I'd felt at the crease for a long time and I thought I got a rough lbw decision off Rana Naved, Sussex's Pakistan all-rounder. The wicket was quick and bouncy and, when it came to my turn, I bowled fast on it, but couldn't get a wicket.

In our second innings, we needed 240-odd on a good pitch and were unable to do it. When I went out, I really wanted us to win the game and for one of the few times in my career I bottled it. I wanted to do it all myself when we started losing wickets, and once I got out in the middle I had a complete breakdown in my thought patterns. I got off the mark pulling one over mid-on and my nerves got the better of me. I was shaking while I was out in the middle. I'd never had that before. I spoke to Stuart Law about it afterwards. There was a lot of attention on me, I wanted to win and I wasn't able to handle it. Our collapse on the third day gave Sussex an important victory and damaged Lancashire's championship hopes. There was a big inquest in the dressing room afterwards and Stuart had a rant, which was good because it showed how much the game meant to everyone.

Now we had a spare day, and before going to Birmingham for the Twenty20 finals I thought we should use the time to practise on the wicket at Liverpool, which was an absolute belter – Old Trafford wasn't available, because an Arctic Monkeys concert was being staged there. That idea wasn't taken up however, and we travelled down to Birmingham without doing any specific Twenty20 practice. We had not played any Twenty20 cricket as a team for a few weeks and it would have been ideal to practice our skills prior to the finals day, which comprises teams playing a semi-final and a final on the same day. Our hopes of success were undermined when Mal Loye, one of our best one-day players, suffered a back problem in the warm-up to the semi-final. We suddenly didn't have an opener, so I volunteered. In hindsight, that was the wrong thing to do because I never really got going before Brad Hodge ran me out and we lost badly to Gloucestershire.

After that, we had a Roses match and were winning the game when Mark Chilton, our captain, brought me back on to deal with the tailenders. I bowled about 10 overs, but started to feel discomfort in my ankle, which was worrying. I'd missed all the West Indies matches and the Tests against India, who were the other summer tourists in 2007, so I didn't want anything to prevent me being recalled for the one-dayers against India.

I was pleased with the way I was bowling and, fortunately, the selectors gave me the nod. When I returned for England for the first match, at the Rose Bowl, I ran in, bowled quickly and could pretty much land the ball wherever I wanted. Despite that, I took just one wicket – I bowled far better that day than I did in the next match at Bristol, when I got five wickets.

The downside was that my ankle was starting to get very sore, which was by now not only worrying but also embarrassing, since I'd only just come back into the side and was bowling well. I didn't want to give in to it – it was a matter of pride. Then my knee flared up after I banged into an advertising board in the field at Bristol, so I missed the next game at Edgbaston anyway. I returned for the following game at Old Trafford but found the footholes jarring. When my ankle plays up, it always follows the same pattern – I start fine and get my first spell out of the way, but when I come back to bowl, I struggle. On this occasion, I swapped ends and it gave way on me. During my last over, my ankle was turning and giving way with every ball. It affected my batting as well, because I couldn't put my foot down properly, and I was caught at backward point as a result.

At the end of the game, I was in pieces. The idea of yet another operation and all the hard work involved with rehabilitation afterwards was almost too much to bear. There are times in your career when you have massive highs, but they don't outweigh moments like that. I remember sitting on the balcony at Old Trafford wrapped in a towel after everyone had gone and I must have smoked six cigarettes. I hadn't had a drink for about two months but I sure as hell felt like one then. I didn't have one, but I didn't want to speak to anyone, I didn't want to do anything because my ankle was done.

England were due to go to South Africa in just a few days to play in the inaugural ICC World Twenty20 tournament. I was booked to make the trip but now I had mixed feelings about it. I wanted to go because I wanted to be involved – and I was trying to kid myself that my ankle might get better, even though, deep down, I knew that it wouldn't. I was also wondering whether I would ever play for England again. The thought that this might be my last trip was powerful motivation.

Before that, though, we had a final one-day match against India at Lord's. I did play, after another cortisone injection, which effectively dulls the pain and gets rid of the inflammation, but I was really wound up. The ankle was affecting my mood on the field and I was getting aggressive and short-tempered. If something didn't go my way, I would be shouting and cursing, which is not me at all. I'm not the biggest sledger by any means. Every now and then I would say a word or two, but I was never abusive, and when I found myself about to sledge Sachin Tendulkar, a player I admire more than anyone in cricket, I knew things weren't right.

Nevertheless, I'd already agreed to go to South Africa, and the injection had got me back on the cricket field, albeit just for a few weeks. The beauty of Twenty20 cricket is that each bowler has four overs only, and I found a way of getting through. I was probably bowling at around 80 per cent of my capability, but still at a decent pace. What I couldn't understand was why I wasn't getting belted all over the place. I got away with a scoring rate against me of 5.80 per over in the tournament, but once again a reflection of how the discomfort in my ankle was affecting me was my having a go at Yuvraj Singh in our final game of the tournament – probably not the best action I have ever taken on a cricket field because he belted poor Stuart Broad for six sixes in the next over! India went on to win the tournament, and by that time it had been decided I wasn't fit enough to carry on to Sri Lanka to play in the one-day series there. I couldn't play as I wanted to, I was in pain and my mood was hardly the best. Sending me home was the right decision.

When I got back, I went to see a specialist in London, and there was talk about stabilising my ankle, which is a procedure usually carried out if you can't walk. There would have been no chance of playing cricket again if they had gone ahead with that. After that consultation, Rooster took it on himself to find the best person in the world to have a look at the problem. At the same time, I had to decide whether I wanted to go through it all over again. There was also the rest of my life to think about and I didn't want to spend it limping because of all the jabs and operations I'd had.

However, Rooster put me in touch with Niek van Dijk, who turns out to be the best person in the world when it comes to ankles. It was a bizarre experience going to see him – I'm probably one of the few blokes ever to visit Amsterdam who wasn't looking for a good time! England doctor Nick Peirce and Rooster came with me and we got off to a terrible start. At the hospital, after I'd signed in and we finally got as far as the waiting room, the consultant's second in command came in to see us. I politely explained that we'd not come to see him, we wanted to see Mr van Dijk, and it was firmly explained to me that we had to go through it with him initially and then Mr van Dijk would take over. Rooster managed to get up this bloke's nose, so Mr van Dijk was summoned. He explained that he had a footballer from Ajax in the next room, another from Inter Milan in the other room, and the only way he could get through it all was to allow his assistant to greet us.

It was quickly evident he had no grasp of cricket, but we talked him through it and showed him videos. At first, I was concerned about the idea of putting my ankle in his hands – he knew nothing about my sport, we were lower down his list of priorities than footballers and we'd upset him by making a fuss. However, the one thing he said straightaway was that he didn't want to stabilise the ankle. He thought that was a complete no go, which conflicted with the other doctor's view. He found the minute bone fragments, which had been there all along, but said they were living, had their own blood supply and were growing in a place where he'd never seen bone before. Everything was starting to fit with my symptoms. I voiced my initial concerns, he set my mind at rest about them and, after a bit of deliberating, I thought, 'What else am I going to do?' and decided to go ahead with my fourth operation.

I knew the rehabilitation would be a lot longer this time, because I'd chatted to Brett Lee, who has had ankle problems, and Rooster had spoken to quite a few different people who had been through the same thing. Mr van Dijk was saying I'd be running in six weeks and playing in eight, and if I'd been a footballer I may have been, but I had a shrewd idea that, for me, it would be five or six months of gym work. I wanted to get the rehabilitation sorted out before I went under the knife, so that I knew exactly what I had to deal with afterwards and could decide what I was going to do and where I was going to do it. In England, pressure to get fit came from the media, the public, everyone. I would have people dipping in and out to do interviews and I found myself saying the same things over and over again. I wanted to get away from all that, but being a cricketer is not like being a golfer, who can do what he wants. I was employed by the England and Wales Cricket Board, so had to do what they said, and I can't fault the support I received from Peter Moores, Hugh Morris, managing director of the ECB, and Nick Peirce the England doctor. The notion of going to Florida came about after a conversation I had with Chubby Chandler. I'd never been to America before and he told me about West Palm Beach and the contacts he had there. A bloke he knew could help us and make sure we stayed at the right places. Once that seed was sown I pursued it, and it was a master stroke.

It goes without saying that the weather in Florida is better than in the Ribble Valley, where I normally do my rehabilitation. Exercises that would have taken me six or seven hours to do at home took three or four hours there. Everything was in one place, whereas in England I have to travel long distances up and down the motorway to all the different venues I use for rehab. The other good thing about going to America was that no one knew who I was, which was terrific.

The first week was difficult, mainly because Rachael didn't like the house I'd found, so we trailed around here, there and everywhere looking for another one, but ended up staying where we were. The place was called Palm Beach Gardens and just down the road there was a golf complex with a gym, clubhouse, restaurant, tennis facilities, swimming pool and everything I needed for my rehab. Shops were nearby and the beach was a mile away. In a climate like that with everything on your doorstep, there's nothing to hold you back and I really dedicated myself to the training. I almost severed contact with home because I also wanted to use the time away to do some soul-searching. I spent a lot of time thinking about the past, the mistakes I'd made, and where I wanted to take my career. For the first two weeks, we were on our own, essentially taking a holiday, and for the next five weeks the ECB paid for Rooster to come out and help with my rehab. Apart from him, no one was chipping away at me, telling me I should be doing this or that. I'd been an international cricketer for ten years, I'd not long celebrated my thirtieth birthday and I was constantly being pulled in different directions. In Florida, I spent time on my own with my family and it was one of the best things I've ever done.

After the World Cup, when my name was often in the paper for the wrong reasons, I'd started thinking about how I was living my life. The only person who was really harmed by the pedalo incident was myself. A lot of people saw it as a bit of fun, but I don't want my kids going to school and hearing about their dad being in the paper after getting drunk on a pedalo. Like any parent, I want my kids to grow up proud of what I've achieved. I don't want people taking the mickey out of them because of what I've done. In Florida, I could relax walking down the street, knowing no one would recognise me and no photographer would suddenly appear to take my picture. It was really nice being able to go out to a restaurant and not have everyone turn around when we walked in.

One of the major things on my mind was whether I could recapture my form. Could I get back to playing as I did, and could I get better? If I couldn't, it wasn't worth the effort. It was something I thought about long and hard. Ego and pride tell you that of course you can get back to your best form at the very least, but it takes a bit more than that, so you start thinking about how to go about achieving that aim. Naturally, I had doubts but I bet the best players in the world have doubts from time to time, especially when they are on their own. How you deal with them is the key to getting back to your best.

While we were in America, I had ringside tickets to watch Ricky Hatton's fight with Floyd Mayweather Jr, but I didn't think going to Las Vegas would have sent the right message if I had been seen on television back home. I got Rachael going about it later, though. When we watched the fight on television, the camera panned over the crowd, picking out celebrities, and focused on Brad Pitt and Angelina Jolie. For a while, I had Rachael believing that our tickets were for the seats next to them!

We were still in America when Duncan's book about his time as England coach was finally published, and I was pleased about that. As far as Duncan and I are concerned, it was a case of two people who didn't get on being thrown together for eight months of the year as part of the England cricket team. We had completely different views on life, the relationship didn't work and it came to an abrupt end after the World Cup, so it was clear he was not going to be very complimentary about me, although I've lost count of the number of times I was injured, or had jabs, while he was England coach and played to help the team. Apart from the odd text message from home, I didn't know what he'd said or about the coverage in the papers, and I didn't look on the internet. I was on another continent and I didn't want to see it. I was enjoying myself and didn't want him spoiling my day. I was determined he wasn't going to come back into my life, or ruin my rehab, just as I was getting back on track. I had an inkling he was going to have a go at me, even though he once said, when the press were on his back, that the weakest way to have a go at someone was in print.

At least by being in America, I was able to avoid the media frenzy caused by his book, and I was back in the UK for just a short period before flying out to South Africa for more rehab. I was also getting to know Peter Moores better. He wanted to be involved with everything about my rehabilitation. When there were meetings about my progress and what I was going to do next, he would attend them and offer ideas, and generally made me feel that he cared about me.

# 12

# FIGHTING BACK

After South Africa, the next step in my rehabilitation was a trip to India in early 2008. Lancashire were sending some young lads for experience, and the England Lions (formerly England A) were going on tour there, so it seemed a good plan to join up with them, at least for the practice sessions. I wanted to go about my business quietly, but the news got out and media attention grew. So I went on ahead of the Lancashire lads, and did some work in the nets with the Lions squad.

Former Worcestershire coach Davie Houghton was the Lions' batting pundit and I worked with him, and also with former Indian captain Mohammad Azharuddin, whom I knew from playing against him when I was younger. I got in touch with him once I arrived in India because I wanted to work with a batsman who was good against spin, which I'd struggled with for some time. My choice didn't go down very well with the powers that be at the ECB because of his track record and links with match-fixing. I'd obviously heard all the allegations, but I didn't know whether they were true or not. I just wanted to talk to someone who could further my game, and saw him as a good person to approach. The Board of Control for Cricket in India had lifted their lifetime ban on him, and he remains enthusiastic about cricket. He is still an unbelievable player. He had me batting in the nets on turning wickets, and he went in there, no pads on, and showed me what he meant. He was fantastic. We spoke about the thought processes required for playing spin, and worked on manipulating the ball into gaps and not just relying on boundaries. He wanted me to move my feet quicker, and I felt much better about facing spin by the time I returned from India.

While in Mumbai, I went to the Academy, which has been set up to help players from all over the world with their game. A lot of counties send young players there, and I continued the work on spin that I had begun with Azhar. I used to be a good player of spin, dominating by coming down the wicket, hitting it straight and just keeping it simple, and I wanted to get back to that.

Practice facilities were a bit mixed, and I got fed up with spending all my time in the nets, so I ended up playing a couple of matches for the Lions, just as a batsman. In the first one, I managed just four runs. When I arrived at the crease, batting at No. 5, we needed around nine an over, but I was stretching against spin and was caught before I'd got going. In my second match, I scored 23, but I was bored to death in the field. I'd forgotten what it was like to play in a match without bowling. I stood in the slips for a while and then I was sent out to the boundary. It was very dull.

When the Lions went home, I joined up with the young Lancashire lads. It was good to spend some time with them and get to know them, although the standard of the facilities went down a notch as soon as the Lions departed. The one game I played with the lads was a bit of a shambles. When we turned up at the ground, they didn't even know we were playing! They watered the wicket, drenched it in fact, and tried to get a team together. So much for playing on spinning wickets when you're in India. When we batted the ball was taking bits out of the top of the wicket, but it dried out a bit and when they batted, they swung off their feet and knocked off the runs.

I was supposed to be a mentor to the young lads, but they helped me probably just as much as I like to think I helped them. It was also a gentle reintroduction to being away for a while. I'd found a new life at home and got into a routine that I was really enjoying – getting up and taking the kids to nursery, still training but just being around a bit more. Daft as it might seem, I had to break that pattern before I got too used to it and started wanting to do it permanently. Those three weeks in India helped me do that.

Back at Lancashire, not many people were around pre-season until we went to Dubai for a tournament in March. I have always enjoyed pre-season trips, with everyone getting together as a squad. Along with the cricket, there's time to enjoy being with each other and to catch up with what everyone's been doing for the winter. I had already done some bowling in the nets at home prior to the trip, and it was a case of continuing to build myself up while we were there. I must admit, though, I was nervous the first time I bowled in a match, in case any of the batsmen came after me. I was bowling at around 75–80 per cent and it went fine until Ben Brown, one of the young Sussex lads wound me up. He came down the wicket and hit me through the covers for four, with a bit of a swagger. So I cranked it up and got him out in the next over. I may have had a word about taking liberties when he walked off!

That was the danger – that I would get wound up enough to forget about the injury and tear in. I had strict instructions not to go at full pace, but it's very difficult when pride takes over. Even in pre-season friendlies, the competitive edge comes out. In the field, I managed to persuade them to put me at extra cover, so I was throwing myself around. It meant something to win these games, having not been involved in a competitive environment for a while. The only slight concern was a bit of stiffness in the ankle. The physio took a look at it, and I phoned Rooster. He reminded me what it was like coming back last time. During this sort of rehabilitation, a few twinges are inevitable and they went away pretty much as quickly as they came.

We returned from Dubai to terrible weather, with heavy rain almost every day making it impossible to practise in the outdoor nets. So we were back indoors, not doing a great deal, chomping at the bit to get going, and with a month to go to the start of the season. That set us back and I'm sure it contributed to the number of injuries we had in the Lancashire squad at the start of the summer. I'm also sure it affected our form because we lost that edge in the month after coming back from Dubai.

While life was a struggle cricket-wise, it was a happy time in the Flintoff household with the arrival of Rocky, our second son, a couple weeks after I returned from Dubai. I missed a friendly against Yorkshire to attend the birth and it was great to be there, although it made me feel all the more guilty about missing Corey's arrival. I actually felt I played a part this time. I was able to hold him when he was born, and phone people up to tell them the good news. I missed that for three weeks with Corey and that's something I'll never get back. After Rocky was born, I got home at around 5.00 a.m., and when Holly woke up a couple of hours later I told her she had a new baby brother. She immediately started crying and said she wanted a sister!

Lancashire had a two-day match scheduled against Yorkshire a couple of days later and I was keen to play because I needed some overs under my belt, but inevitably it rained. I wouldn't say I felt rusty with my bowling when the season began – when I'm fit, I'm always confident I can land the ball where I want to – but I was perhaps a little under-cooked. I could have done with a few more overs, a few more miles in my legs to build up my stamina, but I wasn't on my own with that. I'd done what everyone else had done in pre-season, so I think nearly all the bowlers were in the same boat when we turned up at The Oval for the first match, in mid-April. I was finding bowling easy as we approached that game, which is always a good sign. I felt I was doing what I'd always done but a little bit quicker and with less effort, which is an ideal combination for any bowler.

The worst thing about that first game was that the wicket was just dead, a real featherbed. I didn't have much luck and beat the bat a few times and only ended up with one wicket. I got through 28 overs and was keen to bowl. I wasn't playing to prove my fitness. I told Stuart Law, our new captain, that I was there to play and would do whatever he asked. It was difficult because there was a lot of press attention, and journalists were asking to speak to me after every day's play, but I couldn't keep doing the same interviews.

I scored 23 in that first match and enjoyed my time at the crease. Surrey had a young fast bowler from Barbados, Chris Jordan, and as soon as he came on they put someone back for the hook, so I thought, 'Here we go,' and expected a few short deliveries. The first ball he bowled to me I was stuck on the crease and edged it for four. I was quite happy with the man back, because I found it easier playing off the back foot and the field suggested I would get a lot of short deliveries and I didn't want to be dragged forward. I got off to a bit of a flier, hitting three fours in an over, and then, feeling fine, I edged one to slip off Saqlain Mushtaq. It was a doosra – the ball that spins the other way – which I picked but I just went a bit hard at it.

That proved to be one of the batting highlights of my early season, and it was followed by a first-ball duck against Somerset at Old Trafford – the first of three at the start of the season but, out of all of them, this was the one I don't think I could have done much about. The ball pitched and left me and at the point of contact I had my bat straight, and then went with it a bit. I held the line and nicked it. Having waited so long to play again, it was probably something that was always going to happen. Unfortunately, we were playing on the other side of the square, and the dressing room seemed to be miles away, which made getting a duck all the more embarrassing. I walked all the way out, took guard, nicked it and walked all the way back. I can tell you, in situations like that, when people have come to Old Trafford to see you play, you don't know what to do with yourself. You don't know whether to smile or just put your head down and get off the field as quickly as possible. The polite claps that follow you in just make you feel worse.

The press attention hadn't abated and me getting a duck made bigger headlines than someone else scoring runs. In fact, it was getting quite embarrassing in the dressing room – someone would score runs or take a few wickets and everyone still wanted to speak to me.

The one consolation was that I was starting to find a good rhythm with my bowling and, with a bit of a wind behind me, I enjoyed pitting myself against Marcus Trescothick and Justin Langer, Somerset's opening pair. The only way we were going to win the game at Old Trafford was by bowling them out in the second innings, and I told Stuey Law that I was going to have a go at Langer. I hit him everywhere, he played at and missed a couple, but I just couldn't get an edge. He tends to wear a few, by that I mean that he gets hit a lot, and he kept chirping at me to put me off my rhythm. I get on well with Justin, so it was half tongue in cheek. He kept winding me up by telling me that I didn't do that when he had the green Australian helmet on. I didn't respond. I just ran in and kept hitting him – I didn't think I had to say much when that was happening! He was trying to get a rise out of me, but I wasn't having any of it. I cracked in the end after bowling one delivery, and gave him a look, but he said, 'Come on Fred, it's not in your nature, give me a smile.' He got me then, and I couldn't help laughing.

It was also a funny situation with Tres. I've enjoyed some great times alongside him with England, and played with him way back in the Under-19s. He is very annoying, though, because he's so good. When he came out to bat, it quickly became clear he had lost none of his ability. He is certainly the best player I have bowled at in county cricket in recent years. Just to prove how good he is, on that particular day, Jimmy Anderson was swinging the ball all over the place and hitting everyone else on the pads, but Tres just dropped that big bat of his and had no problem at all. To be honest, I had forgotten how good he was until I saw him play again that day. Some of his shots were brilliant. He just stood there, so composed, and spanked me for two fours on the bounce. It's such a shame he is no longer available for England. Everyone went on about my absence when I was out injured, but for my money Tres is the biggest loss of the lot. He was such an important player in both the Test and one-day sides.

In the Friends Provident Trophy, we won a game against Scotland at the Grange before returning to Manchester to play Durham at Old Trafford. I was caught in the deep off Paul Collingwood, going for a boundary, when we were chasing victory, and, if I'm perfectly honest, I was caught by a fielder I didn't see! I had a look around, thought deep midwicket was open, hit it and started running. It was only then that I realised a man was there, running over to take a good catch. It's the sort of thing you see club cricketers doing and I was very embarrassed about it afterwards – it was just as well we won the game.

Our next match was against Scotland at Old Trafford. I remember talking to Mike Watkinson, the Lancashire coach, after we'd beaten them up at the Grange, and dominated the game, wondering how come we'd lost to them twice in recent years. That conversation came back to haunt me because we lost again at Old Trafford. I had a funny exchange with Colin Smith, one of their batsmen. I'd hit him on the head and came down the pitch to make sure he was all right. I asked him twice how he was and he didn't say anything in response. I thought he was ignoring me, so I told him I'd do it again if he was going to be like that, and went back to my mark. A couple of balls later he got down the other end and apologised to me, saying he wasn't trying to be funny – he just couldn't speak because his jaw hurt too much!

After that humbling experience, we played Durham in a championship match at Old Trafford, which everyone was saying was like a Test match because we had all our England players in the team and they had Harmison and Collingwood. We struggled in the first innings and I got another first ball duck. I had a feeling it was going to happen. The ball nipped away and I followed with my hands. I didn't really know what to think about my form. I was pleased with the way I was bowling, but the batting was a real struggle. I was working hard in the nets, but couldn't get past my first ball out in the middle.

I'd travelled to Old Trafford on my motorbike that day, and one of the things they tell you when you do your test is not to ride your bike when you're emotional. I was extremely fed up in the dressing room and thought I'd better not ride back, so I asked Jimmy Anderson to give me a lift home. When Durham started their innings, a howling gale was blowing and Jimmy bowled into it from the executive-box end, taking four wickets. When it came to my turn with the ball, I let go of a little frustration, too, we bowled them out that night and I felt fine to ride my bike home after all.

I was still not improving with the bat, though, and failed to make much of an impression in the second innings. Afterwards, I sat in the dressing room for ages, still wearing my pads. Looking back, I was probably putting too much pressure on myself. I had been out of top-class cricket for the best part of a year and I was trying too hard to get my form back. When I was bowling, I was doing it with a smile on my face because I knew what I wanted to do, whereas I was a bit tense with my batting.

Lack of prowess with the bat was not my only worry. Midway through the match, I had started to feel discomfort in my side. I was running in hard, out of frustration at my failure to score any runs, and bowling very quickly. Halfway through a spell of around seven overs, I eased back a bit, and probably bowled as fast but with more control, and that was when I started feeling my side. I pulled a side muscle a few years ago and it felt as though someone had shot me, but on this occasion all that happened was that I felt a bit stiff, so I thought nothing of it. It was only when I woke up the following morning that I realised something was wrong. My side was not only very stiff, but also painful. I bowled that morning but not as I wanted to, and I asked to go off after about five or six overs.

It was the worst possible timing for an injury. Kirk Russell, the England physio, and a few other people from the ECB were coming up to see how I was getting on with my ankle. I told the Lancashire physio I was feeling something but not to say anything, which was probably the wrong thing to do but I thought it might settle down. I went back on to the field and as soon as the game was finished I went straight to the hospital to have a scan. When the results of that came through, I was told to go for an X-ray and alarm bells rang. A scan is supposed to read your soft tissue, so I asked why an X-ray was needed – a suspected stress fracture of a rib was the answer, and the X-ray did indeed show early signs of a stress fracture. If I had carried on playing, it would have developed into one and I'd have been out for around three months. Rooster arranged for a specialist to have a look, and he confirmed I had a small tear in one of my rib muscles.

It was a massive blow after all the hard work to get back playing again. I'd built myself up to play in the First Test against New Zealand at Lord's, starting the following week on 15 May. The selectors were picking the team that weekend, which was one of the reasons the ECB people had travelled up to Old Trafford to have a look at me. I was also very keen to play at Old Trafford the following week in the Second Test. I'd been working for five months to get back to play for

Lancashire and England, and now another injury would keep me out for a further six weeks. I said to Rachael that I wasn't sure I could do it yet again. It just seemed to be one thing after another. I quickly got over that, though. I'd come so far and gone through so much on and off the field in the previous few months that a side strain was not going to stop me trying to get back playing again.

I tried to keep my fitness up by cycling, but the problem was I couldn't get out of breath because then everything pulled around the injury. Missing Lord's was hard, but missing playing the Test at Old Trafford was even more difficult. I didn't know it then but I was not to play another Test at my home ground.

I went to Old Trafford earlier in the week and saw the stands being set up and the burger vans arriving, and felt the anticipation. On the first day I had lunch in my agent ISM's box, but I hated it and just wanted to get out of there as quickly as possible. For the first time in my career I felt genuinely jealous, which is not a word I like using. I wasn't jealous of the players, and it's not a case of wanting England to do badly without me, but I wanted to be in that team, to take a wicket in front of 15,000 fans at Old Trafford and have a chance of raising my bat, and I wanted to be in the dressing room after a win. Not being able to do that really hurt, but as much as I hated not being part of the Test, those sort of feelings also drive you to get back, and they spurred me on to return later that summer. One of the reasons I'd gone to Old Trafford at the start of the week was to have a chat with Geoff Miller, England's national selector, and Peter Moores, and I came away feeling better. Peter made me feel a part of the squad and gave me the impression he wanted me back in the team. Being around the dressing room was difficult, though. I was in there the day the lads turned up for treatment. Michael Vaughan said I could come up whenever I wanted, but I didn't want to sit up there watching the match and getting in the way.

I was sidelined for the rest of that series, and for the one-dayers against New Zealand, while I gradually built up my fitness with Lancashire. Once again, I was struggling to score runs, but chasing a low score against Sussex at Hove, Stuart Law promoted me up the order. I had a bit of a dip, played some good shots and some bad shots, and just swung off my feet to win the game, scoring 62 off 59 balls. I felt so much better for scoring runs, and from that innings, progressed to batting properly again, rather than just playing a few shots. Halfway through that match, I found out that I wasn't going to be in the squad for the First Test against South Africa at Lord's in July, which was a disappointment but at the same time a relief. Speculation about me being included had been non-stop. Once it became known I wasn't in, everything settled down for a while. Helping to win a game for Lancashire gave me a great deal of satisfaction, and when we got on the coach to go back home to Old Trafford that night, I remember feeling much better about myself and my game than I had for quite some time.

The run scoring continued in my next match, against Hampshire at the Rose Bowl. I got a good ball in the first innings from left-armer James Tomlinson, of whom I had not heard – and the thought flashed through my mind that I was going through a stage of getting out to people I didn't know. He had a bit of a funny action and angled one across me, but I edged it behind and the match progressed in a similar manner to the game at Hove. I finished unbeaten on 39. Neil Mallender was one of the umpires at the Rose Bowl and he wished me luck in the next Test at Headingley. I told him I didn't know if I was playing yet, but he assured me I would be.

I was asked to go to Lord's after we had beaten Hampshire to link up with England, who were training there before the First Test. Unfortunately, the weather didn't let us train outside, and we were restricted to the indoor nets, but I managed to make an impression by hitting Ian Bell on the helmet with one delivery. He suffered no ill effects, I'm pleased to say. It was good to be invited down by Peter Moores, and Michael Vaughan was happy for me to join in, so that was an indication that I wasn't far away from a recall.

England drew that opening Test, despite dominating it for most of the match, and I was called up for the Second Test at Headingley. It almost felt like my debut again because it had been so long since the last Test I'd played, in Sydney many months before. It was good to get back into the dressing room. Things move on pretty quickly without you. I've seen that when other players have left, or had periods out of the team, and then come back. Little things change, such as the humour. I wanted to get back in the thick of it, but I had a lot of nerves to go with the excitement of playing for England again.

# 13

# CHANGING THE GUARD

Interest in my return to the England team was overshadowed by the selection of Nottinghamshire seamer Darren Pattinson for his first cap, which was regarded as controversial. The fuss about his call-up centred on the fact that he was born, and had played most of his cricket, in Australia. I had played against him earlier in the season in a Twenty20 match at Old Trafford, but I didn't know him to speak to before meeting him at breakfast on the morning of the Second Test. Darren didn't know any of us particularly well, so he was a bit quiet, but we made an effort to include him in all the chatter. It must have been very hard and I felt for him when he was made the scapegoat for our poor performance. He was picked to play in a Test match for England and he did all right. Once you've been selected, all eleven of you are trying to win the game. How or where you've been to get to that point doesn't matter.

I wasn't in the greatest form I'd ever been in with the bat, but I was starting to feel more confident. In international cricket you have time to build up to a game, and know who you're playing against. I know it sounds strange but I'm sure if I tried to play league cricket now, I'd be useless, because my game's just not equipped for it. I know it's at a lower standard than the cricket I'm used to, but because the pitches are different you have to adapt your game to be successful. I love playing for Lancashire, but in county cricket I didn't know the bowlers or a lot of the people I was playing against. You get to know the opposition at international level because you play against them so much. The more I batted at Headingley, the better I felt, probably more so in the second innings when I batted for over two hours to score 38. I was also pleased with my bowling, without producing anything special, but the South African batsmen were so patient. They ground us down and outplayed us. It wasn't the comeback I was hoping for. I wanted to come in and make a difference, and play a part in an England victory, but it wasn't to be. None of my debuts, or restarts, at every stage of my career, have been sparkling, and this one was no different.

I kept my place for the Third Test at Edgbaston, starting at the end of July, and again I was pleased with the way I batted. We had fallen into a bit of trouble and I was batting with the tail – I've gained quite a lot of experience of that over the years. Sometimes batting with the tailenders frees you up and I was hopeful that together we could get England up to a decent score. Unfortunately, after a terrible mix-up with Jimmy Anderson, I ran him out. I held my hand up for that, and then, next ball, Monty was run out going for a two when there was an almost easy three. I was fuming, the red mist came down and I just carried on running to the dressing room. The last thing we needed was a couple of unnecessary run-outs and I'm afraid I didn't wait for Monty.

# ENGLAND v SOUTH AFRICA
## (2nd Test) at Headingley 18–21 July 2008

### England

| | | | |
|---|---|---|---|
| A.J.Strauss c Boucher b Morkel | 27 | – c Boucher b Ntini | 0 |
| A.N.Cook c Boucher b Morkel | 18 | – c Amla b Kallis | 60 |
| *M.P.Vaughan c Smith b Steyn | 0 | – c Boucher b Ntini | 21 |
| K.P.Pietersen c Smith b Steyn | 45 | (5) c Boucher b Kallis | 13 |
| I.R.Bell b Kallis | 31 | (6) c de Villiers b Morkel | 4 |
| +T.R.Ambrose c Boucher b Ntini | 12 | (7) c Boucher b Steyn | 36 |
| A.Flintoff c Boucher b Steyn | 17 | (8) c Kallis b Morkel | 38 |
| S.C.J.Broad c de Villiers b Morkel | 17 | (9) not out | 67 |
| J.M.Anderson not out | 11 | (4) lbw b Steyn | 34 |
| M.S.Panesar c de Villiers b Morkel | 0 | – b Steyn | 10 |
| D.J.Pattinson c Boucher b Steyn | 8 | – b Morkel | 13 |
| l-b 6, w 6, n-b 5 | 17 | B 4, lb 11, w 2, n-b 14 | 31 |

| | | | |
|---|---|---|---|
| 1/26 2/27 3/62 4/106 5/123 | 203 | 1/3 2/50 3/109 4/123 5/140 | 327 |
| 6/150 7/177 8/181 9/186 10/203 | | 6/152 7/220 8/238 9/266 10-327 | |

Bowling: *First innings* – Steyn 18.3-2-76-4; Ntini 11-0-45-1; Morkel 15-4-52-4; Kallis 8-2-24-1. *Second innings* – Steyn 28-7-97-3; Ntini 25-7-69-2; Morkel 22-4-61-3; Kallis 17-3-50-2; Harris 15-5-35-0.

### South Africa

| | | | |
|---|---|---|---|
| N.D.McKenzie c Flintoff | | | |
| b Anderson | 15 | (2) not out | 6 |
| *G.C.Smith c Strauss b Flintoff | 44 | (1) not out | 3 |
| H.M.Amla lbw b Pattinson | 38 | | |
| J.H.Kallis b Anderson | 4 | | |
| A.G.Prince c Ambrose b Pattinson | 149 | | |
| A.B.de Villiers c Flintoff b Broad | 174 | | |
| +M.V.Boucher b Anderson | 34 | | |
| M.Morkel b Panesar | 0 | | |
| P.L.Harris c Anderson b Panesar | 24 | | |
| D.W.Steyn not out | 10 | | |
| M.Ntini c Pietersen b Panesar | 1 | | |
| B 2, l-b 19, w 1, n-b 7 | 29 | | 0 |

| | | | |
|---|---|---|---|
| 1/51 2/69 3/76 4/143 5/355 | 522 | (for 0 wkts) | 9 |
| 6/422 7/427 8/511 9/511 10/522 | | | |

Bowling: *First innings* – Anderson 44-9-136-3; Pattinson 30-2-95-2; Flintoff 40-12-77-1; Broad 29-2-114-1; Panesar 29.2-6-65-3; Pietersen 4-0-14-0. *Second innings* – Broad 1-0-8-0; Pattinson 0.1-0-1-0.

Umpires: B.F.Bowden and D.J.Harper
South Africa won by 10 wickets

South Africa had a strong, patient batting line-up, and if we were to remain in the game after being bowled out for 231, the pressure was on us to bowl well. We got early wickets and then Jacques Kallis came out to bat. He has been their key batsman for as long as I can remember. There was a lot of talk afterwards about the sightscreens at Edgbaston not being good enough, and certainly Kallis kept complaining that he was not picking up the ball when I bowled from the Pavilion End. I've had situations like that myself when I'm batting. If you get something in your head, it can totally take over and you start worrying about that more than watching the actual ball.

I'd started to get some rhythm back in my bowling after delivering a lot of overs at Headingley. You can't always be bowling at full pace, and there are times when you just need to concentrate on getting the right line and length and try to frustrate the batsman. There are other times, though, when you know you have to go for the jugular, and Kallis's arrival at the crease in that first innings was one of those occasions. I thought I'd got him out earlier than I did with a low full toss, which hit him square on the boot, but umpire Aleem Dar didn't give it and that fired me up a bit. I chuntered at Aleem for the rest of the over and, fortunately, got my man in the next one.

Our little battle caused a fair bit of comment in the press. Some of the newspapers were claiming it was like Allan Donald's famous duel with Michael Atherton at Trent Bridge all those years ago, but I didn't sense that myself – I just wanted to get one of South Africa's best batsmen out. Maybe it was because

I was out in the middle with the ball in my hand, but I didn't find my set-to with Kallis anything like as tense as the Donald–Atherton duel. On that occasion, I was sat on the balcony as a nervous debutant, willing Athers to stay out there so I didn't have to bat against a fired up Donald!

They say cricket is all down to fine lines and that was certainly the case in this Test. Paul Collingwood ended a bad run of scores by hitting a determined century, which was full of character and typical of him, and we battled well to set South Africa a victory target of 281. A couple of decisions didn't go our way. Monty was denied an appeal for lbw against South African captain Graeme Smith, who also punched one to short leg that wasn't given, and I'm sure we'd have won the Test if either of them had gone our way. Instead, despite getting some early wickets, Smith scored an unbeaten century to wrap up the victory and the series for South Africa.

The game finished on a Saturday evening, and not many of the lads went home. Instead, we stayed at the hotel in Birmingham and had a few drinks at the bar. I had a chat with Peter Moores and assistant coach Andy Flower, and Michael Vaughan was there with his wife Nichola. I had no inkling of what was on his mind. It was only when a few of the other players had gone that he told me he was giving up the captaincy. It was a bit of a bombshell for me, and certainly not something I was expecting. I know we'd been beaten by South Africa, and he'd had a lean time of it with the bat, but I wasn't expecting him to resign. I didn't know what to say, and I don't think he wanted me to say anything. He just wanted to tell me why he was going. I shook his hand and wished him luck. He was going to make an official announcement at a press conference the following morning.

He came past when I was lying on the floor in the hotel reception shortly after breakfast. It's not what you think. I hadn't stayed in the bar all night. I was playing with my kids when he came over, smartly dressed, ready to go off to the press conference at Loughborough. I shook his hand and wished him luck again, with Holly and Corey still jumping on me, and it was only when I watched the press conference on TV later on that I realised just how much he had been suffering. I didn't see it live because Rachael and I took the kids to the cinema to see *Kung Fu Panda*, but we went for a coffee afterwards and they were showing re-runs of the press conference. It was then I saw how emotional it was for him. I know how much it takes out of you, and it was probably worse for him, having done it for such a long time and been so good at it. He has been the best captain England have had in my time as a player, and from what I experienced, it was a miracle he did it for so long. Only those who have done the job, and realise that you take it off the field with you at the end of the day, can really appreciate how difficult it is.

I know exactly what he went through because of what happened to me in Australia. When things aren't going well, being captain can be such a lonely place. I think the big surprise, though, was that none of us knew what was happening to him. He was so constant in the way he dealt with everything. Whether we were winning or losing, he always had that aura of calmness about him. When you're performing and the team's winning, being captain is the best job in the world. When I led the team in India and we won that last Test match in 2006, there was nothing better. If you perform as a player as well, you can do no wrong. I don't know if it's an English trait but as soon as you start losing, you can see people start to withdraw and to apportion blame, and ultimately the buck stops with the captain. I'm sure he felt that, and with hindsight, he probably felt isolated from the players.

In my opinion, his decision to resign as captain was incredibly selfless. I'm sure, given his record, if he'd wanted to, he could have hung on for the Ashes in 2009 and had another crack at the Australians. I think he put his family first, and realised it wasn't the right thing for them, him or the team. I have known him for a long time. We went on A tours together, and on our first senior tour to South Africa in 1999–2000. We were never best mates, like myself and Harmy, but I've spent time with him socially, at golf functions and football and things like that, and he is a good bloke.

It was a sad couple of days, but sport is a harsh world and as a professional sportsman you have to move on. There was no time for sentiment because we were due to play South Africa in the final Test at The Oval and we couldn't afford to mope about.

If Michael's decision to resign was not a big enough shock, I later found out that Paul Collingwood was also stepping down as England's one-day captain. That left England needing two captains at the same time, but I hadn't really thought about who was going to replace them. I got a phone call from Peter Moores just as we were going in to see the film with the kids that afternoon. I had a bucket of popcorn in one hand and was trying to stop the kids running around all over the place with the other when the phone rang. Peter asked me what I thought of Kev and I think Robert Key's name was also discussed, but Kev was the obvious choice as they were looking for someone who would play all forms of the game. I had already told Peter the night before, when Michael announced he was resigning, that if I was in contention I didn't want to be considered. I didn't think it would be right for the team or for me. I had learnt from my experience in Australia that taking on the captaincy was a commitment too many, when I'm also trying to contribute to the side with the bat and ball. I am far happier as one of the senior players who can be in the thick of things in the dressing room, helping out where needed, and I didn't want to be detached in any way, shape or form from that. I think it's inevitable that the captain becomes slightly set apart. I didn't enjoy it previously, and wasn't prepared to put myself through that again.

I tried to speak to Kev after we came out of the cinema but we kept missing each other. I left a message offering my advice to him about the captaincy. I told him that as good a job as it is, the kudos and the honeymoon period don't last long before reality sets in. I advised him to think hard about it, not to make a decision on a whim, and to make sure his mind was clear when he made the decision. I don't know whether he listened to my advice or not, but I think his mind was already made up. The England captaincy is a hard job to reject and I think it was a job he wanted to do.

We did speak again before the Test began at The Oval. He addressed the side as the new captain two days before the start. I've played under a few captains now and they all have their different ideas of how to run the team. You listen to them and try to take what they say on board, but the bottom line is that my job in the team doesn't change no matter who is in charge. Whoever I'm playing for, I'm playing for England, and a change of captain does not alter that. He wanted the senior players to play a big role within the dressing room. That included Harmison, who had been recalled for the final Test, and me, but it was not much different from the role I'd performed within the team under Michael Vaughan's captaincy. I feel very comfortable doing it. I can be mates with people and share in all the jokes and banter in the dressing room, but I can also help out the younger players. I'm better suited to that role than leading the side and tossing the coin at the start of the match.

The only concern with Kev taking over as captain was whether it would affect his own game. He is our best batsman and if we were to be successful under him, we needed him to continue performing as a batsman. There were similar discussions when I took over as captain about whether I would be able to perform as an all-rounder and also lead the side. We shouldn't have worried too much about Kev, though, because he went out and scored a century in his first match. After that, we thought he'd be all right!

Whenever there's a change of captain, in any side, the team has a heightened air of excitement about it. The new captain is very keen to get things right from the word go, and that gets through to the players, resulting in extra energy about the dressing room and on the field. Players want to impress and that was certainly true in Kev's first match. I was really pleased we'd won the game, but at the same time I did spare a thought for Michael Vaughan. Very few captains go out on top, and when Kev took over the reins everyone was talking about a new dawn and a rejuvenated side. You could see at Michael's press conference how much the job had meant to him and how much he had given to it, and it seemed he had been forgotten.

The new captain obviously dominated events throughout that Test, but the big thing for me about the game was the return of Harmy to the team. He was given the first over of the match and could have had a wicket with his first ball, but Alastair Cook dropped Smith in the gully. When Harmy bowled that first over, it was a turning point. I was stood at second slip, a long way back, and the ball was still fizzing through. Everyone was looking around and nodding their heads as if we knew we were on to a winner. We won the game quite easily in the end. Kev's century ensured we had a healthy first-innings lead and we completed the victory on the final afternoon. I think at the start of the summer everyone had expected us to win the Test series and struggle in the one-day series, which followed, but winning that final Test changed the momentum for both us and them.

We prepared for the one-dayers by going to play Scotland in Edinburgh. The game was washed out, but we realised that Ryan Sidebottom was struggling with injury. Harmy had retired from one-day international cricket before the last World Cup, but he seemed to enjoy the final Test so much that the conversation came around to him as a possible replacement. I spoke to him on the phone as we travelled to Headingley for the first match of the series, told him what had been said, and he went away to have a think about it. I didn't want to influence his decision, although he knew I'd love him to return, and he spoke to his dad about it. When he agreed to come back, it gave a big lift to the whole team.

Before the game, Kev asked me where I wanted to bat and I told him as high as possible. He put me in at No. 5 and I was quite happy with that. Statistically, it's one of my best positions. I was worried that he might ask me to bat at No. 7 or 8. I hadn't played for a while and hadn't got a big score since returning to the England side. The difference between batting at No. 5 and lower down the order in one-day cricket is that you usually have time to build an innings before having a go at the end.

We started off quite slowly and Kev and I ended up batting together. The situation dictated that we batted for the last few overs and tried to ensure we were there at the end. I was nervous before I went in because I was playing in a batsman's position. It was suddenly a lot of responsibility, particularly as I didn't have any big innings to boost my confidence. At the same time I was confident I could do it, and determined to enjoy it, and the result was my best innings for some time. I was finally out in the last over for 78, which did a massive amount for my confidence and helped us reach a competitive total of 275 for 4. Harmison continued his revival by claiming a wicket with his fourth ball to dismiss Smith, and the way he celebrated, leaping around the place, you could tell how much it meant to him.

We travelled to Trent Bridge one-up in the series and confident of beating them again. The wicket had no demons and South Africa made a bit of a meal of it, struggling against our pace. I don't think Harmy, Jimmy Anderson, Stuart Broad or I dropped below 85mph that day. Stuart got five wickets but it was the combination of all four of us that hit them hard. We showed real aggression and bullied them out for 83 to win the second match quite comfortably. As a team, we were on a real high and couldn't wait to get at them again.

I was starting to get more confidence in my batting and we were more confident as a team. That was borne out by another convincing victory at The Oval. The wicket there is great. You always seem to get value for shots and this game was a case in point. We all batted consistently to reach a total just short of 300, and Samit Patel, who had been brought in to the squad at the start of the series, got five wickets. That win secured our series triumph.

In the next match, at Lord's, I suffered a back spasm and couldn't move properly, but fortunately it rained not long into the game and I was able to get off the field for a bit of treatment and an anti-inflammatory injection. While the rest of the lads were warming up, I bowled for half an hour in the middle, which is something I never normally do, to see if I could bowl away the pain. If I stood still, or moved slowly, I was struggling, but when I was bowling it seemed to be better. It's amazing how the body works – I was able to find a good rhythm and claimed three wickets, and we finished off another win with a bit of a flurry at the end.

After the game, I sat on the balcony, a bottle of beer in my hand, feet up, shoes off, still in my playing kit, and just looked out at a deserted Lord's. I don't want to sound emotional, but after all the hard work I had put in to get to that point, winning the man-of-the-match award at Lord's where we had just won to lead the series against South Africa 4–0 was a special moment. It had been a long journey but, just then, all the ups and downs seemed worthwhile.

We went to Cardiff hoping to wrap up the series 5–0, but the weather was wet from the moment we got there and the game was washed out almost as soon as we started. It did not dampen my spirits, though. I really enjoyed the end of that summer of 2008 and that series. For the first time I can ever remember, I got all my shirts signed. I gave away a few of them to sponsors and beneficiaries, but I did keep one for myself, because just playing in that series was an achievement for me. I was in such good form and spirits at the time that, if I'd had my way, we'd have carried on playing for a few weeks longer, but I also knew what sort of schedule we faced in the next eighteen months. The team needed a rest.

As soon as the season was over, the family and I went on holiday to Dubai. I was able to get away from cricket completely, but trained in the gym every afternoon when the kids were in bed. After that, we had a day at home before flying out to Antigua for what I would certainly regard as one of the worst trips of my England career.

# 14

## STRUGGLING TO COPE

I had my reservations about the Stanford association even before we flew out to Antigua and they were just compounded once we arrived. Several months earlier, the ECB had signed a deal with American billionaire Sir Allen Stanford for England to play a series of Twenty20 matches against his Superstars team, which were effectively the West Indies. Antigua was the venue, the winners would take home US$20million and the losers would walk away with nothing. I think ECB chairman Giles Clarke was trying to prevent some of us being tempted by the money on offer in the Indian Premier League (IPL), but it was a complete circus from start to finish. The series had no bearing on why I want to play for England. The big mistake was turning up as England when we should have gone as an English side. We should have gone as an England XI or KP's Superstars – anything but England. We all found it difficult to come to terms with that, and maybe it would have been better to be up front about it from the beginning. All the talk about England helping the development of West Indies cricket was absolute rubbish. We should have come out and said that we were there as mercenaries, playing for money. It was nothing to do with playing for England or helping Caribbean cricket. The sole purpose was to play one Twenty20 match for US$20million. I struggled with that concept and I think most of the lads felt the same. I don't play for England for money and the whole Stanford concept didn't excite me.

The amount of money on offer for the winners was mind-blowing – US$1million for each player in the side with the rest to be shared between the non-playing members of the squad, the backroom staff and, in our case, the ECB. If we'd won and danced around in celebration, everyone would have accused us of only caring about the money, and if we'd just shaken hands with the opposition and walked off, people would have said we didn't appreciate what a fortunate position we were in. In terms of public perception, we couldn't win either way.

I was also uncomfortable being a plaything for an American businessman. The cricket was a sideshow and we were just puppets. The trip didn't seem to be popular with anyone, not in the dressing room, and most of the publicity was negative. There was also a certain amount of arrogance on our part, thinking we could fly out to the West Indies on the Friday, play warm-up games on the Sunday and the Tuesday, and the following Saturday take on a team that had been practising for six weeks and training like no West Indies team has ever trained before. The belief seemed to be that we would just turn up and win, collect the money and go home. I thought that was unbelievable. Whoever put that itinerary together wasn't living in the real world. By the time we left Antigua, I think we were united in our determination to do things differently next time, should there be a next time. A few months later, Stanford's business empire collapsed, so that trip was the first and last of its kind.

From the word go things weren't right. We were put in an all-inclusive resort, which may have been very nice for a holiday but wasn't conducive to preparation for a multi-million dollar cricket match. That was just one thing that made this series different from any other England trip. Another was that we were told we would have to pay for all our own flights if we won. That never happens for a series against India or New Zealand. We were under contract to the ECB and were required to go to Antigua as part of our job – or have a pretty good reason for opting out – but it was not treated as a normal England trip. If it had been, surely we would have trained harder for it and it would have meant more.

What really annoyed me was that the press seemed to blame the players for the whole situation. It wasn't the players who welcomed Stanford with open arms when he flew his helicopter into Lord's to announce his involvement with English cricket. Yes, the players would have benefited hugely if we'd won the game, but participation was not our decision. The whole episode is one to forget in my opinion. The whole thing was just a big ego trip for Stanford. He had to be told not to walk into our dressing room without permission, and then he was seen with some of the lads' wives and girlfriends sitting on his knee. A few of the lads were not happy about that and I don't blame them.

We were due to go to India in early November to play seven one-day internationals and two Tests, and just about the only plus-point about the Antigua fiasco was that we were able to spend time practising together before the tour – although I was concerned the whole time that I would be injured and miss a proper series, one you could be proud to take part in for England. I was operating at about 70 per cent and my ankle was hurting because I hadn't bowled for a while. The only bowling I'd done was in the indoor school at Old Trafford, where the surfaces are soft, and I'd gone from that to bowling on rock-hard surfaces in Antigua. As it happened, we scraped through our two warm-up matches against Middlesex and Trinidad, and then got absolutely hammered in the big game, but we didn't feel despondent. The West Indian players celebrated for ages afterwards, understandably, and good luck to them.

As if the Stanford series wasn't bad enough, we then set off on the trip from hell to get to India for the start of the one-day series. I rarely look at itineraries when I'm away, I just take it as it comes, so I was a bit surprised to learn we weren't leaving until the Tuesday and had to stick around for three days. I tried to change flights and looked at every possible option, but I just couldn't do it. I think KP must have better contacts than I do because he managed to get a flight on the Sunday morning. The rest of us were stuck in Antigua. That was just the start of our troubles. On the Tuesday we flew to Barbados, where we had a five-hour wait for our plane to Gatwick. Once we arrived there, we were taken by coach to a hotel near Heathrow Airport and spent another day there. Our next leg was a flight from Heathrow to Dubai and then, finally, we got a flight from Dubai to Mumbai for the start of the India tour. We left our hotel in Antigua on the Tuesday at 8.00 a.m. and arrived in Mumbai on the Thursday at about four in the afternoon. It's not as if the Stanford trip crept up on everybody – we'd all known about it for months. Surely earlier flights from Antigua could have been booked, and an easier journey to India arranged? We were supposed to be elite international sportsmen preparing for a tough tour.

I didn't sleep at all throughout the journey, other than for about an hour and a half from Dubai to Mumbai, so I went to bed almost as soon as we arrived in India. I went to sleep at around 5.00 p.m. and didn't get up until it was time for training the following morning at around 9 or 10. Of course, my body was still all over the place, and the second day I was in the gym at five in the morning. I got my clocks wrong and thought it was six, so I was pounding the running machine around the time most nightclubbers are getting in!

I had said goodbye to Rachael and the kids once we got back to England, so this was my first trip without the family in a while and being without them was hard during those early days of the tour. If you think about it too much, or let it get you down, it will really play on your mind, so you just have to try to concentrate on what you're doing. It helped that we were in India, and particularly in Mumbai, which is a city I have always loved.

Our first warm-up match went well for me. I scored my first century for England since the Ashes series of 2005 – not against the strongest of opposition, but a hundred is a hundred and I don't have enough of them not to enjoy another one. We won convincingly, but in the next match lost to a slightly stronger Mumbai XI, which was disappointing to say the least. We were keen to get on some sort of roll before we met India. We were playing for England now and should have nailed that Mumbai XI, but instead we were bowled out for 98 and lost by a humiliating 124 runs.

Despite that embarrassing defeat, we were still upbeat going into the first one-day international in Rajkot. A couple of months earlier, we'd hammered South Africa 4–0, so our confidence was high, but there was also an element of stepping into the unknown for some of our lads. India had just beaten Australia in a Test series so were really up for it and caught us out. Virender Sehwag and Gautam Gambhir set it up for them and then Yuvraj Singh came in to bat with the pressure on him, having not scored any runs for some time – it was just our luck to face him when his place was on the line. People can criticise us for not bowling as well as we could have done, but when someone plays as well as he did that day, there is not a lot you can do. It has to be one of the best one-day innings I've ever seen. He completely smashed us and by the time the innings was over, he had hit an unbeaten 138 and helped India score 387 for 5, which was a massive total. We came off the field shell-shocked. I don't think any of us could believe what we'd just seen. The wicket was flat and the ground was tiny, but the performance was very special.

It just showed what a huge effect playing Twenty20 cricket

and the Indian Premier League was having on some of the Indian players, and we were getting left behind. We saw it in the West Indies with the way Chris Gayle played and we definitely saw it in this series against India. Batsmen such as Yuvraj had definitely moved on because of their experiences in the IPL, and so had the bowlers. Zaheer Khan and Harbhajan Singh had both developed from playing in the IPL.

After losing so heavily, we had a frank meeting before the next match in Indore, and went into it with high hopes of levelling the series. These games were giving us our first experience of the batting powerplay, which India were exploiting superbly. The rule governing powerplays had been amended in October 2008, just prior to the tour. The first 10 overs continue to be automatically subject to fielding restrictions, but the two further blocks of five overs are now brought into play, one by the fielding captain and one by the batting captain. Previously, both sets of five had been brought in at the discretion of the fielding captain. The new powerplay system has changed my life. Under the old system which was changed shortly before the tour, you'd think you had bowled pretty well if you'd gone for less than 40 off your 10 overs, but now you've done well if you're gone for less than 60. I usually bowl five overs in the first powerplay at the start of the match, when the batsmen are going to get after you, two more in the batting powerplay, and three more at the death, when the batsmen take more risks and come at you again – I'm like a sacrificial lamb! To make things worse, we managed to meet Yuvraj on another of his good days and he hit us for another century, and then took four wickets. We had clearly played him into a golden run of form and it signalled the start of a long, hard one-day series for us.

The third match in Kanpur on 20 November was a terrible advert for cricket. We started late, and a few adjustments were made for that, but there was still no chance of finishing it before the light closed in. The break between innings should have been shortened, but the officials kept it at forty minutes. When we started, everyone knew we would struggle to finish. All it needed was a bit of common sense, but that seemed to be lacking all round. Mahendra Singh Dhoni, India's captain, said afterwards that, given the choice, he would have bowled first, because he knew the game wouldn't be finished. At least, we were starting to play a little better, and we did put them under a bit of pressure at 34 for 2, chasing a Duckworth Lewis target of 198. We weren't favourites but we were in with a sniff of winning, which is more than could be said of the previous matches.

In the end, we lost again, but instead of being upset, I think most of us in the dressing room were angry about the decisions that were made about the game. Everyone wanted to go to see the match referee and umpires and tell them what we thought, but we all knew that was not the way to handle it. Kev expressed his concerns on everyone's behalf in the press conference after the game, but we were still annoyed when we left for the next match in Bangalore and another rain-affected encounter.

The difference this time was that the rain helped us. We

were not bowling well and India were racing along at 81 for 1 after 14 overs when the rain intervened. We just weren't at the races and both Kev and I had a few choice words to say in the dressing room. It was clear that once we resumed it would be a reduced game, and this was where India's greater experience with the IPL came to the fore. Sehwag hit the first ball after the second rain break for six, and both Yuvraj and Yusuf Pathan did the same to get them to a good total. We all thought our best chance of winning was a shortened game, but we got off to a bad start and barely got a run for the first few overs. Owais and I managed to get things going again, and I hit one of the biggest sixes I've ever hit off Harbhajan onto the roof of one of the stands. I stood there, trying to look as though it was deliberate, when in fact how far I'd hit it was just as big a surprise to me as to everyone else. We never recovered from our slow start, though, and ran out of steam to lose the match and series. That left us facing an uphill battle to avoid a 7–0 whitewash in the remaining three matches.

India were playing so well I think it had got to the stage where none of us really thought we could beat them. We spoke about treating the final three games as a separate series, which would give us something to aim for, but I found it hard to subscribe to that. We were trying to take positives out of a situation when there were few to take. We did play better in Cuttack, posting a competitive score of 270 for 4. Kev hit a superb century, but once again India proved to be that much better than we were. Sehwag and Sachin Tendulkar smashed us everywhere in a 136-run opening stand, and in the end they won with several overs to spare. It was more of the same, really.

There was no doubt that India had moved on as a team. England need to improve in the conditions on the subcontinent if we are going to develop as a one-day team. It's no good saying that India are used to it and are really good on home soil because the next World Cup is in India. We have to get better and the only way we can do that is by playing there more often.

# 15

# ATTACK ON MUMBAI

On the coach back to our hotel in Bhupenswar, our troubles on the pitch were placed in vivid perspective. We were quiet on the bus because we'd just been beaten and were trailing 5–0 in the series, and then news started to filter through about an incident in Mumbai, affecting the Taj Mahal Palace Hotel, where we had stayed just a few weeks before during the early stages of the tour, and where we were due to stay again in two weeks' time. I found out from my Blackberry and immediately went to the front of the bus and had a quiet word with Peter Moores and Reg Dickason. By that time the rest of the lads had heard about it, either through phone calls, text messages or just by looking at their Blackberrys. At first we didn't really know what had happened. Was it a bomb? Was it a plane crash? Questions were being asked, and assumptions made, and when we arrived back at our hotel, security seemed to be tighter. Perhaps I imagined there were more guards around, or maybe I just noticed them because of what had happened. There was a different mood about them, though, and a different mood around the hotel.

I went to the bar with Peter Moores and a few of the lads, and watched the scenes coming through on the television. It became clear that terrorists had attacked the Taj Mahal Palace Hotel and the Oberoi Hotel, and had taken hostages. We all sat there in a state of disbelief at what we were seeing – people shooting from cars, fires blazing in the hotel. Leopold's café, which was just around the corner from the hotel, had also being affected. I know there was coverage of the incident back home, but in India we were watching extremely graphic images. We saw dead bodies; we saw people getting shot; we saw everything pretty much as we would have done had we been standing there on the street.

At that stage you start phoning home. I spoke to Rachael, who was understandably worried after hearing what had happened, and rang my mum. I don't normally ring my parents while I'm on tour, but this was different. Mum was in tears and worried sick that we were caught up in it. Most people at home didn't have any idea how far Bhupenswar was from Mumbai. As it happens, it's quite a long way, but that doesn't stop people at home worrying, and it was unsettling for all of us that night. There was a lot of talk in the bar about what was going to happen to the rest of the tour and whether we would be going home. The television was tuned to one of those rolling news stations, and all the scenes kept being played over and over again until they got some new footage. For me, the feeling was similar to when the twin towers were attacked in New York. Back then I watched the whole incident unfold on television at home. I remember watching live as the second plane hit the towers and the sense of disbelief, that this cannot be happening. In India, we were all wondering whether those attacks were just the start, and what else would happen. What brought it home for a lot of us was something quite trivial – the fact that we still had various belongings at the hotel in Mumbai. I had a suit carrier and other bits of kit, which are irrelevant when you think what happened that night, but it did make us think how close we were to it all. Later, we discovered that Shaun Udal and the rest of the Middlesex team had been due at the hotel in a couple of days for the start of the Champions League.

Over the years, we've stayed at the Taj Mahal Palace every time we've been in Mumbai and got to know the staff quite well. Harmy and I ate in the Japanese restaurant every day and that's apparently where the attacks started. It turned out that a member of the staff, who could easily have served us during our time there, had been one of the terrorists. Some of the counter staff, who couldn't do enough for you and were all smiles every time we went in there, had been killed. My thoughts drifted back to the day we left the hotel and I had a bit of a row with one of the guys at the reception desk. Internet charges had been listed on my bill, but since I didn't have a laptop with me there must have been a mistake, and so I told him. He questioned me about it and I ended up having a bit of a go back. Now I felt so guilty, thinking he could have been caught up in all that mayhem but hoping he was OK. I still don't know to this day.

Rumours came out about the terrorists targeting westerners, and British and American passport holders in particular. Apparently, one bloke pretended he was Dutch so they wouldn't shoot him. A security guard who had been with us in South Africa a few years earlier led an escape from a restaurant, and it doesn't take long for you to start wondering what you would have done in that position. What would have happened if we had been in reception after coming back from dinner and someone had run in shooting? Would I have got involved and tried to help out, would I have tried to escape or would I have hidden in my room when I heard gunshots? It was all a bit too real for us, and a hell of a lot of things went through our minds that night.

I stayed in the bar after 4.00 a.m. because I just couldn't tear myself away from the images we were seeing. When I finally went to bed I have to admit I was a bit spooked walking to my room. Our hotel was based on the Thai model, with plenty of bushes and archways and little gardens, and the route back to my room was quite eerie. In my heart I knew nothing was going to happen to me, but my mind was racing and I was conscious of it being very dark. I didn't sleep much. As usual, Steve's room was next to mine and that night the adjoining door stayed open. I don't think we spoke – I switched on the television – but we were both upset by what was happening.

The following morning at breakfast, everyone had an opinion of what we should be doing, and Kev, as captain, never seemed to be off his phone. The consensus among the lads was definitely that we should go home. We wanted to get out of the country. The Indian team were staying at the same hotel, and the players I spoke to were of the same opinion. They didn't think the series should continue.

After breakfast, we adjourned to the team room. The remaining two one-dayers were cancelled but what about the two Test matches? Not long into the meeting, we were told about the financial implications if we didn't stay. They told us about the money they would lose by not playing the Test series, and they emphasised the impact that would have on cricket in England, on county cricket and grassroots cricket. Basically, they were telling us that if we went home, some lad in Preston might not be able to play cricket. From the word go, I thought that trying to put that sort of pressure on us was wrong. The finances of the ECB are, of course, important but we are employed to play cricket – not to take risks beyond the call of duty.

We'd been through similar meetings at the 2003 World Cup, with the Zimbabwe issue, and based on my experience then, I was wary of the ECB's judgement in these matters. They never seem to understand the impact these situations have on your family, who are worried to death about what is happening. It would be good, for them and us, to know that your employers regard your safety as their first priority.

The ECB's desire to forge closer links with the Board of Control for Cricket in India had been widely publicised. The Indian organisation had become very powerful with the success of the IPL and the launch of the Champions League Twenty20 tournaments. It was also an open secret that the

ECB wanted to get the Indian players over for their own Twenty20 tournament in the next few years, and I got the impression they were frightened to death of jeopardising that. I asked them outright whether this was about money and they denied it, but I wasn't convinced then and nothing that has happened since has persuaded me otherwise.

Along with several others in the squad, I was hoping to be offered a contract to play in the IPL in India in 2009, and I knew if I didn't stay to play in the Tests now, that was unlikely to happen. The IPL's tournament was subsequently moved to South Africa because of a clash with India's elections, which raised security fears, but at the time we didn't know that would happen. In my eyes, going home was the right thing to do, whether possible IPL contracts were put at risk or not.

When that first meeting broke up mid-morning, the overriding feeling among the lads seemed to me to be in favour of going home, and I think attempts were made to get us on different flights out of Bhupenswar. Then another idea was mooted about flying to Abu Dhabi for a holding camp instead. I told the management straightaway that if I was leaving India, I was going home. I couldn't see the point of going to Abu Dhabi.

We had another meeting a few hours later, when it quickly became clear that the ECB had changed their stance. They started off by taking the players' views into account, but by the time we went into the next meeting, late in the afternoon, that had changed again. They were trying to dictate to us, which immediately got my back up and I told them straight that I would make my own decision. I voiced my opinion in the meetings, as did Harmy, because we'd both been through all this before with the ECB. I felt quite sorry for some of the support staff. They were in the same difficult position as we were, but I think some of them felt they were a little more dispensable. Let's face it, it's a lot easier to get rid of one of the backroom staff than it would be an opening batsman, a wicketkeeper or an all-rounder. They were fearing for their jobs if they took a similar stance to some of the players.

I also felt sorry for Hugh Morris, who was co-ordinating the talks as the Managing Director of England cricket. I've always had a good relationship with Hugh and he was getting strong conflicting views from all angles, from the players and, I'm sure, from above at the ECB. I told him I was quite prepared to speak to Giles Clarke directly in a conference call, and I would have been happy to do so, but I never got the chance to talk to him from start to the finish of this whole affair. Peter Moores was also put in a tricky position because he was trying to keep everyone happy. He was obviously employed by the ECB, but he wanted his team to be happy. It was an impossible position for him.

By the time we got to that third meeting of the day, pressure was really being put on us but a few of us remained adamant we were going home. I wasn't prepared to go to Dubai or Abu Dhabi to be put in a meeting room for three or four days, as we were in South Africa in 2003. Once it became clear that enough of us were taking the same stance, the message from the ECB was that we could go home but an England team would be returning to play the two Tests. The future of the ECB's relationship with India was dependent on them persuading as many players as possible to go back.

We got on a plane to Bangalore the following day to join the guys who had been based at the Academy there, and stayed the night in a hotel before catching a flight home. I called a team meeting in the hotel to talk through the situation. Kevin was very keen to play the Tests and some of the lads were against it, and they gave their reasons. Kevin left after about half an hour to have a massage while the rest of us continued our discussion. At that stage, most of the lads didn't want to come back. Stories about the terrorists targeting westerners didn't help. A few of the lads were genuinely scared. How were we to know they wouldn't target a cricket team? Our fears were justified a few months later when the Sri Lanka team bus was attacked in Lahore on the way to the ground to play a Test against Pakistan. We were very high-profile westerners and it didn't make sense for us to put ourselves in a vulnerable position. If I was that way inclined, I'd have joined the army and had a real go. I wouldn't be playing cricket.

Over the years, I've learnt how these things work when players are put in this position, and it's not always easy to stick to your principles. There are always members of every team whose places are not secure because they've not been playing well, and other players may be making their way in the team. They find it very difficult to go against the wishes of the ECB because they don't know what the consequences might be, and are in a far more difficult position than more established players, such as myself.

When I got home, I turned off my phone. The ECB knew where I stood. I spoke to Harmy and was in constant touch with Neil Fairbrother, but otherwise I tried to keep away from it all. Then on the way back from shopping in the Trafford Centre I stopped for some lunch and turned my phone on. Hugh had been trying to get hold of me, so I rang him back. Sean Morris, the Professional Cricketers' Association chief executive, also came on the line to tell me he was in on the call. Sean was answering the questions I was asking Hugh when I thought he should have been looking after players interests. I was asked again if I would go back and I told them that once I'd seen the security report I would make an informed decision and not before. They asked, if all of them – Hugh, Sean and Reg – thought it was safe to go back, would I then, and again I refused, repeating that I didn't need them to make decisions for me.

This carried on for some time in phone calls, with changing hypothetical scenarios, and eventually they called to ask if I would go to Abu Dhabi for a training camp. I had no reason to turn down a training camp, and then they asked me if I would go to India if the security report came back saying it was safe, and again I refused to commit without sight of it. This time they said they would get back to me to let me know if they were prepared to let me travel on that basis. I phoned Peter Moores at this point and told him my feelings on the issue. He was sympathetic to my point of view but at the same time he was trying to put a squad together to go back to India, and that was his top priority. I told him that if I went to Abu Dhabi, I would practise and prepare as if I would be on the plane to India.

Peter asked me to ring Kev, which I did. The conversation was a bit strained. Kev said a lot of the lads had agreed to go back and asked why I wouldn't do the same. I explained to him that I'd been in a similar position before and I wasn't prepared to make a decision until I'd seen the security report. He also told me they'd get back to me to let me know whether they thought they could take me to Abu Dhabi or not, at which point I sought legal advice on my position. During all this process, I'd offered to go to London, or anywhere else, to talk to Giles Clarke or David Collier face to face and explain my position, but from start to finish I never got the chance to talk to them. I asked if either of them would be going to Abu Dhabi to talk to the players, but apparently they couldn't make the trip.

I was eventually given clearance to go to our training camp in Abu Dhabi, which had been strengthened by members of the performance squad, just in case any of the senior players decided they would not fly on to India. I travelled from Manchester with Jimmy Anderson, Sajid Mahmood and Adil Rashid, and all the squad met up in Dubai. I still sensed a strong feeling among the players that we shouldn't be there, and I felt for some of the young lads because this was the first time they'd been through something like this. When you become part of the England set-up, you are put through media training but nothing prepares you for having to make a decision about terrorist attacks. Everyone seemed to be asking everyone else what they were going to do.

We arrived on the Thursday night and, since the idea was to prepare as if we were going to play the Test series, it was decided among the squad not to talk about it formally until the Sunday night, by which time Hugh, Sean and Reg would have arrived from India with the security report. No light relief was provided by my birthday celebrations because Saturday was a national holiday and none of the restaurants I wanted to go to were open. We practised all day Saturday and Sunday and then came the moment of truth. The press were circling in the hotel lobby – and cameras were everywhere – all waiting to find out what would happen.

Reg sat at the front of the meeting room with Hugh and Sean Morris. Reg and Hugh both presented their reports and said they thought the security was good enough for us to return. All the way through I was thinking to myself how unreal the whole situation was. If you'd brought someone in off the street without telling them what it was about, they would have thought we were preparing for a war. All the talk was about the number of armed guards, the way they were going to block off the hotels, how we were going to travel, the police escorts and so on. It was more like a briefing for Jack Bauer before he headed out on a mission in the television series *24* than a meeting to discuss playing a couple of Test matches. The emphasis on guns did very little to reassure me. In India I wanted to be able to mix freely and play cricket, although in the circumstances I realised that wouldn't be possible, but I didn't want to be around all those guns. A lot was said about London being on high alert, and how the terrorist attack could have happened there. The ECB insisted the terrorists were not killing westerners, despite the group who claimed responsibility for the attacks saying the opposite. We were going around in circles.

Then we were told the big difference between deciding not to go to Pakistan for the Champions Trophy the previous year and feeling reassured about going back to India was the mode of killing. In Pakistan the terrorists favoured suicide bombers, who cannot be stopped, but in India they just shot people, and if you have enough people facing them, you can stop them! Now I'm no expert in these things, but the whole thing seemed just crazy to me. They were basing their argument on how people were being killed. They didn't seem to think that the fact we were even talking about different modes of killing was at all alarming.

The venues for the two Test matches were to be changed. Originally, we were going to play in Ahmedabad and Mumbai, and they talked about moving the First Test to Chennai, because Ahmedabad was close to the Pakistan border, but then the Second Test was going to Mohali, which is similarly close. Whether they thought we didn't know geography or were stupid I don't know, but the discussion just got crazier and crazier. They reckoned that since Mohali was hilly, it would be too much effort for the terrorists to come over and attack. I'd already been asked during the week at home whether I'd be prepared to play a one-off Test in Mumbai with all the proceeds going to charity. In an ideal world that would have been brilliant for cricket and the Indian people, but in reality there was no chance of it happening. I was dubious about going back to India at all, never mind returning to the scene of the terrorist attacks. Some would say it was probably the safest place in India at the time, but that doesn't stop you fretting.

By this stage of the meetings, you could see the performance squad lads looking around and their faces were an absolute picture. You could almost see their jaws dropping, and there were nervous giggles from some of them around the room. Eventually, the discussion got to the type of security being laid on for us. We were told the police and commandos allocated to guard us were the best available, but were not as well trained as their equivalents in the UK, which wasn't that comforting. If a question was asked that Hugh, Reg or Sean couldn't answer, they went temporarily deaf and moved on to the next one. Throughout the meeting, they said that anyone who had made the decision to go could leave whenever he wanted, and people were walking out. Some of the performance squad lads got out of there as quickly as they could. About six of us were left in the room and we were being pressed for a decision. I told them I couldn't give them one. They had to give me some time to digest what we'd just been told. I wanted to make one or two phone calls and I promised to come back to them within the hour. I went back to my room, sat on my own for five or ten minutes, then phoned Rachael. She said whatever I decided to do, she would support my decision. She didn't want me to go, but we talked about what would happen if I didn't go. We knew there would be a fall-out from the press and I'd be putting my career on the line, not to mention a lucrative

IPL contract, but she said that no matter what decision I made we would get through it. Even if I never played for England again it would not matter to her or the kids. Finances didn't come into it. It was important I made the decision for myself.

I spoke to Neil Fairbrother and he couldn't believe I was in this position again, and then Harmy came to my room and we just sat there and smiled at each other as if we couldn't believe what was going on. We knew we had to say we were going. There was no way out of it. If the other lads who had stayed behind in that meeting had voiced their concerns sooner, I would really have pressed for us not to go back. I felt that the ECB had put pressure on the lads individually, and had they spoken up earlier, I would have gone around to each of their rooms and talked to them, shown them support. If they were putting aside reservations about going back because of their careers, I'd have taken the hit for all of them, but I didn't get the feeling that anybody would make a stand until it was too late.

After thinking about it long and hard, I was clear about my reasons for agreeing to go back – my team-mates were going and I wanted to stay loyal to them, and I didn't want to go through all the fall-out from the press, with people outside my door affecting not just my life, but my family's life again. I wouldn't say the IPL played a major part. I wanted to be able to look Harmy and all the other lads in the eye and have them know I was going back for the right reasons, and not because I was chasing IPL money. I would have given it all up for Jimmy Anderson and the rest of the lads. To be able to look them honestly in the eye, for me, is not something you can put a price on. These people are more important than money will ever be.

Although Harmy and I laughed and smiled at each other, I felt as though I'd lost. I was being backed into doing something I didn't want to do. In the meeting room with the other guys who had to make their decision I told them exactly what I thought. I said I was proud to play for England and I told them the reason I was agreeing to go back was for my team-mates. I assured Peter Moores I would not be a problem and that I would play cricket to the best of my ability. There would be no chuntering in the background or anything like that. Then I turned to Hugh and told him again that I was proud to play for England, but I was embarrassed by my employers. Time after time after time I'd been put in this position. I let rip at Hugh, not to have a go at him but because I wanted him to pass my feelings on to the ECB.

Everyone assembled at the Irish bar at the hotel. I didn't say much to begin with. Most of the lads were there, waiting to find out what the final few of us had decided. They asked me what I was going to do and I just nodded my head. I remember getting quite upset when I was talking with Mark Saxby, the team masseur, because I felt I had betrayed myself, and I hated the idea of putting my family through three weeks of worry. I felt I was being forced to do something I didn't want to do. I'd gone with it and it didn't feel good. I had a pint of Guinness and then the alarm bells started ringing. I could have drunk myself into oblivion, which I've done in the past when things have been bad just to forget about it and put myself in a better mood for a while. I could have got leathered, but I didn't want to do that, so I just went to bed and got ready for the next day's flight to Chennai.

# 16

# RETURNING TO INDIA

We weren't quite sure what to expect when we arrived in Chennai – how many armed guards we were getting and how good they were going to be. The previous lot had been taking photographs and asking for autographs, and we wanted to know if they were going to be like that or more professional. When we got off the plane, it was like a military procedure. We were shepherded into a holding area, and then marched out of the airport in a line, armed guards either side. It was a great photo opportunity – Kev walking out smartly, two blokes either side of him with guns, and this is a cricket tour. The area was supposed to be closed off with nobody there, but was it heck! Harmy and I walked out together and there were a lot of press and cameramen. The first thing I saw was cameras – five guys all taking photographs of me. As we boarded the bus, a bloke with a TV microphone, live on some station or other, was saying they didn't think Harmy or I would be coming.

On the bus, we closed the curtains, on the grounds that you can't be too careful. Lots of things went through my mind on the journey to the hotel. When we got there, guards were everywhere, some running alongside the bus with their guns pointing up. Inside, more armed guards stood by the lift. I had a guard outside my room, which I was slightly concerned about because no one else had one. He stood there with some rifle or other, but my room was opposite a fire escape, so I was hoping he was there because of that and not because some fat lad from Preston was a big target. So there we were. Back in India. That night fireworks and firecrackers went off near the hotel and I was straight up to the curtains, wondering what it was. A lot of the lads mentioned it the next day.

On the way to the ground for training we were accompanied by escorts, ambulances and everything else that goes with it. When we got there, the security closed in on us. At the hotel, the guards were 100 yards away. At the ground, they started off 50 yards away, then it was 25 yards, 20 yards and then they were holding hands in a line in front of us. It was like a guard of honour with blokes holding guns. On a daily basis, we had at least fifty guns around us, which is very scary. It's not normal. We walked through the guard of honour and an armed guard would open the door. We walked down the corridor and armed guards were there, too. An armed guard would open the dressing-room door, and if you walked through to the seating area, more armed guards were stood in front of that. Yet more were stationed around the pitch, while other blokes walked around checking for bombs. This is all for a practice session! It made you wonder whether it was worth all the trouble. I remember Kev saying in a press conference that we wanted to go back and rub shoulders with the Indian public, but the only people I rubbed shoulders with were armed guards. I didn't see any of the Indian public.

The Chennai Test was written up as an amazing match, with Sachin chasing down the runs on the final day, but what did it matter? Cricket was secondary to everything else that was going on. For the Indian public it was perfect – the son of Mumbai, the biggest name in cricket ever, hitting the winning runs. What could be better? Not for us, though. We were just fodder. We started well and were on course for a major first-innings score, but in India it is a lot easier to score off the new ball, and it gets harder and harder. We were dismissed for 316 and it took me nearly an hour and a half to score 18. I went into my shell and played for the next day, but I should just have teed off. I could have got 18 off eight balls and saved everyone the hassle of having to watch that.

We bowled well when they started their innings and Graeme Swann, on his Test debut, was unbelievable. He got two wickets in his first Test over and I was delighted for him. He had waited 10 years to play Test cricket and then got Gambhir and Dravid in his first over. He should have played a lot more. Seeing some other people playing for England, he has probably been tearing his hair out, but he never got a look in. Sportsmen are supposed to be all the same, schooled to say and do all the right things and behave in a certain manner, but Swanny doesn't do that. He is what he is. He's been the same since he was a schoolboy, and you've got to love him for that, but I don't think Duncan could relate to it.

Swann's efforts helped us claim a 75-run first-innings lead, and another century from Strauss and a determined hundred from Collingwood enabled us to declare 387 runs ahead with around four sessions to bowl at India. We had 29 overs on that fourth evening, which played a huge role in deciding the outcome of the match. If we'd bowled well, we would have been in the box seat to claim victory on the final day, but we didn't do that. We fed Sehwag's cut shot and he hit a quickfire 83 to help them reach 131 for 1 at the close, needing just 256 to win on the final day on a wearing wicket. Sehwag played well, but if someone bowled short and wide at me I'd be happy, and I'm not as good as he is.

We got Dravid early the following morning, but he was struggling so much at this stage I think we all fancied bowling at him. That brought Sachin to the crease for his big moment. I love bowling at Dravid and all the Indian batsmen. It brings out the best in you, but with Tendulkar, when I bowl at him, I actually want him to respect me. I hold him in such high esteem and he's such a good player I want to make it hard for him. I want him to walk off that field thinking that Flintoff is a good player, he can bowl. I want to impress him. The more he got into his innings, the better he played, and he played brilliantly. He started to look like Sachin at his best. He is a humble, quiet man, very mild-mannered. He's just the best role model in cricket. What happened next was almost inevitable. Yuvraj came in and hit a few around, but it was Tendulkar they all wanted to see and it was a fantastic story – Sachin scores the winning runs and walks off with the whole crowd shouting his name. The man from Mumbai won the Test match after everything that had happened.

## INDIA v ENGLAND
## (1st Test) at Chennai 11–15 December 2008

### England

| | | | | |
|---|---|---|---|---|
| A.J.Strauss c & b Mishra | 123 | – | c Laxman b Harbhajan Singh | 108 |
| A.N.Cook c Khan b Harbhajan Singh | 52 | – | c Dhoni b Sharma | 9 |
| I.R.Bell lbw b Khan | 17 | – | c Gambhir b Mishra | 7 |
| *K.P.Pietersen c & b Khan | 4 | – | lbw b Yuvraj Singh | 1 |
| P.D.Collingwood c Gambhir | | | | |
| b Harbhajan Singh | 9 | – | lbw b Khan | 108 |
| A.Flintoff c Gambhir b Mishra | 18 | – | c Dhoni b Sharma | 4 |
| J.M.Anderson c Yuvraj Singh b Mishra | 19 | | (10) not out | 1 |
| +M.J.Prior not out | 53 | | (7) c Sehwag b Sharma | 33 |
| G.P.Swann c Dravid b Harbhajan Singh | 1 | | (8) b Khan | 7 |
| S.J.Harmison c Dhoni b Yuvraj Singh | 6 | | (9) b Khan | 1 |
| M.S.Panesar lbw b Sharma | 6 | | | |
| l-b 7, n-b 1 | 8 | | B 10, lb 13, w 2, n-b 7 | 32 |

1/118 2/164 3/180 4/195 5/221    316    1/28 2/42 3/43    (for 9 wkts dec) 311
6/229 7/271 8/277 9/304 10/316            4/257 5/262 6/277 7/297 8/301 9/311

Bowling: *First innings* – Khan 21-9-41-2; Sharma 19.4-4-32-1; Harbhajan Singh 38-2-96-3; Mishra 34-6-99-3; Yuvraj Singh 15-2-33-1; Sehwag 1-0-8-0. *Second innings* – Khan 27-7-40-3; Sharma 22.5-1-57-3; Mishra 17-1-66-1; Yuvraj Singh 3-1-12-1; Harbhajan Singh 30-3-91-1; Sehwag 6-0-22-0.

### India

| | | | | |
|---|---|---|---|---|
| G.Gambhir lbw b Swann | 19 | – | c Collingwood b Anderson | 66 |
| V.Sehwag b Anderson | 9 | – | lbw b Swann | 83 |
| R.S.Dravid lbw b Swann | 3 | – | c Prior b Flintoff | 4 |
| S.R.Tendulkar c & b Flintoff | 37 | – | not out | 103 |
| V.V.S.Laxman c & b Panesar | 24 | – | c Bell b Swann | 26 |
| Yuvraj Singh c Flintoff b Harmison | 14 | – | not out | 85 |
| *+M.S.Dhoni c Pietersen b Panesar | 53 | | | |
| Harbhajan Singh c Bell b Panesar | 40 | | | |
| Z.Khan lbw b Flintoff | 1 | | | |
| A.Mishra b Flintoff | 12 | | | |
| I.Sharma not out | 8 | | | |
| B 4, l-b 11, n-b 6 | 21 | | B 5, lb 11, n-b 4 | 20 |

1/16 2/34 3/37 4/98 5/102    241    1/117 2/141 3/183    (for 4 wkts) 387
6/137 7/212 8/217 9/219 10/241            4/224

Bowling: *First innings* – Harmison 11-1-42-1; Anderson 11-3-28-1; Flintoff 18.4-2-49-3; Swann 10-0-42-2; Panesar 19-4-65-3. *Second innings* – Harmison 10-0-48-0; Anderson 11-1-51-1; Panesar 27-4-105-0; Flintoff 22-1-64-1; Swann 28.3-2-103-2.

Umpires: B.F.Bowden and D.J.Harper
India won by 6 wickets

Throughout the one-day series I'd had a bit of a battle with Yuvraj. He was playing really well and I was trying to wind him up, not in a malicious way, but just to try to get to him so he would make a mistake. During the first innings of the Test, forty minutes of chuntering paid off when he went for the bait in a big way and I caught him at slip off Harmy. In the second innings he wouldn't look at me. It was funny, actually. He'd clearly been told to cool it. He knew and I knew he'd been told, but he wouldn't look at me at all. I'd say something and he would walk away. Yuvraj has got one of those daft smiles, and he couldn't hold it in. He just couldn't get rid of that smile of his. He played superbly in the second innings, but the one thing that made playing that Test almost worthwhile for me came right at the end. As we were walking off, the Indians came over to shake our hands, and as Sachin shook mine – it was probably because he'd scored a hundred and played a great game – he said, 'Thanks for coming back. Thanks for coming back to India.' That struck a massive chord for me, particularly coming from him.

After that, we moved on to Mohali, where the security was similar and the guards just as heavily armed. We were never going to get a full game in there at that time of year, just before Christmas. It's cloudy in the morning, so there's always a delayed start, and it's cloudy in the evening, so we have an early finish. It would have taken one of the teams to collapse badly for there to be a result. We had a good crack at it, though. I was pleased for Dravid when he scored a century, his first for a while. I'd played with him in that Rest of the World side in

Australia about four years earlier, and got to know him. Like many of the Indians, he's just a brilliant man. It's different when we're playing against them, but generally I don't like to see the world's best players stuck in the sort of rut that he was in. His place in the side was being questioned, he was getting a kicking in the press and it was good to see him silence his critics with a century.

We ended up with a 150-run deficit and I managed to score 62 – I came out of my shell a bit and tried to play a few shots. To be honest, when Kev was at the other end, I was just a spectator. The ball was reverse swinging and I think I was late on just about every one that Ishant Sharma bowled, and he is not an express bowler. Kev was flicking them here, there and everywhere. He helped me through my difficult time. Kev is obviously a very gifted player but he often doesn't get credit for his thinking about the game. He was telling me the things that had helped him – areas to hit, or tactics to try against left-arm seamer Zaheer Khan.

I got out to the last ball of the day, partnering Jimmy, who had come in as nightwatchman. As a nightwatchman, you're supposed to protect the batsman at the other end and keep the strike, but Jimmy took the single instead. In his defence, we shouldn't have been out there because it was pitch black. Darrell Harper, the umpire, wouldn't tell me if it was the last over or not, and also personal pride takes over. I'm not having Jimmy Anderson fending the ball off for me. I can do it myself, or couldn't, as it turned out! Sachin was fielding close to the wicket and said, 'Come on, Freddie. Play a big one. Go for a big one off the last ball.' I was facing leg-spinner Amit Mishra and I knew it was a googly, with the field placings. I should have come down the wicket and hit it out of Chandigarh, but instead I had a bit of a nibble at it and got out. I was annoyed with myself and stomped off. Later, in the dressing room, I told Jimmy, 'It's fine, mate. Nothing to do with you.'

In the end, India declared and the game was fizzling out towards a draw to such an extent that Dhoni took off his wicket-keeping gloves and bowled an over. One thing that sticks out for me from that Test was the presentation. I was disappointed with the Indian team. Kev was speaking and they all started pouring Pepsi over each other. Kev was trying to thank everyone, the crowd, the Mohali authorities, and five yards away it was like a wrestling match. Dhoni was being drowned in Pepsi, Ishant Sharma was on the floor, and all these other kids were throwing Pepsi at each other. It just showed a lack of respect.

I was glad to get home on Christmas Eve morning. I had bowled a lot of overs and was physically and mentally goosed. I was in bed by 8.30 or 9.00 p.m. I was just so knackered, and so happy to be home, even more so than usual. I was looking forward to enjoying time with the family, knowing I had a few weeks off before we were due to fly out to the West Indies. We had come through an even tougher tour than normal in India and I was hoping for a relaxing time at home.

That peace was shattered when the news broke in the media that Peter Moores and Kev weren't getting on. I'd had a chat with Kev in Mohali about it, and he'd told me that he would prefer a new coach to take us forward. He said he didn't want Moores or assistant coach Andy Flower. I told him I would support him as a player and as my captain, but I couldn't support him in this. I had come through the Duncan Fletcher era, working for a coach I didn't get on with, but I had a very good relationship with Peter and I wasn't prepared to jeopardise that. I had no problems with him. It was left at that and I was none the wiser until New Year's Day, when we were invited round to Neil Fairbrother's house. His father-in-law showed me the *Daily Mail* with all the stuff about a breakdown in the relationship between Kev and Peter. I had not read any papers since I got back until that day and I thought, 'Here we go.' It all kicked off over the next few days.

I was nothing to do with it, and I didn't have a problem with either Kev or Peter, but before I knew it, all the players started getting phone calls from the ECB asking our opinions. I said I thought the two of them should sort it out. I was asked to phone Kev and talk to him about it, but I didn't. I told the ECB that it wasn't my business. It was for them to sort out, and then I started getting dragged into it all. The media were writing that I had turned against Kev. How anybody could think I was trying to undermine him after watching the way I played for him during the one-day series against South Africa and in India, I don't know. I remember bowling my 27th over against India in Mohali at 94mph, and people were questioning my commitment to the captain! That really annoyed me because it was untrue. I didn't want to be England captain, so why would I want Kev out? The media have tried to build up a story about Kev and I not liking each other, but that's rubbish. We're not close friends, but I respect him enormously.

I found out the ECB had decided to sack both Kev and Peter after a walking trip with Lancashire. We went up to Windermere and the chat on the bus was all about what was happening with England, and I kept telling everyone I didn't know. The Lakes were the best place I could have been. There was no signal on my phone, I was up some mountain or other and no one could get hold of me. I found out what had happened when we got back down from the peak. It was bizarre. I had to feel for both of them. Everything Kev wanted happened, but he didn't get put at the helm, and from Peter's point of view, he did nothing wrong but got fired.

The next time I saw Kev was at Loughborough shortly before we flew out to the West Indies when Andrew Strauss had been appointed captain. I had a chat with him and explained what had happened from my perspective. I wanted to make sure he knew where I stood and told him I didn't want either of them to go, reiterating that I'd had a good relationship with the coach. I was up front about it.

Some newspapers had been tipping me to become captain again, which was way off the mark. I hadn't been consulted about the captaincy at all before Strauss was appointed and I didn't want to be asked. I was better off looking after my own game and trying to help the younger players. I think I know myself better now. I was happy playing.

# 17

# A FRESH START

After all the turmoil of the events in Mumbai, returning to India before Christmas and the controversy over the ECB's decision to appoint a new coach and captain, it was almost a relief to get back to cricket in the early months of 2009.

We flew out to the Caribbean in late January for our tour of the West Indies, hoping to build some momentum leading into the bigger challenge of the Ashes series later that year. St Kitts, one of the smaller Caribbean islands where we stayed initially, was good for all the lads except me because I managed to strain my side early in the trip. I began feeling a little stiff during one of the early net sessions, but thought nothing of it. It was only when I batted during our first three-day match that my side started to get very sore and I began to think maybe something was wrong.

For as long as I've known him, Rooster has always told me to report any pain in my side straightaway, because for a bowler it can be potentially very serious. So I mentioned it and, after the game, I was flown to Jamaica for a scan, courtesy of Big Arthur. During our time on St Kitts, Big Arthur looked after us brilliantly. He ran the hotel where we were staying and wanted to make sure St Kitts was shown in a good light. He arranged everything for us, meals in restaurants, everything, and in the absence of the relevant medical facilities on the island, he organised a private plane to fly me to Jamaica and back.

The scan showed no significant damage, but the stiffness prevented me playing in the only other warm-up match before the First Test, so by the time we arrived in Jamaica I hadn't had any cricket at all, really. There was nothing I could do about it but I felt very under-prepared, particularly with the bat – the bowling always tends to look after itself.

The days before the Test had been dominated by talk in the media about the auction for the Indian Premier League in Goa. A few of us were involved and we were obviously interested in what was happening, but it wasn't as big a talking point in the dressing room as some of the papers would have you believe. The auction was held the night before the Test and it was a strange situation to be in. It's very hard to put a value on yourself without looking like an idiot. What if I'd put myself down for a huge total and no one had bought me? Neil Fairbrother sought advice and we decided to put a reserve price of US$950,000. As it turned out, Kev and I went for the same figure – US$1.55 million. Ravi Bopara, who was due to join us for the one-day leg of the West Indies tour, Paul Collingwood and Owais Shah also got contracts.

I found out the staggering amount I'd gone for by ringing Neil, who was in Goa as my representative. I couldn't believe it when he told me how much Chennai had paid for me. I was so stunned I had to go and sit on the balcony of my room to try to compose myself. It is an amazing feeling to know that someone has paid over a million dollars for you to play Twenty20 cricket, and it took some time before it sank in.

Unsurprisingly, when the rest of the lads found out about it the next day, a fair amount of mickey-taking ensued. It even extended on to the field of play. Chris Gayle, the West Indies captain, kept teasing me while he was batting on the second day by calling me a million-dollar cricketer, and asking me what I was going to spend the money on. That was one of the few lighter moments of the First Test. We just didn't perform. We were favourites to win the Test series before it began, and I think that, as a team, we thought we should win it. It's often hard to deliver when everyone expects you to win, though, and sometimes it's much better to be regarded as underdogs.

We found it difficult from the very first morning in Jamaica. Andrew Strauss, having won the toss, chose to bat first and there's no doubt we should have got a bigger total than the 318 we scored. As it was, we did well to get even that. Kevin showed that losing the captaincy had had no impact on his batting by cracking an excellent 97, Matt Prior scored runs down the order and I contributed 43, which I was quite pleased with, considering the amount of cricket I had played in the build-up.

We actually did quite well to limit them to a 74-run first-innings lead after bowling them out for 392. Stuart Broad claimed 5 for 85, and as a bowling unit we performed well together. The great thing about the 2005 team was that we would bowl in pairs and not release the pressure at any time. Harmy and Matthew Hoggard would open up and then Simon Jones and I would come on and keep the batsmen under pressure consistently – that's the best way to get wickets at this level. Despite centuries from Gayle and Ramnaresh Sarwan, we felt reasonably pleased that they had not claimed a bigger first-innings lead.

I still don't really know what happened when we began our reply and were bowled out for 51. It wasn't a pitch that was doing all sorts. Jerome Taylor did bowl well for his five wickets, but it wasn't a 51-all-out pitch. The ball with which Taylor dismissed Kev was a fantastic delivery, an inswinging yorker that few batsmen in the world would have kept out, and after that we just seemed to collapse. When I was batting at the other end, I couldn't quite believe what I was seeing, and by the time Harmy came out to bat with me towards the end, our main goal was to try at least to make them bat again, because by then the game had gone. I started swinging a bit and hit Sulieman Benn, their leg spinner, for a couple of fours, but it did nothing but delay the inevitable.

Losing the Test so badly was hard enough, but the following day I found myself back in the *Sun* newspaper for the wrong reasons. Harmy and I had been invited to join an ITC travel group for dinner on their boat, and to answer a few questions to entertain the group of cricket fans they were taking around the Caribbean. We didn't think there was anything wrong with that, so we went along, had a couple of glasses of wine and were helicoptered back to our hotel early the following morning.

Kevin Pietersen quickly took to his new role as captain and guided England to wins in the final Test and the one-day series against South Africa.

The shock of the terrorist attacks in Mumbai, including on the Taj Mahal Palace Hotel, hit us all. It led to heightened security and much discussion about our return to India.

Andy Flower (*left*) and Andrew Strauss were appointed as the new coach and captain before we went to the West Indies.

I was embarrassed for Sir Viv Richards when the ground that bears his name was clearly not ready for Test cricket, and the match had to be abandoned shortly after it started.

The IPL experience with Chennai in South Africa was enormously enjoyable.

Visiting First World War graves was extremely moving. Adil Rashid and I study the headstones during our pre-Ashes trip.

Matt Prior (*left*) and Peter Siddle both made impressive starts to the series in Cardiff.

Jimmy Anderson (*left*) and Monty Panesar deserve all the credit for hanging on in those last overs and earning a draw.

The catalogue of injuries I have had over the years, including my right knee problems, forced me to announce my retirement from Test cricket before the match at Lord's.

Andrew Strauss led the team superbly throughout the Ashes series. He captained well and was also our leading run-scorer.

Taking five wickets for the first time was a good way to finish my final Test at Lord's, and helped England win their first Ashes Test there for 75 years.

I could not believe how well Jonathan Trott played in scoring a century on his Test debut – particularly in a match with the Ashes riding on it.

Stuart Broad's spell after lunch on the second day at The Oval swung the final Test firmly in our direction.

My unlikely run-out of Ricky Ponting set us on the way to regaining the Ashes. The urn's fate was sealed when Graeme Swann claimed the final wicket of the match, dismissing Michael Hussey.

Finishing my Test career with an Ashes victory was the perfect way to end, particularly as my family was there to share the moment with me.

We didn't think anything more of it until the following day when the *Sun* wrote a big story about us being on a free booze cruise, which just wasn't true. I had a call from Hugh Morris, media relations officer Andrew Walpole and Straussy asking me about it. I told them that I may have been involved in scrapes in the past, but this wasn't one of them. They accepted my explanation and we moved on to Antigua for the next Test.

I had started feeling a twinge in my hip towards the end of my overs in Jamaica and dismissed it as another niggle, but to be on the safe side, I didn't do too much before the Second Test. We practised at the Recreation Ground, which is Antigua's traditional old cricket ground. The authorities preferred to stage the Second Test at the Sir Viv Richards Ground, which had been purpose-built for the 2007 World Cup. We played a bit of football during the warm-up and I felt the hip problem kick in again, so took the build-up quite easy. I bowled a bit and it niggled a little, but I still thought it was nothing more than a twinge.

Part of the problem was that I hated to admit I was injured again. I've had so many injuries I just don't want to give in to them. I'm almost embarrassed when I give in to an injury, and I was hopeful of getting through this one. I didn't think it would prevent me from playing a full part in the Test, but it didn't turn out that way.

We didn't visit the Sir Viv Richards stadium until the day before the game, and as soon as we got there we could see that the outfield was awful. It was so sandy it was like a beach – everyone passed comment on it – but that's where we were playing and there wasn't a lot the players could do about it. We practised on one of the pitches alongside the Test wicket and noticed we were digging up the outfield as we ran in to bowl even then. Nothing much had changed when we arrived the following day for the start of the Test. We won the toss and batted, and once the game got started, all the fuss appeared to die down. The first couple of balls were about shin high and Strauss didn't seem to have too much trouble with them, so at that stage I think the two opening bowlers probably feared the worst. To my mind, Fidel Edwards made a bit of a meal of the pitch, I thought the sand would perhaps have an influence on the game a bit later as it dug up – nobody was expecting the authorities to cancel the Test during the first morning of the game, not long after it had started.

We were sad about what had happened, although I'm sure the West Indies were quite happy to keep their 1–0 series lead. I know Sir Viv Richards was embarrassed about the situation. I have always looked up to him, and to have given his name to a ground that was such a complete shambles was terrible.

There were also the fans to consider. A lot of people had spent their hard-earned money to go to Antigua to cheer us on and the match had been abandoned before lunch on the first day. As a team we hung around afterwards, signed autographs and chatted to people in the crowd. There was a real feeling of anger among the fans about it all. One couple said they had been saving for ten years to make the trip and saw fifteen minutes play. We felt pretty bad about it.

Word came through later that day that a new Test would

start in a few days' time at the Recreation Ground, which we were all pleased about. I would have been quite happy to play the Test there from the start. During our practice sessions, the ball had flown through with plenty of pace. We also doubted whether there would be time to prepare a proper wicket, which gave more chance of a result, and if the ball started moving around, we thought we were the better equipped team to deal with it – how wrong we were.

Maybe the West Indies were also influenced by that thinking because they put us in to bat after winning the toss and we declared on 566 for 9. I was just about the only member of our line-up not to get runs. I was out second ball to Jerome Taylor, who bowled me a ball that shot along the floor and knocked over my off stump. There wasn't much I could have done about it. My hip was still a problem, though, and I started struggling from my second or third spell with the ball. We bowled well as a team and managed to dismiss them for 285 to claim a 281-run first-innings lead, but Strauss decided not to enforce the follow-on. As I've already said, I think that as a general rule enforcing the follow-on is overrated. Unless you're playing against a terrible team and you're confident of bowling them out in the second innings in not many overs, it can be a very tough ask of your bowlers.

Still, having decided to bat again, I thought we made some strange decisions. We were all those runs ahead and chose to send Jimmy Anderson in as nightwatchman on the third evening after Straussy fell early in our reply. Jimmy does a valuable job as nightwatchman for the team, and his batting has improved tremendously, but he is not going to be as effective as a recognised batsman when you're looking for quick runs in order to declare and give yourself more time to bowl the opposition out to win the game. The other decision I found strange was sending me out to bat when we were 482 runs ahead. I had been put down the order to No. 9, since my movement was limited because of my hip problem. I couldn't move to play my shots, and I didn't want any pain-killers then because I wanted to save them for when we bowled. The inevitable happened – I was out for a duck and was furious when I got back to the dressing room. My kit went everywhere when I came in. We were over 400 runs ahead and we sent a cripple out to bat!

We finally set them a victory target of 503 and, although I was in pain by then, I somehow managed to get through 15 overs. I couldn't get going, I just couldn't move my legs. Once I got to my delivery stride I could get the ball down using the strength in my shoulder, but when I started following through I was in agony. I thought I was going to bowl them out, so I kept going. I had some painkillers and thought I'd just give it a go. I ran in and tried to get through it, and it worked to some degree, but it was getting worse and worse.

The problem turned out to be a tear in the muscle that goes from your hip to your back. It's quite a fat muscle and Rooster told me it takes something special to tear it – trust me to do it! I managed to get through the game but we weren't quite able to force the victory. Last-wicket pair Daren Powell and Fidel Edwards survived for about 10 overs before bad light ended play. I dropped one in the gully in the second to last over, which I don't think many people picked up on. I was struggling and couldn't get down low enough to take the catch. Everyone in the team was shattered because we knew we had missed a good chance to level the series.

In Barbados, which was the venue for the next Test, I had yet another scan and was diagnosed with a grade two tear of the muscle. All sorts of talk followed about the possibility of being able to play in ten days' time, but I knew it was a serious injury and would take longer than that to heal. I didn't go to the ground to watch the lads in their two-day warm-up match against a Barbados Cricket Association XI because I didn't want to get in the way. I stayed at the hotel with the holiday-makers. They were all interested in how I was getting on, so I was constantly being approached, which was not the ideal situation in which to work on my recovery. After a few days, I asked the team management if I could go home to work on getting fit again, and they agreed. I knew I could get more done at home, working with Rooster all day, than I could sitting around a luxury hotel in Barbados. Rooster thought it was a four-week injury, which would give me time to recover and come back for the one-day series following the Tests.

As it happened, I returned to the Caribbean after around ten days at home but did not return to playing until the third one-day international, by which time I had missed our defeat in the Twenty20 International. I was also absent for the opening one-day international in Guyana, when West Indies coach John Dyson called his side off, thinking they had won under the Duckworth Lewis method. His error allowed us to celebrate an unexpected one-run victory.

There was a chance of me returning for the second one-day international in Guyana, which we lost, but we decided to err on the side of caution and I waited for the next game in Barbados. It was our worst performance of the series. The West Indies won comfortably after bowling us out for 117. Several of us were out, caught hooking, although I thought mine was a slightly unlucky dismissal because I was trying to paddle Dwayne Bravo around the corner and got a top edge that carried all the way down to fine leg. It still didn't look good when several other members of the team had got out to short balls.

We needed to win the next game, again in Barbados, to remain in the series, but it was rain-affected and ended up almost like a Twenty20 match. They batted all their overs but after another rain shower we were set a target of 135 from 20 overs, which we passed with some to spare after an outstanding innings from Strauss. I was pleased we had set up a series decider in St Lucia, but I wasn't really enjoying the trip. I think it was partly because I had gone home and come back, and had not really settled back on to the tour. It was also because I wasn't quite fit enough to play. No one likes being on tour when you're not in the running to be selected. Also, there was a funny atmosphere around the squad. It had been a long tour, we had been beaten in the Test series and we were initially behind in the one-day series.

With all that on my mind, the obvious didn't occur to me – that the media would pick up on my first visit back to St Lucia since the pedalo incident. Despite their attentions, I actually enjoyed that final week of the tour. I didn't go anywhere near Rodney Bay, scene of my run-in with the pedalo. We stayed at a place up the coast and instead of being given hotel rooms, we were given two-bedroomed flats, which was a nice change.

I shared my flat with Harmy. Neither of us were having the best of times, but we came to the conclusion that there was no point in being in St Lucia if we weren't going to enjoy it, so we decided to make our own fun. We had some time off the day after we arrived and had a little party in our flat. We ordered in some wine, got a few of the lads around and had a great afternoon. In the evening, we went out to meet former England spinner Norman Gifford, who was hosting a tour group of fans. I got to know him very well when he ran the England Under-19s many years ago, and since he has done a lot of work at Durham, Harmy knows him well, too. Harmy and I had just decided to enjoy ourselves. We weren't going out and getting hammered every night, but we entertained ourselves. We sat on the beach, chilled out around the room, invited people around and made an effort. That was what made it an enjoyable week.

By the time we got around to playing the series decider, I think we were ready to play, but the match did not start well for me. I was anxious to make some runs, because in my only previous innings in the series I'd got a duck. Just when I thought it couldn't get any worse with my batting, Shivnarine Chanderpaul made a brilliant one-handed diving catch to dismiss me for just 3. Shiv is a brilliant batsman but I don't think even he would say he's one of the best fielders in the world, so when he pulled off a catch like that, I knew my luck was out!

That match underlined to me what a strange game cricket can be. I didn't think I bowled particularly well in the match, but I ended up with 5 for 19 and a hat-trick when I've bowled much better in other games and not got a wicket! I bowled slightly differently from the way I do normally. I was bowling into the wind and I delivered cutters for the first time in my life. I tried to run my fingers over the ball to impart a little spin, thinking it might bounce a little more, and it worked. I came back at the end, when they were struggling to keep up with the rate anyway, and claimed the wickets of Denesh Ramdin, Ravi Rampaul and Sulieman Benn in successive deliveries – it was just one of those days when things went right for me with the ball. I hadn't practised bowling cutters, but they just seemed to work.

It's funny with bowling because I do need to work on my variations. I have got a slower ball, but I think it's a case of not knowing when to use it rather than not being prepared to bowl it. I have always found with bowling that if I sit down and think about what I'm trying to do, I can usually do it, and that was the case with the cutters.

We were all looking forward to getting home, but it wasn't straightforward. Talk about having to wait a couple of days for a connection from St Lucia to Barbados, where we were due to pick up our flight home worried me. We were due to travel back on the Saturday (4 April), which would get me back in good time to attend Rocky's christening on the Sunday lunchtime. There was no way I could miss the flight home to England, so I had no choice but to hire a plane to get me from St Lucia to Barbados. It wasn't a flash, luxury private jet. It was a propeller-type plane and I took Harmy, Kevin and Jimmy Anderson with me. Jimmy was coming to the christening. As it turned out, the lads landed in Barbados not long after us, so it was a complete waste of money, but I couldn't run the risk of missing the flight. I finally got home at 11.30 on the morning of the christening and had just enough time to walk through the door, say hello to everybody, dive in the shower and get to the church. It was a lovely day and I was able to catch up with all my family and friends in one hit.

# 18

# RACE FOR THE ASHES

I was at home for four or five days before travelling to South Africa for my first taste of the Indian Premier League. In hindsight, I think it would have been better to arrive a couple of days earlier to get to know my new Chennai team-mates, but I wanted to spend the time with my family. The IPL games had been moved to South Africa because of security concerns in India – the dates clashed with the Indian general election. Despite my recent reservations about returning to India with England, that was a disappointment to me because I wanted to experience the atmosphere of the IPL in India, with the passionate Indian fans and the excitement they bring.

I've never been an overseas player for anyone, or played for any team other than Lancashire and England, so I didn't know what it would be like. Going into a dressing room full of strangers at that stage in my career was very odd. Most of the side were from India, of course, and as well as their names I had to learn the way they do things, which is not the same as the way we do them in England – different culture, different approach. I've played for the same two teams all my career and, naturally enough, have got used to the way Lancashire and England warm up, practise and prepare for games, but Chennai did things differently, and not knowing too many of them made the adjustment that much harder. If I'd spent ten days prior to the tournament with them and got to know them a little better, it would have made all the difference. I was only just getting to know a few of their names when it was time to leave.

I remember my first net session with them the morning after I arrived. They must have been wondering what they'd signed! They were so good and I was very nervous. MS Dhoni was captain. Suresh Raina from the India team was playing for us. I knew Matthew Hayden quite well from playing against him in the Ashes. New Zealand all-rounder Jacob Oram was there, and South Africa's Albie Morkel joined us a few days later. I would have liked more preparation for the tournament and next time around I will be practising somewhere before I go, if not arriving early to get my game in order.

It was a definite move out of my comfort zone and I did find it hard. Getting to know different people quickly was a challenge in itself, and having such a big price tag didn't make it any easier. The amount made me feel a little uncomfortable, bringing its own pressures.

Our first game in the tournament was against Mumbai Indians in Cape Town. I was nervous beforehand, anxious to make a good impression, and having to bowl my first over to Sanath Jayasuriya wasn't the best way to ease into my IPL career. I also had Sachin Tendulkar dropped at slip by Hayden.

It was the easiest catch ever. I was frustrated by that because I thought that if I'd got Sachin out in my first game, Chennai would start to think they hadn't done too badly in signing me. Unfortunately, I was confronted with a left-hander I knew nothing about, and Abhishek Nayar, whom I had never even seen before, just kept launching me. I didn't seem to have an option against him. I tried a bouncer and he spliced that to the short boundary for six. I conceded 22 runs in the over, and as it turned out, that over probably cost us the game because we lost by 19 runs, so I wasn't feeling too flash after that.

The thing I have realised about Twenty20 cricket is that there are stages in the game when it's incredibly difficult to stop batsmen coming at you. The last two overs of the powerplay are just horrendous for the bowlers, because the batsmen really go for you, and bowling at the death is just the same. My short stint with the IPL showed me the areas where I can definitely improve in that form of the game. I need to work on subtle variations with the ball because you can't just rely on a yorker or a bouncer.

For most of my time in South Africa I hung around with Hayden. He's never been the most popular player around the world, not least with England players, but I've never had a problem with him. He's big and brash, but underneath he's a big soft lad. He's also reached the latter stages of his career. He's always been a fierce competitor but now he's playing in the IPL for fun. Of course he still wants to win, but he enjoyed himself while he was in South Africa as well, and did a lot of surfing. He kept talking about surfing, using various surfing terms, and in the end I had to tell him I hadn't a clue what he was going on about. I'd grown up in Preston so never saw any waves when I was a kid! The way Hayden approached the IPL and played during the tournament was a lesson. If you can play with that much freedom, you're going to do all right.

Our second match in the tournament, against Bangalore Royal Challengers in Port Elizabeth, was built up as the big match because it pitched me against Kevin Pietersen. It was billed like two prize-fighters facing each other. The question I kept being asked was how were we going to react to playing against each other. I suppose the interest was only natural, particularly as we haven't faced each other that much in county cricket – in just one match that I remember, when he was playing for Nottinghamshire.

As soon as I came in to bat, Kev brought himself on to bowl at me. He said afterwards that he thought spin might be the best way to go against me. If anyone else had tried to bowl the ball he delivered first up, I would have tried to hit it over the pavilion. It was right in the slot, but because it was Kev, I just turned it for a single. There was no way I was going to get out to him! I was not going to spend the next few years in the dressing room being ribbed about it! Unfortunately, I didn't get to bowl at him because Murali got him out, but it was great to be involved in a win for my new team. What that match, and the IPL in general, showed up was that, as far as Kev and I were concerned, we still had some way to go in Twenty20 cricket. We have both got big contracts and potentially we can do really well in it, but you could see the difference in the lads who were playing in their second year of the tournament compared with us. They were really good. I was pleased that Ravi Bopara did so well, but again he has played a lot more domestic Twenty20 cricket than we have and it showed. The game against Bangalore was probably my best game for Chennai because I didn't get collared when I was bowling and managed a quick 22 at the death when I was batting.

Talk to any fast bowler around the world and they will tell you they have niggles and pain in some part of their body. It's just a part of the job. So, despite my history of injuries, when I started feeling my knee while I was in South Africa, I thought it was a minor blip and didn't bother to tell anyone. It wasn't like the hip injury I sustained in the Caribbean. This just felt like a stiff knee and it wasn't even every day, just now and then. It started getting worse after the Bangalore game and I was in a bit of pain in the warm-up for the next match against Delhi Daredevils in Durban. The England medical staff were in constant contact with the guys at Chennai, and when I felt something at the back of my knee, I was sent straight for a scan the day before the game. Two radiologists looked at it and both immediately said I needed an operation. When I phoned Rooster, he thought I was taking the mickey, but the scans went off to England for further examination and they confirmed what the radiologist in Durban had said.

I played the game against Delhi because I knew it was going to be my last one before going home for an operation and I knew I could get through it. In hindsight, I should probably have not bothered because I got smashed again, this time by A.B. de Villiers. Mentally I was shot because of the disappointment of having to go for yet another operation. My head was all over the place at the thought of it, and at the prospect of having to grit my teeth through yet another period of rehabilitation – and the Ashes were looming on the horizon. I also knew I was going to get a kicking in the press for getting injured while I was with the IPL. I have no regrets about that, though, because had I not been in South Africa I would probably have been playing for Lancashire and it could have gone just as easily then.

As soon as I got back home, I had the operation. I wanted to give myself as much time as possible to recover and to play enough cricket to make sure I was right for the Ashes. I have met a number of surgeons over the years through all my various injuries, and they are mostly very matter-of-fact, very confident. This time, I immediately liked the guy as well. Andy Williams comes across as a very normal bloke. He explains everything and doesn't treat you like a fool if you don't understand what he's talking about, and he listens to what you've got to say. I had a lot of confidence in him. He told me that the one thing he didn't want to find was any bone damage in the knee, but told me not to worry because the chance of that happening was one in a thousand.

When he came to see me afterwards, I asked him if everything was all right, and even though I was still a bit groggy from the anaesthetic, I could tell it wasn't. He said he would speak to me upstairs once I'd come round properly, and later in his office he told me the tear in my ligament had been repaired, but he had found some bone damage, which meant the healing process would take longer. Instead of four or five weeks, it could take seven or eight weeks – a setback but not a disaster. There were still around ten weeks before the Ashes started, so I had time to complete my rehabilitation, play some cricket and still be all right for the First Test in Cardiff.

It came as a surprise to be named in England's squad for the ICC World Twenty20 tournament, which was due to begin just five weeks later at the start of June. Usually, when a statement goes out from England, you are shown it beforehand, so you know what is going to be said, but this time I was just announced in the squad. I understand why I was included. If you're in the squad to start with, a replacement can be brought in if you don't make it, but you can't just be added later while those originally named are all fit and well. So if by some miracle I had recovered in time, I wouldn't have been able to play unless I was named in the original squad. That said, I was pretty confident I would not be fit for the start of the tournament and told the England management so. Once they realised I was unlikely to make the tournament, Adil Rashid was named in my place.

Normally after an operation I get very down at the thought of all the hard work I have to go through to get fit again, but this time the incentive was massive. I knew if I was fit, I would have a good chance of playing in the Ashes again and that thought kept me going through all the weeks working with Rooster. It was still hard work. For the first two weeks I was sat on the couch in the house with an ice machine on my knee. It even went to bed with me and was set for intervals throughout the night to compress my knee. I was also on crutches for two weeks, but Rooster insisted that I did leg weights and exercises on my quads. While I was injured and immobile they were wasting away, so I was on the couch doing leg work pretty much as soon as I got back home after the operation.

Midway through June, I returned to action with Lancashire, against Durham. They had the best attack I played against that summer next to Australia – Harmison, Graham Onions, Mitch Claydon and Callum Thorp. Harmison and Onions did most of the damage. It was a good wicket to bowl on and I got Harmy out twice, but he got his revenge by bowling me off an inside edge in the first innings. I was a bit unlucky because the edge went on to my pad and then on to the stumps, but I was hanging back a bit in my crease against Harmy if I'm honest. He does run in when I'm at the crease for some reason, but perhaps because I've faced him so much the nets over the years, I'm used to his pace. He gets me out nearly every time without question, but when I get back to the dressing room and I'm asked how he's bowling, I always tell them he's not that quick – I usually get a few glares later when Harmy has been flying the ball past their noses!

We were chasing 274 to win in the final innings. Ian Blackwell had just swung at the ball during his 74 in their second innings, which gave them a good lead, and Peter

Moores told me to try to do the same when we batted. I didn't have the same success as Blacky, though, and was caught at mid-on by Claydon off Onions for a duck and we lost convincingly. It was one thing for Chanderpaul to make a one-handed diving catch, but now Claydon was doing it!

My next match was against Hampshire at Liverpool and I was given an opportunity to bat up the order for a change. Tom Smith, who had been opening the batting for us, was injured and Mal Loye came in and opened, so I asked Peter Moores if I could bat at No. 3. I played all right in the first innings and was going along well until I reached for one off Dimitri Mascarenhas, who has a habit of getting me out, and was caught at slip for 12. I played a lot better in the second innings and scored a half-century before being bounced out by Dimi, although I maintain I wasn't out. I went to hook him but I got through the shot too early, the ball hit me on the back and spooned up. I was given out caught.

That match was the first time I'd played against my old mate Dominic Cork since he was snapped up by Hampshire. I did not agree with Lancashire's decision to release him the previous summer because I believed he still had something to give. Durham had played Hampshire recently, so I asked Harmy what was the best way to get Dominic out. He told me to bowl short at him, and hit him on the gloves or the head, and then bowl the next one outside off stump. He said that Dominic would nick it behind and that was exactly what happened. When Cork walked out to bat, I asked him how we were going to do it. 'Are you going to get out before the bouncer or after,' I inquired, and it proved to be after, just as Harmy had said it would be. It did not have a great bearing on the overall result, though, because we were beaten again.

Although the results were not going the right way, I felt I was getting better in every game I played, particularly with the ball. In each match, I started off with a quick spell but then found it hard to come back with another. I was physically fit but not match fit, so bowling spell after spell after spell was hard but I was improving.

After those two matches, we switched back to the Twenty20 Cup and lost again at Liverpool, this time to Leicestershire. I found my range in my last match for Lancashire before I assembled with England for a pre-Ashes training camp. I had not been to Derby since 1999 and was pleasantly surprised at how they had spruced up the ground. It was the best pitch I had played on in a long time. It had pace and was good to bat on. I had batted at No. 3 in the previous game, but Peter Moores and captain Glen Chapple wanted VVS Laxman, Lancashire's overseas player, to open the batting and I would come in at No. 5 to give us some momentum towards the end.

As it turned out, I went out to bat in the seventh over and got a four away early on before they brought Garry Park on to bowl. I had faced him the year before when he was at Durham, and I went down the pitch to tell VVS I was going after him. He wanted to know why I was so keen on facing him and I explained he had got me out the previous year despite playing most of his career as a wicketkeeper. I thought he had basked in the glory a bit about that, so I really went for him and took a few runs off his next over. I ended up scoring 93 off 41 balls and Lancashire won by 56 runs to secure their passage into the Twenty20 Cup quarter-finals. It was a good way to say goodbye before reporting back to the England camp.

# 19

## THE GREAT ESCAPE

Our initial instructions from England were to assemble at the National Performance Centre in Loughborough for meetings about the Ashes and some training, but we were then told to meet in London from where we travelled by Eurostar to France and on to Belgium. From our base in Ypres, we were to visit First World War graves and battlefields. It was a very different way of preparing for the Ashes, but Andy Flower, who had been appointed England's permanent coach as a replacement for Peter Moores at the start of the summer, was keen for us to go.

On our first day, we attended a service to commemorate those people who had lost their lives in the First World War, laid wreaths at the Menin Gate and visited war graves. As I went around reading the gravestones, for some reason I found it even more moving if the grave was of a solider from Lancashire or Lancaster. I know that's wrong but I suppose it's natural to feel more of an affinity with someone from your home territory.

We rounded off an emotional day with a team function. Part of the purpose of the trip was to have a good time as a team and that evening we did. We had a meal, went to a bar afterwards and had a late night. Next morning I missed the bus and was absent for the first activity of the day. I wasn't the only one who was late down but I was the only one who missed the bus. I'm sure if Harmy had been there, he'd have come and got me because he knows what I'm like. The other lads said they tried ringing my room to alert me the bus was about to leave, but I must have slept through the calls. The unfortunate thing is that I missed the visit to the trenches, which was the one part of the trip I was really looking forward to. I had read Sebastian Faulks' book *Birdsong*, which is all about the First World War, and I wanted to see for myself the horrendous conditions the troops had to suffer.

I was there for the next part of the day, which was really the main reason for the trip – a team meeting with Steve Bull, the sports psychologist we have used extensively in the past. So in the great scheme of things, I had just missed the first hour of the day. I know I was in the wrong and I apologised to Andrew Strauss and also rang Andy Flower. I'm sure it didn't go down well with the management but it wasn't a catastrophe either, in my opinion. My big concern was that it might be interpreted as showing disrespect to First World War veterans, which I certainly never intended. I also apologised to the team. I probably should have done that on the morning of the meeting with Steve Bull, but I just wanted to be involved and I didn't think the timing was right.

On our return, we headed for Birmingham to prepare for a three-day warm-up match against Warwickshire, and it was there that James Avery, one of the team's media relations officers, told me the press had got wind of what happened. I was disappointed it had got out because it meant Strauss and Hugh Morris had to answer questions about me at the press conference, and I was also upset with myself. In the weeks leading up to that point, I had been getting up at all sorts of hours to train in order to be ready for the start of the Ashes, and here I was all over the papers for missing the bus after a team-building night out. I was gutted. The ironic thing was that just as the papers were writing about what had happened in Belgium, we were being given a talk by James and Andrew Walpole, the team's other media relations officer, about the dangers of playing in such a high-profile series and how our behaviour away from the matches could also be reported.

At least I had a match to concentrate on, although it was an awful game for anyone who came along to watch. Edgbaston was one of the Test venues, but we were playing on a bad wicket with a 20-yard boundary on one side against a young Warwickshire team. By contrast, Australia were getting a really good run-out against England Lions a few miles down the road in Worcester. In my opinion, we should have played against the Lions and had a really good run-out, instead of a poor, low-key, three-day match. The one thing I took from the match was good bowling practice. I think the events of the previous few days got to me and I bowled very quickly, but it was not the best way to prepare for an Ashes series.

The match finished on the Friday and we were due to assemble again in Cardiff on the Sunday night, ready for two days of training leading into the Test. Rather than go back home, Rachael booked us rooms in a castle somewhere near

Bristol to stay for two nights with the family, which was a lovely break. We took the kids to the beach at Weston-super-Mare and let them have rides on the donkeys. It was a lovely way to relax before switching on for another Ashes series.

The start of most Ashes series is usually full of hype and expectation, with people predicting the score and everyone having an opinion of what's about to happen. Normally, you can't avoid getting caught up in it, but on this occasion I managed to escape it all. After the Belgium trip, I was determined not to read any papers during the build-up and to remain oblivious of everything going on. I wanted to stay relaxed after those couple of days with the family, and I don't think it had quite sunk in that I was going to be playing in the Ashes again.

It was quite a strange experience for us all, really. Cardiff was a new Test venue and we didn't know the ground, the conditions or the facilities any better than the Aussies did. Everyone was very friendly. The staff on the gates, Roger the dressing-room attendant, they all made us feel very welcome. If I had a criticism, it would be about the wicket, which was slow throughout the match. The first day was very tense – in the dressing room, out on the field, among the crowd. Despite that, and perhaps because there was no history of playing Test matches in Cardiff, or maybe because there were a lot of Welsh people in the crowd unsure about whether they should cheer for England, the atmosphere wasn't as you'd expect for an Ashes Test match. It didn't really get going until the final hour of the final day when the crowd and everyone else was counting down the overs and minutes to see if we could hold out.

The tension before the start of the match was amazing, particularly in our dressing room. I love playing for England, and you want to win every match you play for your country, but there is no doubt that an Ashes series stirs up emotions you don't feel very often. You can see it having an effect on the Aussie players, too. It's high-pressure stuff and it's interesting to see how people react. It will bring the best out of some players, while others just shrink with the responsibility of it all. We had four players in our line-up – Ravi Bopara, Matt Prior, Stuart Broad and Graeme Swann – who had never played an Ashes Test before, and I did try to pass on some of my experiences to them. I've had some of the best and worst times of my career in Ashes series, and I wanted to warn them about it, which I tried to do in the team meetings. I also spoke at the end of the first day. Strauss, as captain, obviously did most of the talking, but I was there to help if needed as one of our experienced players. We were also aware that building up the Ashes too much might be counterproductive, making our players feel constrained and affecting their freedom to play. The Ashes mean so much to so many people, but as players it was important to remain as relaxed as possible. There is a fine line between alerting people to what it can be like and making them so tense about the occasion they struggle to perform.

For all that, I think players on both sides were just relieved to get the first day over with. So much had been said and written about the series, it was a big relief just to play. During practice before the game started, Graeme Swann snapped at me. I've known Swanny for many years and he's normally up for a bit of banter and a bit of a laugh. We were practising our slip catching and he dropped about three so I joked with him, 'Unlucky, Swanny. They're not easy, these, are they?' He came straight back at me and told me to go away in not very polite terms. That was an indication of how tense we all were on that first morning. By the end of the day, we had reached 336 for 7 – we had lost two more wickets than we wanted to, but to score that many runs on the first day on a slow pitch was a bonus. We had got ourselves into a strong position at tea and Kev was going well, so to lose four wickets in the final session was a bit of a setback, and both sides probably thought they were in the game.

When I walked out to bat with Matt Prior we had slipped to 241 for 5 and the day could have gone either way, but he is the type of player that I seem to feed off when I'm batting. Geraint Jones, our 2005 Ashes wicketkeeper, was a similar player. They are both quite aggressive, very strong playing the cut shot, and both pull anything short. I like batting with players like that and I enjoyed batting with Matt. We were both going well and added 86 off 95 balls when I fell to the seventh over with the second new ball. I had decided to go out there and be positive, take it to them and play my shots. I achieved that but I was disappointed with the timing of my dismissal, not long before the end of the day. Peter Siddle, Australia's aggressive seamer, bowled the ball just outside off stump, and if I was bowled that ball again I would still attempt to drive it. On this occasion, it nipped back a bit and I chopped it on to my stumps for 37. I'd taken a few risks during my innings anyway, and you're never going to get away with all of them.

You would never have known it was Swanny's first Ashes Test match the following morning when he began his innings. We wanted to get over 400 and he combined with Jimmy Anderson in a superb 68-run stand, which eventually got us up to 435. I'd had a bet with Jimmy that if he scored 30 I would buy him a case of Cloudy Bay, which is a lovely white wine from New Zealand. He got to 26, tried to hit a four over the top and was caught at mid-on. Back in the dressing room, he admitted that he was trying to reach his case of Cloudy Bay in style.

We all thought that our total was a good effort, but on that wicket we knew we would have to bowl well to prevent Australia taking a first-innings lead. During our innings, not many balls had swung or seamed. Playing against some countries, you would be confident of taking control of the match if you scored 435, but not against Australia. When they started their innings midway through the second morning, I was pleading with Straussy to let me have the new ball and have a go at Phil Hughes, their dangerous new opener. He had scored a lot of runs playing for Middlesex earlier that summer, but Harmy had roughed him up the previous week playing for the Lions against Australia at Worcester, and had told me to bowl around the wicket at him and bowl short. If I did that, Harmy did not think Hughes would last six balls. A lot of people don't give Harmy credit for being a thinking bowler, but I can tell you he is.

I wanted to get at Hughes and when I got the chance after lunch, I bowled him a bouncer with my first delivery and followed through down the wicket. I introduced myself to him and told him, 'I'm going to be all over you for five Test matches

– if you play five.' Being a young lad he came back at me, but I just smiled at him every time he played a bad shot. He kept trying to chirp at me, but there was no point in responding because the damage was done – he was more interested in playing me than in playing the ball, and he wanted to show people he could dominate me. He wasn't out there for many more overs before he nicked one behind and was off. I wasn't trying to sledge him or get personal. I just wanted to let him know that I'd seen what Steve had done to him and what I was going to do to him. All he wanted to do after that was come after me, and it distracted him from playing his own game.

That success was our only breakthrough for another 70 overs. Ricky Ponting had come in to the match with very few runs under his belt from the Worcester game and was looking terrible at the crease, but you have to take your hat off to him for the way he played in that First Test. He is obviously a highly talented player, but he is also mentally tough. He is gritty when he needs to be and knuckles down to the needs of his team. The glaring difference between the two teams in the First Test was that we wanted to play shots and were a bit excitable, and when some of us got into the 30s or 50s or 60s, we started showing off, but Ponting just plays the same way all the time – that's what the great players do. That's what Tendulkar does, that's what Kallis does. They just play at the same pace. They don't go through the gears and start messing about, and when they get to a hundred, they just keep batting and batting.

Simon Katich surprised me. He was incredibly disciplined but he played some shots as well. After we finally got through their top order, we were confronted with Marcus North, who had played for a few weeks at Lancashire a few years earlier as a temporary overseas players. He was a nice lad, but didn't do much for Lancashire, so when he marched out I was thinking, 'Here's another one gone!' How wrong can you be! He scored a hundred and played really well, and then Brad Haddin came in and rolled off a century. We were starting to wonder if anyone else fancied one. I think we were all pretty relieved when they declared 239 runs ahead with just over four sessions for us to bat out the game.

It was disappointing to lose two early wickets to tired shots before tea on the fourth day, but I think we got a bit hung up on the idea of rain, which was forecast to wipe out most of the fourth day. It was mentioned in meetings, it was mentioned in general conversation, but it didn't rain as much as everyone thought it was going to. If I've learnt anything from my previous battles with Australia, it's that no one does you any favours against this lot. You have to be prepared to do the job yourself, to do the hard work and not rely on the weather or anything else. By the time any rain fell, we'd already lost those two wickets, which made the task for the final day that much more difficult.

The pitch on that final morning had not got any worse, and we knew we had made a bit of a meal of playing against Nathan Hauritz, their off-spinner, who claimed three wickets in our first innings. That didn't stop us continuing in the same vein for a period in the second innings. He claimed two wickets before lunch to increase the tension, but we had to believe, as a team, that we could bat out 90-odd overs. We didn't want a repeat of Adelaide a couple of years previously, when we failed to bat out the game or score runs. We had to score some runs and Paul Collingwood is brilliant in that situation. He just gets his head down and bats, and between us we batted for over 20 overs. I found it very hard because Hauritz was lobbing them up – every time the ball left his hand all I could think of was hitting him into the river, and every time I made sure I didn't do anything stupid and just blocked it. I was desperate to have a big swing across the line at him, but I couldn't do it because of the situation. I was finally out after nicking a ball from Mitchell Johnson, their left-arm seamer, which was a decent delivery. I had been working with Dean Hills, our new batting coach whom we had poached from Australia, on lining up the angle when facing a left-arm seamer. We'd been using the bowling machine, and the idea is that you should play straight, or play to mid-on or mid-off, to minimise the chances of nicking the ball behind. This was one of the first times I had not followed that plan and I was out edging low to Ponting at slip.

Both Stuart Broad and Swanny provided further support for Colly. While he was at the crease we knew we had a chance of saving the Test, but he finally edged one to slip with what turned out to be forty minutes remaining, and the responsibility of keeping the Aussies out fell to Monty Panesar and Jimmy. For a time, the dressing room was quite relaxed, because for most of us our match was over and not a lot was expected of the two guys out in the middle. The closer we got to the close, though, the more tense the situation became. Jimmy's batting has improved no end after the going over he got from Fidel Edwards during the previous winter. After that, he thinks nothing can be as bad, so he gets in behind the ball. From the moment Monty walked out to bat, you could just sense he was up for the challenge, defending with a lovely flourish and not shirking any delivery.

Sitting up on the balcony, we were counting down the overs. As we got closer, I think someone started looking at the laws of the game to work out how long our pair had to bat for and whether Australia could bowl extra overs. We sent our physio, Steve McCaig, running on with 12th man Bilal Shafayat, and they both got a roasting from Ponting for being out there and trying to waste time. I don't think anyone could have been too critical of what we were doing, however, and I'm sure Australia would have done exactly the same in our position. I seem to remember a few changes of gloves out in the middle in 2005 at Old Trafford, when they were clinging on for a draw. It's almost expected. You also have to bear in mind that up on the balcony, we were tearing our hair out at Jimmy and Monty. Normally in that position, the batsmen out in the middle will waste a little time to reduce the number of overs they have to face by chatting between deliveries, going down the wicket to do a bit of gardening with their bat, or, as the Aussies did, calling for a change of gloves, but we had nothing like that from them.

At the end, there was no question of us celebrating getting out of jail. I remember Australia celebrating at Old Trafford, and the West Indies did the same during the previous winter, but we didn't want to celebrate a draw. We were happy to move on to Lord's still level in the series. Jimmy and Monty were, quite rightly, delighted because they had battled through, and it was their moment, but on the balcony we just shook each other's hands.

# ENGLAND v AUSTRALIA
# (1st Test) at Cardiff 8–12 July 2009

## England

| | | | | |
|---|---|---|---|---|
| *A.J.Strauss c Clarke b Johnson | 30 | – | c Haddin b Hauritz | 17 |
| A.N.Cook c Hussey b Hilfenhaus | 10 | – | lbw b Johnson | 6 |
| R.S.Bopara c Hughes b Johnson | 35 | – | lbw b Hilfenhaus | 1 |
| K.P.Pietersen c Katich b Hauritz | 69 | – | b Hilfenhaus | 8 |
| P.D.Collingwood c Haddin | | | | |
|   b Hilfenhaus | 64 | – | c Hussey b Siddle | 74 |
| +M.J.Prior b Siddle | 56 | – | c Clarke b Hauritz | 14 |
| A.Flintoff b Siddle | 37 | – | c Ponting b Johnson | 26 |
| J.M.Anderson c Hussey b Hauritz | 26 | (10) not out | | 21 |
| S.C.J.Broad b Johnson | 19 | (8) lbw b Hauritz | | 14 |
| G.P.Swann not out | 47 | (9) lbw b Hilfenhaus | | 31 |
| M.S.Panesar c Ponting b Hauritz | 4 | – | not out | 7 |
| B 13, l-b 11, w 2, n-b 12 | 38 | | B 9, l-b 9, w 4, n-b 11 | 33 |

1/21 2/67 3/90 4/228     435    1/13 2/17 3/31 4/46    (for 9 wkts) 252
5/241 6/327 7/329 8/355 9/423 10/435    5/70 6/127 7/159 8/221 9/233

Bowling: *First innings* – Johnson 22-2-87-3; Hilfenhaus 27-5-77-2; Siddle 27-3-121-2; Hauritz 23.5-1-95-3; Clarke 5-0-20-0; Katich 2-0-11-0. *Second innings* – Johnson 22-4-44-2; Hilfenhaus 15-3-47-3; Siddle 18-2-51-1; Hauritz 37-12-63-3; Clarke 3-0-8-0; North 7-4-14-0; Katich 3-0-7-0.

## Australia

| | |
|---|---|
| P.J.Hughes c Prior b Flintoff | 36 |
| S.M.Katich lbw b Anderson | 122 |
| *R.T.Ponting b Panesar | 150 |
| M.E.K.Hussey c Prior b Anderson | 3 |
| M.J.Clarke c Prior b Broad | 83 |
| M.J.North not out | 125 |
| +B.J.Haddin c Bopara | |
|   b Collingwood | 121 |
| M.G.Johnson | |
| N.M.Hauritz | |
| B.W.Hilfenhaus | |
| P.M.Siddle | |
| B 9, l-b 14, w 4, n-b 7 | 34 |

1/60 2/299 3/325 4/331     674
  (for 6 wkts dec)
5/474 6/674

Bowling: *First innings* – Anderson 32-6-110-2; Broad 32-6-129-1; Swann 38-8-131-0; Flintoff 35-3-128-1; Panesar 35-4-115-1; Collingwood 9-0-38-1.

Umpires: Aleem Dar and B.R.Doctrove
Match drawn

# 20

# A FAREWELL TO LORD'S

Getting the First Test out of the way without defeat was a big bonus for all of us. I don't know how many times we've started a series against Australia and lost the First Test, so to travel to Lord's still level in the series was a major improvement. Also, we had seen what Australia had to offer. They had dominated that First Test, and their batsmen were outstanding, but we had escaped with a draw and now knew there was nothing major to worry about. There was no Shane Warne in their line-up, no Glenn McGrath, and Brett Lee was injured. Mitchell Johnson's impressive record over the previous year suggested he was a fine bowler, but he was struggling to come to terms with the conditions. Ben Hilfenhaus and Peter Siddle bowled well in Cardiff, but there was nothing to fear as there had been in previous series against them. Rightly or wrongly, getting out of Cardiff unscathed almost felt like a victory, and we prepared for Lord's in good spirits.

While the team were approaching Lord's with confidence, I was concerned about my right knee again. It had ballooned to the size of a beach-ball. I had started to feel it during the second innings in Cardiff, and although I was fine when I was bowling, I was struggling in the field and starting to get very worried about it. I had the obligatory scan on the Saturday night in Cardiff to determine how bad it was, and the radiologist put the fear of God into me, pointing out problems right, left and centre. She told me I had a tear in my ligament, and my knee joint would need surgery necessitating a six-month lay-off. I left the hospital that night in pieces. I thought my career was over. I was already considering my future in Test cricket and had made up my mind to announce my retirement from that side of the game officially before the next Test, but the way she talked to me I thought I'd be lucky to play cricket, or even walk, again. It was not the message I wanted in the middle of an Ashes series when I should have been concentrating on nothing but beating Australia.

To say I was a bit flat going back to the hotel was an understatement, and on the back of that I changed my plans. Originally, I was going to go home from Cardiff, but instead I went straight to London because I had another appointment with the surgeon, Andy Williams. Apparently there were things going on with my knee, but I just wanted to finish the series. I had three jabs to get me through, with cortisone injections outside the joint.

Had I not already made the decision to retire from Test cricket at the end of the summer, and had it not been an Ashes series, I wouldn't have gone down the route of cortisone injections. However, these were my last few Test matches and I wanted us to win the Ashes back so badly, I was prepared to do anything it took to get on to the field. A lot's been said about cortisone and its after-effects, but I don't think I'm going to escape unscathed, anyway. I've already been told I'll get arthritis in my knee when I'm older, and a few cortisone injections are not going to affect that one way or another. As well as a stiff knee, I'm guessing I'll have a stiff ankle, bad back and all the other things that go with being a professional cricketer – I'm hoping for big medical advances in the next thirty years to sort me out!

I had the three injections all in one session, two in the back of my knee and one in the front. The local anaesthetic lasted five or six hours and once that had worn off my knee was very sore. The following day at Lord's I didn't do much other than bat. Cortisone takes four or five days to kick in, rather than providing instant relief, and I wanted to give my knee time to settle down a bit before I bowled again.

That was also the day I officially informed England of my intention to retire from Test cricket at the end of the Ashes series. I'd talked to Chubby Chandler, Neil Fairbrother and the people close to me about my intentions, and the consensus of all the forthcoming advice was that there would come a time when it felt right to make the announcement. When I was having those injections, that moment came. I didn't really want to make the announcement just before the final Test at The Oval and have some big send-off. I was keen to get the news out there so everyone knew of my intentions. Anybody who has followed my career knows that I have had injury after injury ever since 2005, which I took to mean my body was telling me enough was enough. I also did not want to wait until after the series was decided and be accused of making a knee-jerk reaction, if you'll excuse the pun, about my future.

Also, speculation had started about what I was going to do next, and people were writing things that simply were not true, so rather than keep answering questions, I thought the best way was to be upfront about it. I didn't want to sell my story and make any money out of a big exclusive. I just wanted to sit down, explain my reasons and get on with playing.

I ended up doing a load of press conferences the day before the Test started, including standing in front of a mass of cameras behind the pavilion at Lord's, answering questions from various TV companies. They kept asking me if I was upset, but the main feeling was one of relief. I wasn't quite sure what I was supposed to say. Was I supposed to thank my mum and dad and everybody who had helped me throughout my career? It was strange because I'm not giving up international cricket entirely. I hope still to play for England in one-day and Twenty20 internationals.

The one thing I didn't want to do was give the press a hard-luck story about being unable to play any longer because of my body. The bottom line is that I'm happy with my Test career. For two or three years, from 2003, everything went right for me, and I've played 70-odd Tests for England. I'd have been more than happy to settle for that when I was first starting out in the game. Between winning the Ashes in 2005 and the 2009 series, I had been in rehabilitation from one injury or another for a solid two years. That's two years of moping around the house feeling sorry for myself, so for my family's sake, and my own sanity, I had to do something. If I'd managed to stay fit throughout my England career, and played in every Test for which I was available, I'd have been England's most-capped all-rounder, but it wasn't to be. I seem to have played the bulk of my career with pain not far away, and I'm proud to have kept going despite that. I was born with a body that struggles to cope with the demands of cricket at the top level, and it was time to listen to it.

Andy Flower and Andrew Strauss were concerned about the announcement causing a distraction to the team and were hesitant about the timing at first. The more I talked to them about it, though, the more they came around to my way of thinking. It was obviously going to be big news for a few days, but I thought that could actually help the team – all the attention would be on me rather than on them. After the way we had performed in Cardiff, I thought that might not be a bad thing, and in the end they were happy with my decision to break the news, and the reasons for it.

Everyone was very kind once the news came out, and people I'd never even met came up to me at the ground, wishing me well and wanting to shake my hand – it was very humbling to realise how much people had enjoyed the efforts I had put in over the years.

Playing a Test match at Lord's for the last time was a big moment for me. I've always loved playing there. It's a special place to play cricket, and I suppose I was looking around a little more than normal, trying to imprint memories. I've tried to savour the experience every time I've played there, but this time was a little different. I wouldn't describe myself as a purist or a traditionalist, but there's something about Lord's that really gets to me. A dinner for Straussy's benefit was held in the Long Room on the Tuesday before the Test started, and sitting there, I just felt so spoilt.

All you have to do is look around and watch the reaction of people walking in to Lord's for the first time to see the effect it has. I had a bit of a spring in my step myself – I hadn't played in a Test at Lord's in three years, this one was against the Aussies, and I felt a sense of freedom that my news was out in the open and I could just go out and play. I decided I was going to enjoy the experience whatever the result, and walking out to bat on that first day just made me more determined. I've never known any atmosphere like the first morning of the Lord's Test back in 2005, when the whole ground seemed to be electric. This wasn't quite the same, because we batted first, but both Straussy and Alastair Cook were excited about it when they came in for lunch on the first morning. Lord's has a special atmosphere you don't get at other grounds. People don't go along in fancy dress as they do at some of the other grounds, and there isn't the chanting from the crowd, but there is a constant buzz of expectancy.

How we started was always going to be important at Lord's, particularly after the way we'd performed in Cardiff. Had we begun badly, the Aussies would immediately have seized the momentum, but Strauss and Cook were both positive. As captain, Straussy led from the front, and the openers' 196-run partnership set the tone for our performance for the rest of that Lord's Test. It helped that Mitchell Johnson was struggling to find the right line and length, and conceded 53 runs in just eight overs before lunch, but our opening pair definitely laid the platform for our victory. When you're seeing our batsmen cutting the opposition bowler for four and getting off to a good start, you just have to enjoy it, but at the same time you don't want to see another cricketer struggle like that, either.

After our promising start, however, we faltered as the first day drew to a close. The ball started swinging towards the end of the day and we ended up losing four wickets for 66 runs in the final hour, finishing on 340 for 6 after Hilfenhaus bowled a really good spell. He comes in very close to the stumps and swings the ball at good pace with no visible change in action, or to his grip, and he gets the odd one to nip back in to you, so you always have to think about how to play him. When you're facing a right-arm swing bowler who moves the ball away from you, there is plenty of opportunity to leave deliveries, because you know they're not threatening your stumps. Hilfenhaus has you thinking because of his ability to bring the ball back in. I think that's the way he dismissed Ravi Bopara, bringing the ball back in to win an lbw appeal, and he got me out with a delivery that succeeds nine times out of ten because of my technique. Once again he ran in close to the stumps and nipped it back down the hill, and I nicked it to Ponting at first slip. The experts would say I had hard hands when I played at the ball, but for me that's exactly where I don't want him to bowl.

We were not too down about our finishing position because Straussy was still there at the close, unbeaten on 149 and looking good, and also we had scored our runs in a positive manner. It was not quite the same as Edgbaston four years previously, when we scored around 400 on the first day, but we had made over 360 in a day. Just like the opening day in Cardiff, we had lost two more wickets than we wanted to lose, but the way in which we had scored the runs and the manner in which we had played was very encouraging.

The second morning did not start as well as we had hoped and we lost three wickets inside the first three overs, including Straussy to the second ball of the morning. One of the big strengths of the England teams I have played in over the years, however, has been their ability to score runs down the order, and we were hopeful in the dressing room it could happen again. If you look back to when Michael Vaughan was captain, the lower order scored runs, with Steve Harmison, Ashley Giles and Matthew Hoggard all contributing to partnerships, and fortunately Jimmy Anderson and Graeme Onions were able to do the same this time. Adding 47 for the last wicket, for a total of 425, was absolutely crucial for the match. To get us well past 400 was a brilliant effort. We were all pretty sure it wasn't a 500-run pitch, but the combination of Strauss and Cook playing so well and the Aussies bowling so badly, enabled us to reach that very competitive total.

Unlike our performance at Cardiff, when Australia's batsmen were able to come back at us hard, this time we followed it up with the ball. We were quite lucky with the weather. They always say at Lord's that it doesn't matter what the pitch looks like, you should always look up to see whether the ball will swing or not. We were fortunate to bat in sunshine when the ball wasn't really swinging, and then to bowl in cloudy conditions, which helped us tremendously.

Jimmy approached the Aussies' innings with tremendous confidence and it showed in his bowling. In my opinion, he has improved tremendously as a cricketer. His talents with the ball are obvious and he has started to make more of a contribution with the bat, but I think he has also matured as a person, gaining in confidence as he's got older. He's always had the ability to swing the ball and he has learned about his craft through playing and bowling more. Everyone was taking the mickey out of him in the dressing room, calling him the new Botham because he was starting to score runs as well, but I know from my own experience that contributing with the bat can also help with your bowling. It doesn't happen to me the other way around, but scoring runs definitely has an effect on my bowling.

Strauss threw me the new ball this time, and as an opening pair of bowlers, I think Jimmy and I complement each other quite well. It's almost the same thing that Onions and Harmison do for Durham – one providing a bit of bounce and aggression, and the other attacking the stumps and really swinging it from the other end.

In the press conference after the game I told Michael Atherton that I had been waiting ten years to take the new ball for England, and that wasn't a joke. I've hardly ever been given it. I remember one occasion in India and Pakistan a few years earlier, but that was because we didn't have any bowlers. I could understand it for the period when Hoggy and Harmy were playing so successfully, and if Harmy came back into the side, I would understand again, and get over it, but in the circumstances, I thought I should be taking the new ball, and I was so pleased to have been given it finally. I know various captains have seen me as someone to call on if things don't go right with the new ball, someone who could possibly block off the run-flow, but one of the things I really pride myself on as a bowler is setting the tone. I pride myself on showing intent in my first over. This time, I think everyone saw giving me the new ball as the obvious move, and I vindicated the choice by conceding just 27 runs in my 12 overs, and 21 of those came in my second spell!

I know people are always going on about me not taking huge numbers of wickets and how few five-wicket hauls I've managed, but I'd like to think that by keeping it tight at my end I help contribute to wickets down the other end. In the Aussies' second innings it was my turn to get the wickets, but in the first innings Jimmy was superb and deserved his four wickets. I can take great pleasure in the man bowling from the other end taking wickets if I'm bowling well at my end.

After the First Test, we had talked about using the short ball more against them. I don't care how good a batsman you are, you're not going to like the ball flying around your head at 90mph. Certain batsmen play it better than others, but I don't believe anybody enjoys it. We thought we could exploit that against Australia and we succeeded during their first innings. Phil Hughes and Simon Katich were both out trying to take on the short ball, as were Marcus North, Brad Haddin and Mitchell Johnson, which allowed us to bowl them out for just 215 and claim a 210-run first-innings lead.

We could have enforced the follow-on and we all thought that was going to happen. I didn't bowl all morning on the third day because I was gearing up for taking the new ball if we made them bat again. That was certainly the plan after the team meeting before start of play, but Straussy changed his mind at the last minute and decided we should bat. We left the field expecting to come back out again to bowl, but I think Strauss made the right decision. I'm not a big fan of the follow-on after what happened at Trent Bridge four years ago, when we enforced it and then had to face Warne and Lee on the final day, chasing down a target.

Both Strauss and Cook played positively again, but the key part of our innings was when Ravi partnered Kev. They are both naturally attacking batsmen, but they restrained themselves during that crucial stage of the match. Australia bowled really well during that period, and if we'd lost three or four wickets then, it would have forced us to rein in a little to make sure we did not let them back into the game. The two of them ground it out and added a crucial 73 runs. It wasn't vintage Kevin or Ravi, but those two performed for the good of the team and made a big contribution to our eventual victory. Their efforts enabled me to come out and just play a few shots, which is how I wanted to play.

There was a lot of discussion about what sort of lead we needed before we declared. I was keen to bowl at them as soon as we could, remembering Antigua when we delayed our decision and they were able to save the match. If you look at the history of the game, nobody has ever chased down 500 in the final innings, so I thought we were pretty safe to declare. Throughout my unbeaten 30, I was enjoying my innings, but keeping my eye on the dressing room for a signal that we were declaring. It was cloudy towards the end of the third day, the lights were on and I wanted to have a bowl at Australia to see if we could get two out before the close. I started chatting to Rudi Koertzen, one of the umpires, just as everyone was considering when to declare and he confirmed that we wouldn't come back on if we went off because of the bad light, so the decision was made to bat on and declare overnight.

It was important to get early wickets the following morning, just to keep Australia on the back foot, and we started well. I had been out in the middle before the start of play with Ottis Gibson, England's bowling coach, chatting about bowling to Katich. One of the things Ottis had noticed about him was that when he played the ball, he played a little bit across himself, which was more or less how I'd got out to Mitchell Johnson. Katich was far more comfortable playing it straight back towards the bowler. We came up with a plan of bowling from wider on the crease, so that the ball would pitch just outside leg stump, but by the time it went past him it would be a foot outside off stump, enticing him to play across and send the ball back in the direction it had come from. When I started my spell, I gestured to Ottis on the balcony that I was going wider with this ball, and with my first delivery I got it to travel pretty much where I wanted, and Katich played it to Kev in the gully. Ottis was on his feet claiming his wicket. It's always good when you make a plan and it comes off.

As for Hughes, I didn't think I was going to get him out with the short ball, despite our success with that tactic against him, but for the second time in a few overs a plan worked to perfection. Hughes was playing the short ball better than he had been playing it before, so I told Straussy I would bowl him a bouncer and follow it up by coming around the wicket to try to get him to nick it behind – and Hughes edged the ball low to Strauss at first slip. A lot was said about whether the catch was clean, but Billy Doctrove, who was standing at square leg, did not refer it to the third umpire, which suggests that he was satisfied it went straight into Straussy's hands. There are some players around the world whose word you might not trust, but Straussy is a stand-up, honest guy. I think that's why Ricky Ponting didn't make a song and dance about it at the time – he realised that Straussy is not that sort of player. The controversy seemed to centre on the fact that it wasn't referred, as Ravi had been in the first innings when he chipped to mid-on but survived on the evidence of the television replay.

There was further controversy after lunch when Graeme Swann had Mike Hussey caught at slip trying to drive out of the rough. We all thought it was a clean dismissal and it was only later we discovered Hussey had not actually hit the ball. It had just diverted out of the footholes outside off stump to the left-hander. What made us all think he had edged it was the way in which he took his dismissal. There was no grimace or frown, or even a bemused expression, as he walked off, which you would normally expect when you've had a bad decision. We took the new ball shortly before the close but were unable to claim another breakthrough and Australia reached 313 for 5 overnight, still needing another 205 for victory.

I had been struggling with my knee since the first innings. I thought I had broken my leg, but my knee was just in bits. I bowled one delivery, felt something go and thought that was it, but I hobbled back to my mark, ran in and it seemed to be all right. When I stopped, it was very sore and I struggled to walk, but I could run, so I didn't think it was too bad and carried on, with the help of some anti-inflammatory injections and painkillers. When I turned up on the final morning, my knee was still sore but I was incredibly excitable. I just couldn't shut up and was rabbiting on all morning. It wasn't nerves, just excitement. Australia needed another 205 runs to win and were five down – I just didn't believe we would not win. Everybody had been a bit tense during the final session of the fourth day and I couldn't understand why.

I bowled a couple of balls and felt all right but had another anti-inflammatory injection to calm my knee down. I spoke to the team before the game got under way and just imagined I was going to take wickets that morning. Neil Fairbrother asked me on the phone if I was going to be OK to bowl and I told him I wouldn't be coming off until we had got them out and won the game. I'd said something similar to him four years earlier, when we went out to dinner during the Oval Test, and the following day I'd got a five-wicket haul, the last time I'd achieved it. When the game started, I was fielding in the slips and told Straussy that I'd be bowling until Australia were all out. He asked me if he had much choice and I told him he hadn't and started running in from the Pavilion End.

An early wicket always helps, especially when you're going to be bowling for a long spell, and getting Haddin out in my first over, nicking the ball to slip, gave me some early momentum. One thing I had managed to achieve in the months building up to the Ashes was to get physically fitter and stronger. That and the adrenalin kept me going. I wasn't tired, despite bowling a 10-over spell, and I was not going to stop. The more I've played, the more I've grown to enjoy bowling, and the irony is that I was probably at my quickest in my final series before retiring from Test cricket. I was feeling so good that day, despite the knee, that I'm sure I could have bowled unchanged until tea.

I was conscious of not getting a five-wicket haul for a long time, and the fact that it would be good to break the sequence at Lord's, but it wasn't of paramount importance to me when we started the day. If we got two wickets, they would be seven down and the game would be almost over, so rather than think about getting a five-for, I just wanted to get a couple of wickets to try to wrap up the win as soon as possible. The real pleasure I took from that day stemmed from winning the match to go 1–0 ahead in the series, rather than getting my name up on the Lord's honours board. It's great to be up there, of course, alongside Sir Ian Botham, and particularly for my bowling. I'm also up there for a hundred I scored against South Africa in 2003, but that was in a game we lost heavily. To get on the board and help England win a Test, especially against Australia, meant so much more. I was so happy when we achieved our first Ashes win at Lord's since 1934 – that's 75 years!

During the winter, I had decided that if any special moments came my way, I would celebrate them with my family. Too often in the past I have gone out with the rest of the lads, while the family have had to put up with me during all the bad times. They see me at my worst, when I'm moody around the house, when I'm injured, and I wanted to spend time with them after winning at Lord's. I stayed in the dressing room after the game and had a few drinks, and then went back to the hotel to be with Rachael, the kids and my mum and dad.

Once we'd put the kids to bed, we went to meet Piers Morgan at a pub his brother runs in Mayfair. I know Piers gets a bit of stick, but through everything that has happened over the last few years, he has always stuck by me and shown his support. We had some fish and chips and a couple of drinks, and had a really good night. When we got up to leave, a complete sea of photographers was waiting for us – I felt like Paris Hilton! It had been four years since I'd received this sort of attention and I'd forgotten what it was like, although the world has changed again since then. There seems to be a lot more intrusion now than there was then. A couple of papers made out I was bladdered when I was nothing of the sort.

I had forgotten about my knee while I was out, but it stiffened up overnight and when I woke up the next day it was a bit of a struggle to get out of bed. Firstly, I was tired, and when I put my leg down, my knee was killing me. I got up early to do some promotional work for Puma, who were filming an advert. During the course of this I was supposed to bowl three balls, but I told them I could only do it off three steps because I was struggling so much. I also had some interviews to do to promote the dinner we were having that evening to raise funds for the AF Foundation, which is a charity we have set up to help children's charities.

It was a fairly hectic day and I barely had time to go back and change before heading off for the dinner. Although I've spoken at several charity dinners, I was incredibly nervous about it, and Rachael was equally tense. She had played a big part in organising the line-up, ringing management companies and persuading Razorlight and Keane to play in the evening. Six hundred people attended and I was probably more nervous about that than I was about playing in the First Test in Cardiff! We were raising funds to help the children's physiotherapy and rehabilitation unit at Alder Hey hospital, so a lot was riding on the evening being a success. I was so on edge I couldn't eat, but in the end it went very well and we managed to raise £250,000 from the auction. All sorts of things were on offer, including caddying for Lee Westwoood the day before the Masters, and dinner with Sir Ian Botham and me, which was advertised in the brochure with the words, 'if you're brave enough!'

## ENGLAND v AUSTRALIA
## (2nd Test) at Lord's 17–20 July 2009

### England

| | | | | |
|---|---|---|---|---|
| *A.J.Strauss b Hilfenhaus | 161 | – | c Clarke b Hauritz | 32 |
| A.N.Cook lbw b Johnson | 95 | – | bw b Hauritz | 32 |
| R.S.Bopara lbw b Hilfenhaus | 18 | – | c Katich b Hauritz | 27 |
| K.P.Pietersen c Haddin b Siddle | 32 | – | c Haddin b Siddle | 44 |
| P.D.Collingwood c Siddle b Clarke | 16 | – | c Haddin b Siddle | 54 |
| +M.J.Prior b Johnson | 8 | – | run out | 61 |
| A.Flintoff c Ponting b Hilfenhaus | 4 | – | not out | 30 |
| S.C.J.Broad b Hilfenhaus | 16 | – | not out | 0 |
| G.P.Swann c Ponting b Siddle | 4 | | | |
| J.M.Anderson c Hussey b Johnson | 29 | | | |
| G.Onions not out | 17 | | | |
| B 15, l-b 2, n-b 8 | 25 | | B 16, l-b 9, w 1, n-b 5 | 31 |

1/196 2/222 3/267 4/302     425    1/61 2/74 3/147   (for 6 wkts dec) 311
5/317 6/333 7/364 8/370 9/378 10/425  4/174  5/260 6/311

Bowling: *First innings* – Hilfenhaus 31-12-103-4; Johnson 21.4-2-132-3; Siddle 20-1-76-2; Hauritz 8.3-1-26-0; North 16.3-2-59-0; Clarke 4-1-12-1. *Second innings* – Hilfenhaus 19-5-59-0; Johnson 17-2-68-0; Siddle 15.2-4-64-2; Hauritz 16-1-80-3; Clarke 4-0-15-0.

### Australia

| | | | | |
|---|---|---|---|---|
| P.J.Hughes c Prior b Anderson | 4 | – | c Strauss b Flintoff | 17 |
| S.M.Katich c Broad b Onions | 48 | – | c Pietersen b Flintoff | 6 |
| *R.T.Ponting c Strauss b Anderson | 2 | – | b Broad | 38 |
| M.E.K.Hussey b Flintoff | 51 | – | c Collingwood b Swann | 27 |
| M.J.Clarke c Cook b Anderson | 1 | – | b Swann | 136 |
| M.J.North b Anderson | 0 | – | b Swann | 6 |
| +B.J.Haddin c Cook b Broad | 28 | – | c Collingwood b Flintoff | 80 |
| M.G.Johnson c Cook b Broad | 4 | – | b Swann | 63 |
| N.M.Hauritz c Collingwood b Onions | 24 | – | b Flintoff | 1 |
| P.M.Siddle c Strauss b Onions | 35 | – | b Flintoff | 7 |
| B.W.Hilfenhaus not out | 6 | – | not out | 4 |
| B 4, l-b 6, n-b 2 | 12 | | B 5, l-b 8, n-b 8 | 21 |

1/4 2/10 3/103 4/111     215    1/17 2/34 3/78 4/120    406
5/111 6/139 7/148 8/152 9/196 10/215  5/128 6/313 7/356 8/363 9/388
                                       10/406

Bowling: *First innings* – Anderson 21-5-55-4; Flintoff 12-4-27-1; Broad 18-1-78-2; Onions 11-1-41-3; Swann 1-0-4-0. *Second innings* – Anderson 21-4-86-0; Flintoff 27-4-92-5; Onions 9-0-50-0; Broad 16-3-49-1; Swann 28-3-87-4; Collingwood 6-1-29-0.

Umpires: B.R.Doctrove and R.E.Koertzen
England won by 115 runs

# 21

# FIGHTING TO BE FIT

It was quickly becoming apparent that the problems with my knee were not going to go away. We had a week off between Lord's and turning up at Edgbaston for the Third Test, so I returned home for more work with Rooster, desperately trying to get my knee down to normal proportions again. Plenty of people were speculating that I wouldn't be fit in time. If truth be told, I probably wasn't fully fit before Lord's and I wasn't 100 per cent fit for Edgbaston either, but I ran in to bowl during practice in the nets, anyway, despite being in some discomfort. I was actually more worried about my condition when I was batting. During the usual throw-downs with Phil Neale, England's operations manager, he pointed out that every time I tried to play a shot, my knee was giving way. It was sore, but I was determined to get through it and, although there were concerns about my fitness, I was included in the team for the Third Test.

I'd be lying if I said I wasn't anxious about how my knee would react to another Test match. I was nervous about what was going to happen in the game. I'd already had three injections before

Lord's and I had another course of Ostenil, which is a lubricant similar to WD40 that helps with the cartilage inside the knee. Rooster had identified an inflamed area at the side of the knee, where three tendons meet. A bursa here was inflamed and adding to my problems, and Rooster suggested I had a cortisone injection into that to settle it down. It didn't take the knee pain away, but it eased the discomfort I was feeling in that part of it – it was just the rest of the knee that was a mess after that! I was also having anti-inflammatory injections in my backside every day and taking pain-killing tablets so I was rattling – but come the day, I was fit enough to play.

I wasn't the only member of England's side struggling with injury at the time. It had already been announced before the Test that Kev would be out for the rest of the series. He had been suffering with Achilles problems during the first two Tests and during the break between Lord's and Edgbaston, it was decided he should have surgery, which would put him out for a couple of months. I'd spoken to him when I heard the news because I know from personal experience how demoralising something like that can be – particularly if it rules you out of an Ashes series. I tried to cheer him up by assuring him he would be involved in future series against Australia and would probably end up winning them for England, but I know he was very disappointed to miss out. His absence gave us a new challenge as a team – could we beat Australia without our best batsman?

There had been heavy rain in Birmingham in the build-up to the Test, so it was no surprise to anyone that we didn't start on time and had to wait until 5.00 p.m. on the opening day to get on to the field. Australia won the toss and decided to bat first with a new opening partnership. They had dropped opener Hughes, who had been clearly struggling during the first two Tests. He is a young player and I think they realised they needed to take him out of the firing line. Shane Watson, their all-rounder, came into the side as their new opener. His record in first-class cricket suggested he was a decent player, and after a few overs, it was apparent he had added something to their line-up. He left the ball really well, which threw us all a bit. We started bowling straighter at him and he clipped a few fours away. I'm not sure we did enough homework on him beforehand, but it took us by surprise that he was playing in the first place. Normally, we look at DVDs of the opposition and have clear plans on how to bowl at each batsman, but I don't think that was the case with Watson.

I opened the bowling and didn't perform particularly well. I was just trying to get the ball down the other end with strength and determination, and probably sacrificed some accuracy because I wasn't getting a great deal of support from my knee. We didn't get off to a good start and they were in a strong position on 126 for 1 at the close of the opening day. Graham Onions helped pull it back by taking wickets with the first two balls of the following day. Jimmy Anderson followed up Onions' early efforts with one of the best spells I've seen him bowl. He was swinging the ball all over the place – got a deserved five-for – and we were very happy to bowl them out for 263, particularly after the start they'd had. Now we had a chance to go on and win the Test and really dominate the series.

We lost a couple of early wickets when Alastair Cook edged behind and Ravi Bopara was bowled by Hilfenhaus. I was starting to feel very sorry for Ravi. He'd had a really good build-up to the Ashes, scoring three successive hundreds, and so was kept at No. 3 when, for such a big series, he would perhaps have been better down the order. Even Kevin had been eased into things a little bit at the start of his Test career by batting down the order. I thought Ravi was thrown in at the deep end to a certain extent, when other, more experienced, players were available to bat in that position. I'm sure he will come again and make the No. 3 spot his own, but at that point, I thought he was better suited to coming in lower down the order.

Ravi wasn't the only one of our batsmen to struggle against Hilfenhaus. Not many people knew much about him when he arrived for the start of the tour, and it was a bit of a surprise that he was chosen ahead of more experienced bowlers, such as Stuart Clark, for the First Test. Since then, though, he had demonstrated his abilities as a swing bowler. He bowls close to the stumps, swings it away, and every so often, sends down a delivery that goes straight on and causes you problems.

Ian Bell had been brought into the England side to replace Kev, which is a virtually impossible task in itself. How do you replace such an instinctive player? One thing Kev brings to the side, quite apart from being our best player, is his ability to allow other batsmen to feed off him. When they are batting at the other end from him and see him whipping a shot from outside off stump through midwicket, it allows them to relax and play their natural game while he plays the way only he can. When he isn't in the side, you realise the impact he has on the rest of the top order. It forced the rest of us to stand up. Bell did well, got a half-century on his return to the side and helped steer us away from trouble after losing those early wickets.

By the time I got to the crease I felt pretty comfortable, despite the earlier misgivings about my knee. I'd played well before at Edgbaston, which always helps your confidence, and I had been working hard in the nets with both Phil Neale and Dean Hills, our Australian batting coach. I'd also been making use of the bowling machine with Dean, and had it set so the ball swung more and came through at a quicker pace than it would out in the middle, the theory being that it would be easier once I got out there.

From the first ball I felt good because I defended solidly and hit it with the middle of the bat. I was facing Mitchell Johnson, who tried to test me out with a couple of early short balls. I ducked under them and managed to avoid getting hit, which is always nice and gives you a boost at the start of an innings. Mitchell came back and gave me a few words, but it was all light-hearted. I get on quite well with him off the pitch, so I gave him a few words back, which seemed to get the crowd going a bit. After that I was determined I wasn't going to get out to him because I'd have looked like a right idiot after our exchange.

I felt OK throughout my innings, and was angry with myself for not going on and making a century. I didn't feel as though I was going to get out and that's what made it all the more infuriating. When they brought on Nathan Hauritz, their off-spinner, I had decided that I would play sensibly against him. If the ball arrived in a suitable area, I would have a go, but otherwise I would be careful with him. The manner of my dismissal was the most frustrating thing of all. I've always said that if I'm going to get out, I'd rather it happened while I'm hitting out, but this time I was trying *not* to play a shot. I tried to hide the bat behind me, out of the way of the ball as it drifted outside off stump, but the ball followed me, glanced off my glove and I was caught at slip for 74. I was furious with myself and must have uttered every expletive going on the walk back to the dressing room.

Both Graeme Swann and Stuart Broad contributed runs further down the order, so we made 376 and claimed a 113-run lead. Given the amount of time lost through rain and bad light, it would have taken an exceptional bowling performance to win the match, but when Australia began their innings on the fourth evening, the two most likely results were either an England win or a draw. We managed to get two early wickets, those of Katich and Ponting. Swann dismissed Ponting with a fantastic delivery that bowled him after spinning back through the gap between bat and pad. Next day, though, any hopes of victory were ended by Michael Clarke and Marcus North, who batted most of the day out, and by the end Australia were comfortably ahead. It was probably just as well we'd lost as much time as we did to the weather, otherwise they would have put us under considerable pressure in our second innings.

## ENGLAND v AUSTRALIA
## (3rd Test) at Edgbaston 30 July–3 August 2009

### Australia

| | | | |
|---|---|---|---|
| S.R.Watson lbw b Onions | 62 | – c Prior b Anderson | 53 |
| S.M.Katich lbw b Swann | 46 | – c Prior b Onions | 26 |
| *R.T.Ponting c Prior b Onions | 38 | – b Swann | 5 |
| M.E.K.Hussey b Onions | 0 | – c Prior b Broad | 64 |
| M.J.Clarke lbw b Anderson | 29 | – not out | 103 |
| M.J.North c Prior b Anderson | 12 | – c Anderson b Broad | 96 |
| +G.A.Manou b Anderson | 8 | – not out | 13 |
| M.G.Johnson lbw b Anderson | 0 | | |
| N.M.Hauritz not out | 20 | | |
| P.M.Siddle c Prior b Anderson | 13 | | |
| B.W.Hilfenhaus c Swann b Onions | 20 | | |
| B 5, l-b 7, w 2, n-b 1 | 15 | B 4, l-b 6, w 2, n-b 3 | 15 |

1/85 2/126 3/126 4/163    263    1/47 2/52 3/137 4/161 5/346

                                      (for 5 wkts)    375

5/193 6/202 7/202 8/203 9/229 10/263

Bowling: *First innings* – Anderson 24-7-80-5; Flintoff 15-2-58-0; Onions 16.4-2-58-4; Broad 13-2-51-0; Swann 2-0-4-1. *Second innings* – Anderson 21-8-47-1; Flintoff 15-0-35-0; Onions 19-3-74-1; Swann 31-4-119-1; Broad 16-2-38-2; Bopara 8.2-1-44-0; Collingwood 2-0-8-0.

### England

| | |
|---|---|
| *A.J.Strauss c Manou b Hilfenhaus | 69 |
| A.N.Cook c Manou b Siddle | 0 |
| R.S.Bopara b Hilfenhaus | 23 |
| I.R.Bell lbw b Johnson | 53 |
| P.D.Collingwood c Ponting b Hilfenhaus | 13 |
| +M.J.Prior c sub b Siddle | 41 |
| A.Flintoff c Clarke b Hauritz | 74 |
| S.C.J.Broad c & b Siddle | 55 |
| G.P.Swann c North b Johnson | 24 |
| J.M.Anderson c Manou b Hilfenhaus | 1 |
| G.Onions not out | 2 |
| b 2, l-b 4, w 6, n-b 9 | 21 |

1/2 2/60 3/141 4/159    376

5/168 6/257 7/309 8/348 9/355 10/376

Bowling: *First innings* – Hilfenhaus 30-7-109-4; Siddle 21.3-3-89-3; Hauritz 18-2-57-1; Johnson 21-1-92-2; Watson 3-0-23-0.

Umpires: Aleem Dar and R.E.Koertzen
Match drawn

My knee was hurting again after the game at Edgbaston, but I was still keen to play at Headingley just a few days later. I turned up for practice and struggled through, although I have to admit I probably wasn't at my best that day. Just before the end of it, I was called over by the two Andrews, coach Flower and captain Strauss, and knew instinctively what they were going to say. They told me they didn't think I was fit enough to play another Test just a few days after my last one, and were worried, particularly, about my movement in the field.

Normally in situations like that I stand my ground and argue my case. I had argued all summer that after more treatment and when the adrenalin of a match situation kicked in, I was able to perform differently and do a job for the team. But this time I just stood and listened to them. There was no point getting into an argument, because they had made up their minds, however disappointing it was for me. From my point of view, having top-scored at Edgbaston, I thought it was worth playing me at No. 7, even if I could get through only 10 or 11 overs. It was not a selfish desire to play – I honestly believed I could help the team.

Contrary to reports in the media, there was no big row with either Andrew. I accepted their decision, even if I didn't agree with it, and I respected their reasons for making it. I spoke to Chubby Chandler about it and then drove out towards Bolton to have a talk with Rooster. I often use him as a sounding board. I was just getting things off my chest. Once again, my career was being stalled because of injury. I had just a few games left, and I was hoping to go out playing my best cricket. That made my omission at Headingley all the more frustrating. The one thing that burns away at me is that I never actually peaked in my career. I was never able to play the cricket I wanted to play. People say batsmen peak in their early thirties and after Edgbaston I felt I'd reached the point where I could kick on again. I was thinking like a batter again, but anyone who has followed my career will tell you that I score runs consistently only when I play a run of games, and once again injury denied me the opportunity.

After sounding off to Rooster, I drove back to the team hotel feeling a lot better. A few hours later we were all woken up by a fire alarm. It started off with a voice coming through the loudspeaker system telling everyone to remain in their rooms. That immediately made me nervous after what had happened in Mumbai, and I started checking for possible escape routes. After a couple of minutes, the fire alarm started going off again, so I gave it a bit longer to see if it was going to stop and then I thought I'd better go outside. Quite a few disgruntled guests had gathered, including the team in their undies. We did wonder at the time whether it was done on purpose, and I think a few Australian fans later admitted to setting it off deliberately to unsettle the team before the Test.

I intended to get to the ground early, even though I wasn't going to be needed for the warm-ups, because I wanted to wish the lads all the best, particularly Harmy, who had been recalled to the side to replace me. However, the traffic around Leeds was snarled, so I missed the drama before the start of the game. Apparently, Matt Prior's back went in the warm-up and at one stage we were contemplating playing Bruce French, the wicketkeeping coach, as his replacement. That would have been an ironic twist to the previous Test, when we gave Australia permission to play reserve keeper Graham Manou after Brad Haddin broke a finger in the warm-up. We had no objections then and I'm sure they wouldn't have minded in the least if England had fielded a 50-year-old replacement for Prior! As it turned out, Matt recovered in time to take his place in the side, but the toss was delayed by 10 minutes.

I was still trying to fight my way through the traffic when we started losing early wickets, and I thought it would be best if I got out of the way and went home instead. On the way, I tried listening to the cricket on the radio for just about the first time ever. I didn't realise how bad the signal for *Test Match Special* is at times while you're driving. I don't know what was worse, England getting off to such a bad start in the match or trying to keep up with it on the radio in the car! I watched a bit more of the game when I got home, but it was horrible to see us being bowled out for 102 on the first day. Harmy caused some brief excitement when he got a wicket with the new ball, but mostly it was painful.

While England were losing at Headingley, I did consider going down to Cornwall, just to get away from things and work on my rehabilitation with Rooster. Four years previously, during the last home Ashes series, I'd done that to try to relax, but this time we decided to stay put and work at home. I spent most of the week getting treatment from Rooster, but on the

## ENGLAND v AUSTRALIA
## (4th Test) at Headingley 7–9 August 2009

### England

| | | | |
|---|---|---|---|
| *A.J.Strauss c North b Siddle | 3 | – lbw b Hilfenhaus | 32 |
| A.N.Cook c Clarke b Clark | 30 | – c Haddin b Johnson | 30 |
| R.S.Bopara c Hussey b Hilfenhaus | 1 | – lbw b Hilfenhaus | 0 |
| I.R.Bell c Haddin b Johnson | 8 | – c Ponting b Johnson | 3 |
| P.D.Collingwood c Ponting b Clark | 0 | – lbw b Johnson | 4 |
| +M.J.Prior not out | 37 | (7) c Haddin b Hilfenhaus | 22 |
| S.C.J.Broad c Katich b Clark | 3 | (8) c Watson b Siddle | 61 |
| G.P.Swann c Clark b Siddle | 0 | (9) c Haddin b Johnson | 62 |
| S.J.Harmison c Haddin b Siddle | 0 | (10) not out | 19 |
| J.M.Anderson c Haddin b Siddle | 3 | (6) c Ponting b Hilfenhaus | 4 |
| G.Onions c Katich b Siddle | 0 | – b Johnson | 0 |
| B 5, l-b 8, w 1, n-b 3 | 17 | B 5, l-b 5, w 5, n-b 11 | 26 |

1/11 2/16 3/39 4/42     102    1/58 2/58 3/67 4/74    263
5/63 6/72 7/92 8/98 9/102 10/102    5/78 6/86 7/120 8/228 9/259 10/263

Bowling: *First innings* – Hilfenhaus 7-0-20-1; Siddle 9.5-0-21-5; Johnson 7-0-30-1; Clark 10-4-18-3. *Second innings* – Hilfenhaus 19-2-60-4; Siddle 12-2-50-1; Clark 11-1-74-0; Johnson 19.3-3-69-5.

### Australia

| | |
|---|---|
| S.R.Watson lbw b Onions | 51 |
| S.M.Katich c Bopara b Harmison | 0 |
| *R.T.Ponting lbw b Broad | 78 |
| M.E.K.Hussey lbw b Broad | 10 |
| M.J.Clarke lbw b Onions | 93 |
| M.J.North c Anderson b Broad | 110 |
| +B.J.Haddin c Bell b Harmison | 14 |
| M.G.Johnson c Bopara b Broad | 27 |
| P.M.Siddle b Broad | 0 |
| S.R.Clark b Broad | 32 |
| B.W.Hilfenhaus not out | 0 |
| B 9, l-b 14, w 4, n-b 3 | 30 |

1/14 2/133 3/140 4/151    445
5/303 6/323 7/393 8/394 9/440 10/445

Bowling: *First innings* – Anderson 18-3-89-0; Harmison 23-4-98-2; Onions 22-5-80-2; Broad 25.1-6-91-6; Swann 16-4-64-0.

Umpires: Asad Rauf and B.F.Bowden
Australia won by an innings and 80 runs

Monday, the day after the Test had finished, we headed down to London for another check-up with the knee surgeon. I don't normally read the papers much, but during the journey I saw Rooster reading *The Times* and noticed a big story about me on the back page. Chubby had already told me he had spoken to Mike Atherton, but I thought he'd just bumped into him somewhere and I wasn't aware he meant an interview. In that piece, Chubby said I was fit to play and it was England that didn't want me, which wasn't strictly correct. I could not describe myself as 100 per cent fit for Headingley, any more than I could for Lord's or Edgbaston, but I did believe I was fit enough to do a job for England.

The article didn't come across very well and during the journey, not surprisingly, I got a call from Andy Flower. I explained I was on a train to London to see the surgeon and would ring him later. When we spoke later that night, I admitted that I did not agree with their decision not to play me at Headingley, but I respected their opinion and he accepted that. The article didn't do me any favours, but I'm sure Chubby was just trying to help and to stick up for me.

The newspaper article and the fall-out that followed with most of the media criticising me, was the start of one of the worst weeks of my career. I can't speak highly enough of Andy Williams, the surgeon. He is clearly at the top of his field and he has a very good manner with his patients. He explained to me the last thing he wanted to do was operate on my knee, and it would be done only as a last resort. I had a frank discussion with him about what it would entail if more surgery was warranted and how long it would keep me out of the game. He told me I would be on crutches for six to eight weeks and possibly unable to play cricket for six to eight months. That was not something I could contemplate. If I was 26 or 27, being out for that length of time wouldn't matter, but I was 31 and I wanted to carry on playing one-day international cricket for England. Things move on quickly in sport and I didn't want to be out for that long because I may not have got back in if the team had progressed without me.

On the way back from London, Rooster showed me a few articles on his computer about the rehabilitation required for surgery of that type. When I got home, I also talked to the medical staff at Manchester City FC – a couple of younger lads there had been through a similar thing. The worry and anxiety affected me as I tried to get my head around what was the best thing to do. I had another long chat with the surgeon on the following Saturday morning over the phone and it was after that when I finally decided to go ahead and have the surgery. The shocking realisation dawned that, without an operation, this could be it for cricket. I was retiring from the Test arena, but I still wanted to play one-day internationals, so I had no other choice. If I wanted to prolong my career, the operation was my only option.

I had to believe I had a chance of playing my final Test at The Oval, and so I needed to put this to bed. I had to get it straight in my own mind what the next step was to be in order to concentrate fully on the Test match and trying to win the Ashes for England. Once it was decided that I would have the surgery on the Tuesday after the Test finished, I could switch my mind away from it. In some ways, it was the best thing that could have happened. I had five more days of Test cricket to play and enjoy, and after that I was booked in for an operation.

I still had to prove my fitness for the final Test when we met up in London, however. I bowled for about an hour in the nets and, to be honest, I wasn't much different from the way I was at Headingley, but I had an injection this time before practice and that seemed to swing the decision my way. I don't believe I was being selfish in trying to get fit for the match. I wasn't after a grand farewell or anything like that, but I did believe I could make a difference to this England team for the final Ashes Test.

# 22

# THE GRAND FINALE

When I met up with the rest of the squad before the start of the final Test, I didn't notice any signs of after-effects from the defeat at Headingley. There had been a bit of a gap between losing that match and assembling again in London and I think the time away helped. No one seemed to be dwelling on what had happened and, as a team, we were keen to make amends.

A draw or a defeat were not options – we had to win if we were to regain the Ashes. We've had some really shocking defeats in my time with England, but historically we're very good at bouncing back quickly from them, and I was confident we could do the same again. In practice before the game, I sensed that everyone was confident of pulling it off. This match was not so much about talent as nerve, and I was sure we could show that.

Despite calls for numerous changes – including suggestions for the return of Trescothick and Mark Ramprakash – the selectors made just two. Jonathan Trott was picked to make his debut and I was passed fit. Ravi and Graham Onions were left out. I was delighted that Steve Harmison retained his place. I wanted my best mate around for my final Test, but I also thought he could make a difference if we were to win the match. Since it was my last Test, I gave a little talk before the game started, thanking everyone for the patience they had shown after all the injuries, always welcoming me back into the dressing room.

In Ravi's absence, Ian Bell was promoted to No. 3. Alastair Cook fell early so it was up to Bell and Strauss to set the platform for a good total, and they both played vital innings. I know from my time as captain that balancing your own game with that of leading the side is not easy and Strauss did it brilliantly throughout the series. He was our leading run-scorer, which is a fantastic achievement considering everything that goes on to distract you as captain. He led from the front all the time. I was equally pleased for Bell, who comes in for a lot of stick about his contribution to the side. In that first innings he played one of his best for England. Usually, Bell is so technically correct that all his shots could come straight out of a coaching manual, but on this occasion he really had to battle for his runs. They peppered him with short balls early on, he took a few blows, but showed his character and still got forward to play his shots.

Trott, whom I didn't know that well before he came into the England squad, looked solid from the word go, which is quite remarkable considering everything that was riding on the match and all the pressure of making his debut. He was unlucky to be run out in the first innings, but more than made amends in the second by scoring a brilliant century to put us firmly in charge of the match. I remember saying to him in the dressing room afterwards, 'Trotty, I'm sorry. I didn't realise you were that good!' From the first ball he faced, he looked comfortable. You'd have thought he'd played 50 Test matches the way he was so composed out in the middle.

I came out to bat midway through the final session on the opening day and I knew what to expect. The crowd gave me a fantastic ovation, which was a lovely gesture, but the time for reflection was later and when I walked out into the middle I was concentrating on helping England towards a competitive total. I knew Australia would come at me hard, last Test or not, and they did not disappoint. Mitchell Johnson came around the wicket and gave me some width so I was able to get off the mark with a four to third man. It was obvious from the way it had played already on the opening day that this was not a normal Oval pitch, where you can win the toss and set your sights on scoring 500. This was more like a 350 pitch, and it was not going to be easy to score runs, so I had to think about how I should best play my innings. I decided to go for my shots and if I could stay around for a while, then we had a good chance of getting a decent score.

Australia did their best to rough me up and I was hit on the shoulder, failing to sway out of the path of one of Johnson's bouncers. Normally I try to have a word back, to show that the hit has not affected me, but this one hurt, so I just stood there, trying not to show the pain. I was determined not to allow the Aussies to think they had got to me, so for the next ball I decided I was coming forward come what may. If Johnson had dug another one in short, I'm sure he would have hit me square on the badge in the centre of my helmet, but fortunately he tried to follow up the bouncer by pitching it up. I was dismissed in Johnson's next over after I went hard at a wide delivery and edged behind. I had reasoned that any opportunity to score I should try to take, so I was going hard at the ball in the hope that it would clear the slip cordon. Instead, I just edged behind and it probably looked a horrible dismissal.

A big feature of this series had been our ability to score runs down the order and once again both Broad and Swann contributed to help us reach 332. As a team we were satisfied with our total, and I thought it put us right in the game. At a Barclays dinner that night I talked about the surface being more like one you would get after four days of a Test match. We had a good spinner in Swann and the pitch was going up and down, so we had more than a fighting chance. Perhaps the only member of England's dressing room not happy was Jimmy Anderson, who was dismissed without score for the first time in his Test career. He was very proud of his record – 55 innings without getting a duck – but as someone who is quite high up on the list of most ducks for England, I couldn't resist a small chuckle.

When Australia started their reply, we wanted some sort of first-innings lead so we could put them under real scoreboard pressure when they batted last in the game. Once again they got off to a good start with Watson and Katich sharing a 73-

run opening stand. Throughout the series, batsmen seemed more comfortable against the new ball than the older one and that was the case at The Oval. I had a couple of early lbw appeals against Watson rejected by umpire Asad Rauf, one of which I thought was definitely out, and got into a bit of a negative mindset about nothing going my way. Fortunately, Broad had one of those days that don't come along very often in a career, and established us in a dominant position for the rest of the match. We had a short rain break before lunch and once we resumed, Strauss turned to Broad and he produced a magnificent spell. In my whole career I've never got five wickets in one spell, but that's just what Stuart did – and he's only 23. He used the conditions and the pitch perfectly, pitched the ball up and made Australia play. They just couldn't cope with him. I was pleased Swann also got some wickets because he had bowled well earlier in the series without getting the rewards he warranted. I pitched in with a wicket at the end to help dismiss them for 160, but the hard work had already been done.

From that position, we could only mess it up ourselves. We were 172 runs ahead with three days of the game remaining on a wicket that was only going to get worse for batsmen, or so we thought. We lost three early wickets before the close of the second day and I must admit I didn't really fancy going out to bat that evening. Once again, Strauss provided stability at the top of the order and was brilliantly supported by Trott to ensure I wasn't needed that night. Strauss is not as aggressive a player as Marcus Trescothick was, but he has taken over Marcus's mantle as the man we rely upon at the top of the order. Ever since Tres announced his retirement from international cricket, we had been looking for another solid opener to take his place. I am sure Alastair Cook will fulfil the role in time, but he is still young and developing as a Test player, whereas Strauss has five years' experience and he provided superb leadership for the team throughout the series. His partnership with Trott was broken only after a rare moment of misjudgment, when he pushed at a wide delivery outside off stump and edged behind.

By the time I arrived at the crease for my final Test innings, which was again marked by the whole ground standing to applaud me as I made my way out to the middle, we were 340 runs ahead and I had a licence to go out and enjoy myself. I was hoping and praying the Australians would not give me a guard of honour as I walked out to the crease. For a start, I didn't think I deserved one. For me, they should be given to truly great cricketers only, such as Shane Warne and Sir Ian Botham. I also thought it would be highly embarrassing and I probably wouldn't have known what to do with myself. In any case, the only reason I could see for the Australians doing such a thing was to put me off! There was one nice gesture from the Aussies – captain Ricky Ponting walked over to me as I took my guard and shook my hand to wish me all the best. You battle hard with these guys over the years, but having the respect of players such as Ponting makes all your efforts worthwhile.

I took guard as I always do and looked around the field

as I prepared to face part-time off-spinner Marcus North, who was providing Australia's spin threat in the Test after they left out Hauritz, surprisingly. I noticed the fielder at midwicket was standing back, which was a big blow to me because that's where I wanted to hit him, but before North bowled the first ball he changed the field and brought the player in. It was perfectly set up for me, so I got down on one knee and slog-swept through midwicket for four to get off the mark. I was determined to be positive and carried on with that thought in mind. I'd seen Beefy before the start of play and he had told me to stop trying to hit through midwicket and try hitting straighter. I think I tried to get too clever and instead of just hitting North over midwicket, I tried to use my wrists and flick him, and instead got a leading edge to long on. As I was walking back I could just imagine what Beefy was saying under his breath about me! I had scored 22 in my final innings, but I wasn't too disappointed. I had given it a go, which I'd been determined to do, and I'd rather get out that way than pushing the ball around. Once again Broad and Swann scored runs down the order and it enabled us to declare and set Australia 546 if they were to win and retain the Ashes.

There was a fair amount of nervous talk in the press after Australia reached 80 without loss at the close, but no team in the history of cricket had chased down that many in the final innings. Ponting would have had to score 250 or more, which admittedly is not beyond him, for Australia even to get close to the victory target. When we started on that fourth morning,

Strauss let me address the team in the huddle before the start of play. I told them if we were patient, the Ashes would come. I tried to explain to some of the younger lads in the team that if we stuck to the plans that had been successful for us during the series, then the win would come – we didn't need to force it. I reminded them that the only way we would struggle was if we started doing things outside those plans. I urged everyone to be calm and not panic, no matter what the situation, and if we did what we'd been doing for one more day, I assured them we would win. By and large, that is what we did, and not for a moment did I doubt we would win – even when Ponting and Hussey were together after we had taken two early wickets. They still needed over 300 more to win, which is a lot of runs in any form of cricket.

Ponting and Hussey were looking good together, though, and it was the only time during that day we seemed to lack a little belief. I had been fielding in the slips less and less during the final Test. It wasn't so much my knee that was causing me problems, but I genuinely didn't think I was going to catch anything. Fielding is one area of my game that has perhaps suffered in recent years because I've been working so hard on my batting and bowling. A lot of the lads practice throwing the ball at the stumps during every practice session we have, but I must confess I haven't done that as much as I should have done.

I had been put at mid-on when Hussey pushed the ball to me and called for a quick single. I knew there was no point throwing at the non-striker's end because Hussey is too quick between the wickets and the angle was tight. I must have noticed that Ponting had hesitated slightly, using my peripheral vision, because I picked up and threw towards the keeper's end, and was as amazed as everyone else in the ground when I hit the stumps. If Ponting hadn't hesitated, he would probably have made his crease, and I doubt he expected me to hit the stumps anyway. In some ways it was the perfect way to finish my Test career – far better than getting a wicket by normal means because it was so unexpected.

Clarke was next out to the crease, but he didn't look his normal self. He had been calm and composed scoring all those runs previously in the series, but he was more like a jack-in-the-box this time – maybe the situation had got to him a little bit. He might have been unlucky to get out, not that we were bothered at the time. Clarke clipped Swann off his legs, hit Alastair Cook's boot at short leg and while everyone wondered where the ball had gone, Strauss picked him up from slip and ran him out.

Once those two had gone, I don't think any of us had any doubts we were closing in on the Ashes. Swann pitched in to dismiss Marcus North and have Brad Haddin caught in the deep. Strauss had done well to keep Harmy back because by the time he was called upon, he was absolutely desperate to bowl. It wasn't his type of pitch but he put in a brilliant spell right at the end. As my final Test match neared its end, I couldn't have asked for anything better than my best mate running in to finish off the game. Siddle spooned one up and I caught it to earn Harmy his first wicket. It was a horrible ball to catch because it looped up and seemed to take ages before it landed in my hands. Stuart Clark clearly didn't fancy Harmy in this mood and guided the next ball straight to Cook at short leg to set the big man up for a hat-trick. As he ran in, I was hoping and praying that Harmy got it because, for me, that would have been the perfect ending, but sadly Hilfenhaus blocked it out.

Swann bowled the next over and then Harmy walked over to me and asked if I wanted to have a bowl. I told him I didn't because I wasn't sure I'd be able to get to the wicket anyway, and also because this was a Test match with the Ashes on the line, not a pantomime. I explained that if I couldn't bowl, the next best thing was for him to run in and finish things off, and suggested he pulled his finger out! It was great to see Harmy happy as the game finished, but for me the moment of victory was full of mixed emotions.

When Hussey clipped Swann to short leg, the ground erupted just as it had done four years earlier. Then, bad light had ended play and we had the draw that reclaimed the Ashes, but the moment of victory was a bit of a blur. This time, it was far more controlled. The first thing I did was walk to the centre and shake the hands of Hussey and Hilfenhaus. I wasn't trying to recreate another Brett Lee moment, but I do believe that this is the way things should be done. I had all night to celebrate with the rest of the team, and for the sake of another 20 seconds to show some respect to the opposition, I thought they could wait.

## ENGLAND v AUSTRALIA
## (5th Test) at The Oval 20–23 August 2009

### England

| | | | |
|---|---|---|---|
| *A.J.Strauss c Haddin b Hilfenhaus | 55 | – c Clarke b North | 75 |
| A.N.Cook c Ponting b Siddle | 10 | – c Clarke b North | 9 |
| I.R.Bell b Siddle | 72 | – c Katich b Johnson | 4 |
| P.D.Collingwood c Hussey b Siddle | 24 | – c Katich b Johnson | 1 |
| I.J.L.Trott run out | 41 | – c North b Clark | 119 |
| +M.J.Prior c Watson b Johnson | 18 | – run out | 4 |
| A.Flintoff c Haddin b Johnson | 7 | – c Siddle b North | 22 |
| S.C.J.Broad c Ponting b Hilfenhaus | 37 | – c Ponting b North | 29 |
| G.P.Swann c Haddin b Siddle | 18 | – c Haddin b Hilfenhaus | 63 |
| J.M.Anderson lbw b Hilfenhaus | 0 | – not out | 15 |
| S.J.Harmison not out | 12 | | |
| B 12, l-b 5, w 3, n-b 18 | 38 | B 1, l-b 15, w 7, n-b 9 | 32 |

1/12 2/114 3/176 4/181        332    1/27 2/34 3/39 4/157  (for 9 wkts dec) 373
5/229 6/247 7/268 8/307 9/308 10/332    5/168 6/200 7/243 8/333 9/373

Bowling: *First innings* – Hilfenhaus 21.5-5-71-3; Siddle 21-6-75-4; Clark 14-5-41-0; Johnson 15-0-69-2; North 14-3-33-0; Watson 5-0-26-0. *Second innings* – Hilfenhaus 11-1-58-1; Siddle 17-3-69-0; North 30-4-98-4; Johnson 17-1-60-2; Katich 5-2-9-0; Clark 12-2-43-1; Clarke 3-0-20-0.

### Australia

| | | | |
|---|---|---|---|
| S.R.Watson lbw b Broad | 34 | – lbw b Broad | 40 |
| S.M.Katich c Cook b Swann | 50 | – lbw b Swann | 43 |
| *R.T.Ponting b Broad | 8 | – run out (Ponting) | 66 |
| M.E.K.Hussey lbw b Broad | 0 | – c Cook b Swann | 121 |
| M.J.Clarke c Trott b Broad | 3 | – run out (Strauss) | 0 |
| M.J.North lbw b Swann | 8 | – st Prior b Swann | 10 |
| +B.J.Haddin b Broad | 1 | – c Strauss b Swann | 34 |
| M.G.Johnson c Prior b Swann | 11 | – c Collingwood b Harmison | 0 |
| P.M.Siddle not out | 26 | – c Flintoff b Harmison | 10 |
| S.R.Clark c Cook b Swann | 6 | – c Cook b Harmison | 0 |
| B.W.Hilfenhaus b Flintoff | 6 | not out | 4 |
| B 1, l-b 5, nb 1 | 7 | B 7, l-b 7, n-b 6 | 20 |

1/73 2/85 3/89 4/93        160    1/86 2/90 3/217 4/220        348
5/108 6/109 7/111 8/131 9/143 10/160    5/236 6/327 7/327 8/343 9/343 10/348

Bowling: *First innings* – Anderson 9-3-29-0; Flintoff 13.5-4-35-1; Swann 14-3-38-4; S.J.Harmison 4-1-15-0; Broad 12-1-37-5. *Second innings* – Anderson 12-2-46-0; Flintoff 11-1-42-0; S.J.Harmison 16-5-54-3; Swann 40.2-8-120-4; Broad 22-4-71-1; Collingwood 1-0-1-0.

Umpires: Asad Rauf and B.F.Bowden
England won by 197 runs

I didn't plan it this way, but the first person I came to after that was Harmy, which was fitting really. We've been through a lot together over the years and although I was emotional for myself, I was really happy for him and the way he had bowled at the end of the match. We joined the rest of the team on the outfield and then went over to shake hands with the Aussies. They are a hard team to beat, but they are also dignified in defeat. Ricky, for instance, must have been hurting like hell because there are not many Australian captains who get beaten twice in England, but he showed what an impressive man he is by congratulating us all.

Eventually, we returned to the dressing room and, just like in 2005, everyone congregated around the table in the middle and started jumping up and down. I sat in the corner and shed some tears. It was not something I expected to happen, but the emotion of the moment got the better of me. I could see the Sky Sports cameras hovering at the entrance to the dressing room, waiting to come in, so I took myself off to the toilets. I stood there by the sink with my head down, needing a minute to compose myself before I went back into the dressing room. I don't know where it came from. Maybe the realisation that I wouldn't be wearing the whites for England again suddenly hit me, but it all came flooding out. When I joined the others I sat near the back and tried to pull myself together before going outside for the closing ceremony.

Just as they did in 2005, the crowd stayed behind, waiting for us to stand on the podium and celebrate our win. It was slightly different from the last time and I didn't quite know what to do with myself. We all walked around the ground and when I looked up at the balcony in the big OCS stand I could see my family. Mum and Dad were there, and Rachael with the kids. It was especially good, knowing they were there to share my last day. The one person who really surprised me while I was on the pitch was Nasser Hussain. I played many of my early years as an England cricketer under his captaincy, and we were never that close. He was a tough captain and I was a young player, so I don't suppose we had that much in common, but it meant a lot to me when he walked over, shook me by the hand, and said, 'You should be proud of your career.'

By the time I got back to the dressing room after doing various interviews on the pitch, all the families had arrived and it was a really good atmosphere. I had photographs taken with the kids and shared a beer with my dad, which was very special because he has been such a massive influence on my career and played such a part in all my success. He got emotional and told me that what made it all the more special for him was the moment two years previously in Melbourne when I broke down on Christmas Eve. Having seen how I suffered then made moments like this so much better. I remember looking around, watching the younger lads in the team enjoying the moment, just as I had done in 2005. The kids were running around and it dawned on me that they were my life from now on. For years I have put every effort into playing Test cricket for England, but now I would get the chance to do normal things with my family – the school run, cooking the kids' tea, things like that.

The feeling of winning the Ashes was different from four

years previously. Back then we had a team that had developed over three or four years and I felt a major part of it. I had played a lot of cricket under Michael Vaughan and alongside Harmy, Matthew Hoggard and Tres, and I knew those lads much better than I knew the 2009 team. Don't get me wrong – I still loved winning the Ashes again, but I don't think I felt as big a part of the team in 2009 as I did in 2005. I had been in and out because of injury, so hadn't played that much cricket with some people in the team, and didn't know them very well. Mind you, that didn't stop me enjoying the night with them. I'd made plans to have a nice meal with friends and family after it all finished, but of course it didn't work out like that.

I went next door to have a drink with a few of the Aussies, and sat around with Siddle, Johnson and Hughes. Shortly before they all disappeared, I had a chat with Ricky for around 10 minutes. It's strange because for all the Tests and matches I've played against him, I'd never really had a chat with him before. He's not only a great player, but he's a really good man. He had his problems early in his career, but he turned that around and now commands absolute respect.

After a while, all the families left to go back to the hotel, and in those situations, time always seems to slip away from you. It didn't feel that long after we'd won the game when it got down to just Harmy and me left in the dressing room, which was a nice way to finish. We got a lift back with Reg Dickason, and I think I was so carried away with drink and emotion that I was talking Egyptian in the back seat! Back at the hotel, the celebrations were in full swing in the suite put aside for our victory party. My parents and Rachael were already there and I think it went on until around 3.00 a.m. On this occasion, I wasn't the last one to leave. Rachael suggested we went to bed around 1.30 a.m. and it was probably a good idea. I could have stayed and drunk a little more, but I didn't want to ruin the next day by being totally wiped out. I wanted to get up and have breakfast with the kids, and I had to bear in mind that the operation had been brought forward a day because the Test had finished early. I'd still had a good night, but it wasn't of 2005 proportions. I woke the next morning with a slightly thick head, but nothing outrageous.

It's funny but I'd temporarily forgotten what it was like immediately after we'd won the Ashes in 2005. The huge interest it generates hadn't crossed my mind much, until I woke up and looked out the window to see fans standing outside the hotel alongside cameramen and photographers. The ECB asked me to do a farewell press conference at the hotel after breakfast. Questions were asked about how good I thought I was, was I a great player, had I fulfilled my talent and things like that. It is always hard to answer questions like that. It is certainly not for me to say how good a player I was, but I told the press I didn't believe I was a great player – that should be reserved for players like Tendulkar, Gary Sobers and Ian Botham. If I'd have remembered at the time, I would have given them a quote from former American President Theodore Roosevelt, which I always thought summed up my approach to the game. It was given to me at a dinner by Jeffrey Archer some years ago and I have included it at the start of this book. I felt incredibly relaxed and at ease answering them. I was happy with my decision, and somehow that final series summed up my career as a Test cricketer, a career I'd started and finished battling with pain and trying to play through an injury. I've always seen myself as a team player, and the 2009 Ashes underlined it for me. I didn't have a sparkling series, scoring just one half-century and claiming eight wickets, but it didn't ruin the enjoyment for me, or the feeling of being involved in a winning team. At that press conference, for the first time in my England career, I didn't have to worry about what the ECB stance was on this or that. I didn't have anyone warning me about the pitfalls of this subject or that, I could just go in there and be myself. I could answer all the questions openly and honestly without worrying about the consequences of what I had to say.

Almost as soon as I'd finished the press conference, Rachael and I decided to go for a walk and have a coffee before I headed off to hospital. It was still crazy out there, with photographers, and people standing outside the window of the coffee shop waving. Earlier in the summer, the senior players had tried to explain to the younger members of the squad that this is what it would be like if we won the Ashes, but it's not until you actually see it with your own eyes that you can comprehend just how much the Ashes mean to people. I am proud to have played a part in two winning Ashes teams and I am proud to have played so many Tests for England. It has been a dream come true for a young lad from Preston, and my Test career has come to a close with many happy memories – not least those scenes at The Oval four years apart.

# 23
# MARKING TIME

I barely had time to celebrate being an Ashes winner again, or to realise I had played my last Test, before I was whisked into hospital for major surgery on my knee. I had been booked in for the day after the Test was supposed to finish on the Monday, but because we finished a day early, the surgery was brought forward.

The operation was a complicated procedure, which involved drilling small holes into my knee to stimulate blood cells to fill the gaps, harden and act as new cartilage. I did a lot of research into this operation, on the internet, and had meetings with surgeon Andy Williams, who was very good at answering all my questions. He told me that several high-profile basketball players in the States, and some rugby players, had played again after having this surgery, and if I wanted to continue my career, it was my only realistic option.

So instead of savouring another Ashes win, just twenty-four hours after I'd walked around The Oval with Rachael and the kids, I woke up in another hospital room after another operation. Rachael drove me home the following day, but it wasn't the most comfortable of journeys because I had to keep my leg up. That discomfort was only the start of what proved to be a very frustrating time for me. Over the years, I have got used to periods of inactivity due to my many injuries, but this time I was unable to move off the couch. It was particularly hard on the kids – Dad was home but unable to play with them.

Whenever you have an operation that keeps you immobile for any length of time, your muscles waste away simply because you're not using them as regularly as you would do normally. To try to prevent this I was given the option of doing three sets of 500 knee bends a day, or using a machine called Continuous Passive Motion, which Andy Williams prescribed. I had to strap myself to the machine for eight hours a day, while it bent my knee up and down in controlled movement. I even had to wear it in bed.

The week after the operation, however, my rehabilitation took a turn for the worse. Rachael and I had gone to Rooster's wedding, but I started feeling a lot of pain. I had to go back to hospital the following day for treatment and was diagnosed as having deep vein thrombosis. Fortunately, it was diagnosed in plenty of time to get the right treatment, and as I was doing very little training then anyway, there was no great disruption to my rehabilitation schedule.

Having retired from Test cricket and had a major operation, clearly my life was going to be very different and we made a decision as a family to have a complete change of scenery and move to Dubai. We had always liked Dubai when we'd visited on holiday, and I wanted somewhere with good facilities for training. It's always easier training when you have the sun on your back rather than the cold of an English winter morning, and the facilities in Dubai are second to none. Rather than have my day disrupted by endless motorway journeys going from the gym to the physios and on to swimming, which would have been the case in the UK, all I had to do was press the right button in the lift in our apartment block to get to the gym. We settled quickly into our life in Dubai and, most importantly, the kids seemed to enjoy the new lifestyle. They liked their new international school and they were able to play on the beach, so it was great fun for them. In fact, we became so accustomed to life in Dubai, I was appointed as an official ambassador with responsibilities for promoting it as a venue for tourism and sport.

I had not been in Dubai long before it became clear that moving overseas would not be the only change in my life. I had been lucky enough to be an England contracted player for most of my international career and there is no doubt the system helped all the players. Before contracts were introduced, there was little time for rest and conserving energy in between series but now the players are looked after well and are given plenty of time to prepare. Having retired from Test cricket, I wasn't really expecting to be offered another contract and I had got to the stage of my life when I knew enough about my body to know when to train and for how long. I didn't want to relinquish control of my life to England and after discussing things with Chubby, we decided it was best to reject the contract. The decision had nothing to do with not wanting to play for England, but now I wasn't playing Test cricket I wanted to explore what it would be like to play in other countries, such as Australia or South Africa. I believed that would, ultimately, help me develop as a one-day cricketer, which would, in turn, benefit England if I returned to play international cricket.

My first goal after undergoing the operation was to be fit for the one-day international series in Bangladesh in late February 2010, but my spell on the sidelines proved much longer than I anticipated. I started to experience soreness in my knee in the New Year and flew back to see Andy Williams to check everything was all right. He was actually very pleased with the knee's progress, but suggested another operation to clean out the debris from the previous surgery, which set me back six months. I was naturally disappointed to face a further lay-off, particularly as it prevented me from playing in the IPL for Chennai, but the fact that Andy was pleased with my progress gave me optimism for the future.

I won't deny there were times when I got very low at the thought of all the hard work ahead of me, but I was determined to come back and play again. I started making strides towards achieving that aim on another trip back to England, when I agreed to take part in Lawrence Dallaglio's cycle challenge from Twickenham to Dublin. My knee was sore after the first day, but it stood up to the challenge, which gave me renewed confidence. It helped that Rooster was on the trip as team physio, because I was able to have long chats with him about my schedule in the coming months.

Another benefit of going on the Dallaglio cycle ride was that I got to know Richard Follett, a physio who works with Rooster. I wanted to give a boost to my training regime, so I paid for Richard, who is a tri-athlete and very knowledgeable about training, to fly out to Dubai and work with me. We started at around eight most mornings and did not finish until four in the afternoon, so they were very active days. Initially, the training was focused on building up my upper body before we moved on to the cross-trainer and the weights. I even began doing some light running, starting in the sea in deep water and gradually getting shallower until I began running on the beach. One of the really good things about this operation, however, is that the specialists have advised me to cut back on my running in training. Instead of doing a lot of running, I will be concentrating on exercises that are specifically designed to help me on the cricket field. The work with Richard helped me enormously. I made big strides in my rehabilitation and could see light at the end of the tunnel for the first time since playing at The Oval.

In April, I became one of the thousands caught up in the travel chaos caused by the volcanic ash cloud. I had returned to the UK for a few days, but was unable to go back to Dubai when UK airspace was closed because of the cloud. I used the unexpected time to join Sir Ian Botham's latest walk for Leukaemia Research. I wasn't able to walk with him, particularly at the pace he sets, because my knee still wasn't up to that, but I was able to help by carrying the buckets around for donations from members of the public. After several days, it became clear the travel situation wasn't going to ease. However, the authorities had re-opened French air-space, so I decided to head for France, making my way to Dover and catching the ferry over to Calais. Sadly, I missed the train to Paris, from where I hoped to get a flight to Dubai, and had a six-hour wait for the next one. I was by no means alone in that situation. Plenty of other people were milling around. I spent the time trying to remember my French lessons from school, or enough anyway to be able to order my breakfast when I got to Paris. By the time I got home, I think my journey had taken me thirty-six hours, but I know there were a lot more people coming back from Europe who had a much worse time of things.

My time away from cricket allowed me to explore other things, one of which was appearing on Sky One's sporting quiz show, *A League of their Own*. It was my first experience of working on a television show and gave me an insight into that world. I had been asked to do it the previous year, but I didn't think I would be available because it was due to be filmed while the IPL was being played. James Corden was the quiz-master, and a very funny man, and the others on the show were Sky presenter Georgie Thompson, comedian John Bishop and Jamie Redknapp. I got on with them all very well, which made the experience much easier for me. It was very different from what I'm used to and I was a bit nervous when we first started filming, but once I got into it, I enjoyed it. A lot more goes into a TV show than I expected and on some days we filmed two episodes, so we could be at the studio from ten in the morning until ten in the evening. Once the initial nerves had passed, I thought I got better with the more shows I did. I was worried about things to say at first, but after a while you realise that, although it takes an hour and a half to film each show, the final edit is only twenty-three minutes long. I spoke to Jamie, who is obviously used to being on TV as a football pundit, but we both realised we are sports people and not comics, so we left most of the gags to James Corden and John Bishop.

I didn't quite know what to expect before I started the Sky programme, but at least it gave me a taste of what television is like, if that is the route I decide to go down in the future. When I do eventually retire from cricket, I want to do something challenging as well as interesting, and finding out what suits me best is all part of this process. For now, though, I want to continue playing cricket. My hope is that the last year of rehabilitation will have been worth it and I can come back and perform as I have done in the past.

# ANDREW FLINTOFF
# CAREER RECORD

# ANDREW FLINTOFF
# IN TEST CRICKET

All records and statistics up to and including
England v Australia, 20–23 August 2009

by Victor and Richard V. Isaacs

# TEST CAREER RECORD

| | M | Inns | NO | Runs | HS | Avge | 100 | SR | 50 | Ct | Overs | M | Runs | Wkt | Avge | SR | 5 | 10 | Best | Econ |
|---|---|---|---|---|---|---|---|---|---|---|---|---|---|---|---|---|---|---|---|---|
| For England | 78 | 128 | 9 | 3795 | 167 | 31.89 | 5 | 61.86 | 26 | 52 | 2457.5 | 502 | 7303 | 219 | 33.34 | 67.33 | 3 | - | 5/58 | 2.97 |
| For ICC World XI | 1 | 2 | 0 | 50 | 35 | 25.00 | 0 | 79.36 | 0 | 0 | 34 | 5 | 107 | 7 | 15.28 | 29.14 | - | - | 4/59 | 3.14 |
| TOTAL | 79 | 130 | 9 | 3845 | 167 | 31.77 | 5 | 62.04 | 26 | 52 | 2491.5 | 507 | 7410 | 226 | 32.78 | 66.15 | 3 | - | 5/58 | 2.97 |

## Series by Series

| | M | Inns | NO | Runs | HS | Avge | 100 | SR | 50 | Ct | Overs | M | Runs | Wkt | Avge | SR | 5 | 10 | Best | Econ |
|---|---|---|---|---|---|---|---|---|---|---|---|---|---|---|---|---|---|---|---|---|
| South Africa in England 1998 | 2 | 3 | 0 | 17 | 17 | 5.66 | - | - | - | 1 | 35 | 5 | 112 | 1 | 112.00 | - | - | - | 1/52 | 3.20 |
| England in South Africa 1999-2000 | 4 | 6 | 0 | 155 | 42 | 25.83 | - | - | - | 2 | 66.5 | 16 | 190 | 5 | 38.00 | - | - | - | 2/31 | 2.84 |
| West Indies in England 2000 | 1 | 2 | 0 | 28 | 16 | 14.00 | - | - | - | 1 | 23 | 8 | 48 | 1 | 48.00 | - | - | - | 1/48 | 2.08 |
| Zimbabwe in England 2000 | 2 | 3 | 0 | 33 | 16 | 11.00 | - | - | - | - | 13 | 5 | 35 | 0 | - | - | - | - | - | 2.69 |
| England in India 2001-02 | 3 | 5 | 0 | 26 | 18 | 5.20 | - | - | - | 1 | 92 | 31 | 189 | 6 | 31.50 | - | - | - | 4/50 | 2.05 |
| England in New Zealand 2001-02 | 3 | 6 | 0 | 243 | 137 | 40.50 | 1 | - | 1 | 2 | 93 | 20 | 313 | 9 | 34.77 | - | - | - | 3/49 | 3.36 |
| Sri Lanka in England 2002 | 3 | 3 | 0 | 42 | 29 | 14.00 | - | - | - | 4 | 107 | 20 | 312 | 6 | 52.00 | - | - | - | 2/27 | 2.91 |
| India in England 2002 | 3 | 5 | 0 | 99 | 59 | 19.80 | - | - | 1 | 3 | 112 | 25 | 357 | 5 | 71.40 | - | - | - | 2/22 | 3.18 |
| South Africa in England 2003 | 5 | 8 | 0 | 423 | 142 | 52.87 | 1 | - | 3 | 7 | 182 | 44 | 592 | 10 | 59.20 | - | - | - | 2/55 | 3.25 |
| England in West Indies 2003-04 | 4 | 5 | 1 | 200 | 102* | 50.00 | 1 | - | - | 7 | 102.2 | 21 | 297 | 11 | 27.00 | - | 1 | - | 5/58 | 2.90 |
| England in Sri Lanka 2003-04 | 3 | 6 | 0 | 143 | 77 | 23.83 | - | - | 1 | - | 97 | 20 | 221 | 9 | 24.55 | - | - | - | 3/42 | 2.27 |
| New Zealand in England 2004 | 3 | 4 | 0 | 216 | 94 | 54.00 | - | - | 3 | 2 | 104.5 | 24 | 291 | 10 | 29.10 | - | - | - | 3/60 | 2.77 |
| West Indies in England 2004 | 4 | 7 | 1 | 387 | 167 | 64.50 | 1 | - | 3 | 5 | 88.3 | 17 | 297 | 14 | 21.21 | - | - | - | 3/25 | 3.35 |
| England in South Africa 2004-05 | 5 | 9 | 1 | 227 | 77 | 28.37 | - | - | 2 | 2 | 201.2 | 42 | 574 | 23 | 24.95 | - | - | - | 4/44 | 2.85 |
| Bangladesh in England 2005 | 2 | - | - | - | - | - | - | - | - | 1 | 36.5 | 5 | 138 | 9 | 15.33 | - | - | - | 3/44 | 3.74 |
| Australia in England 2005 | 5 | 10 | 0 | 402 | 102 | 40.20 | 1 | - | 3 | 3 | 194 | 32 | 655 | 24 | 27.29 | - | 1 | - | 5/78 | 3.37 |
| ICC Super Series Test in Australia 2005-06 | 1 | 2 | 0 | 50 | 35 | 25.00 | - | - | - | - | 34 | 5 | 107 | 7 | 15.28 | - | - | - | 4/59 | 3.14 |
| England in Pakistan 2005-06 | 3 | 6 | 0 | 125 | 56 | 20.83 | - | - | 1 | 3 | 140.1 | 21 | 409 | 13 | 31.46 | - | - | - | 4/68 | 2.91 |
| England in India 2005-06 | 3 | 5 | 0 | 264 | 70 | 52.80 | - | - | 4 | 3 | 105 | 23 | 336 | 11 | 30.54 | - | - | - | 4/82 | 3.20 |
| Sri Lanka in England 2006 | 3 | 5 | 2 | 47 | 33* | 15.66 | - | - | - | 4 | 128.5 | 23 | 354 | 12 | 29.50 | - | - | - | 3/52 | 2.74 |
| England in Australia 2006-07 | 5 | 10 | 1 | 254 | 89 | 28.22 | - | - | 2 | - | 137 | 18 | 481 | 11 | 43.72 | - | - | - | 4/99 | 3.51 |
| South Africa in England 2008 | 3 | 6 | 2 | 113 | 38 | 28.25 | - | - | - | 3 | 123 | 31 | 328 | 9 | 36.44 | - | - | - | 4/89 | 2.66 |
| England in India 2008-09 | 2 | 3 | 0 | 84 | 62 | 28.00 | - | - | 1 | 2 | 84 | 14 | 206 | 7 | 29.42 | - | - | - | 3/49 | 2.45 |
| England in West Indies 2008-09 | 3 | 4 | 0 | 67 | 43 | 16.75 | - | - | - | 2 | 62.2 | 19 | 151 | 5 | 30.20 | - | - | - | 3/47 | 2.42 |
| Australia in England 2009 | 4 | 7 | 1 | 200 | 74 | 33.33 | - | - | 1 | 1 | 128.5 | 18 | 417 | 8 | 52.12 | - | 1 | - | 5/92 | 3.23 |

# Test record at each ground

| Ground | M | Inns | NO | Runs | HS | Avge | 100 | 50 | Ct | Overs | M | Runs | Wkt | Avge | 5 | 10 | Best | Econ |
|---|---|---|---|---|---|---|---|---|---|---|---|---|---|---|---|---|---|---|
| Lord's, London | 10 | 14 | 2 | 429 | 142 | 35.75 | 1 | 3 | 3 | 332.4 | 75 | 1017 | 31 | 32.80 | 1 | | 5/92 | 3.05 |
| Edgbaston, Birmingham | 8 | 13 | 2 | 550 | 167 | 50.00 | 1 | 3 | 8 | 230.2 | 42 | 745 | 22 | 33.86 | | | 4/79 | 3.23 |
| Trent Bridge, Nottingham | 7 | 12 | 0 | 300 | 102 | 25.00 | 1 | 1 | 6 | 234 | 39 | 761 | 17 | 44.76 | | | 3/52 | 3.25 |
| Headingley, Leeds | 5 | 9 | 0 | 254 | 94 | 28.22 | | 3 | 3 | 152 | 37 | 387 | 9 | 43.00 | | | 2/55 | 2.54 |
| Kennington Oval, London | 5 | 8 | 0 | 296 | 95 | 42.28 | | 3 | 3 | 141.5 | 31 | 442 | 12 | 36.83 | 1 | | 5/78 | 3.11 |
| Old Trafford, Manchester | 3 | 5 | 1 | 115 | 57* | 28.75 | | 1 | 4 | 129 | 25 | 384 | 13 | 29.53 | | | 4/71 | 2.97 |
| Punjab CA Stadium, Mohali, Chandigarh | 3 | 5 | 0 | 205 | 70 | 41.00 | | 3 | 1 | 104.2 | 25 | 280 | 7 | 40.00 | | | 4/96 | 2.68 |
| Antigua Recreation Ground, St John's | 3 | 4 | 1 | 116 | 102* | 38.66 | 1 | | 1 | 64.2 | 16 | 188 | 4 | 47.00 | | | 3/47 | 2.92 |
| Kingsmead, Durban | 2 | 3 | 0 | 65 | 60 | 21.66 | | 1 | 1 | 70 | 19 | 178 | 5 | 35.60 | | | 2/66 | 2.54 |
| Newlands, Cape Town | 2 | 3 | 0 | 54 | 22 | 18.00 | | | | 53.1 | 8 | 141 | 6 | 23.50 | | | 4/79 | 2.65 |
| Sabina Park, Kingston, Jamaica | 2 | 3 | 0 | 113 | 46 | 37.66 | | | 3 | 49 | 14 | 117 | 3 | 39.00 | | | 2/72 | 2.38 |
| St George's Park, Port Elizabeth | 2 | 3 | 0 | 89 | 42 | 29.66 | | | 3 | 52.5 | 8 | 174 | 8 | 21.75 | | | 3/72 | 3.29 |
| Sydney Cricket Ground | 2 | 4 | 0 | 146 | 89 | 36.50 | | 1 | | 51 | 7 | 163 | 8 | 20.37 | | | 4/59 | 3.19 |
| The Wanderers Stadium, Johannesburg | 2 | 4 | 0 | 83 | 38 | 20.75 | | | | 60.1 | 15 | 181 | 3 | 60.33 | | | 2/59 | 3.00 |
| Adelaide Oval | 1 | 2 | 1 | 40 | 38* | 40.00 | | | 2 | 35 | 5 | 126 | 3 | 42.00 | | | 2/44 | 3.60 |
| AMI Stadium, Christchurch | 1 | 2 | 0 | 137 | 137 | 68.50 | 1 | | | 28 | 3 | 123 | 2 | 61.50 | | | 2/94 | 4.39 |
| Asgiriya Stadium, Kandy | 1 | 2 | 0 | 35 | 19 | 17.50 | | | | 39 | 8 | 100 | 3 | 33.33 | | | 2/60 | 2.56 |
| Basin Reserve, Wellington | 1 | 2 | 0 | 77 | 75 | 38.50 | | 1 | | 26 | 10 | 33 | 1 | 33.00 | | | 1/24 | 1.26 |
| Woolloongabba, Brisbane | 1 | 2 | 0 | 16 | 16 | 8.00 | | | | 35 | 6 | 110 | 4 | 27.50 | | | 4/99 | 3.14 |
| Eden Park, Auckland | 1 | 2 | 0 | 29 | 29 | 14.50 | | | | 39 | 7 | 157 | 6 | 26.16 | | | 3/49 | 4.02 |
| Gaddafi Stadium, Lahore | 1 | 2 | 0 | 12 | 12 | 6.00 | | | 1 | 36 | 8 | 111 | 1 | 111.00 | | | 1/111 | 3.08 |
| Galle International Stadium | 1 | 2 | 0 | 1 | 1 | 0.50 | | | | 40 | 12 | 74 | 4 | 18.50 | | | 3/42 | 1.85 |
| Iqbal Stadium, Faisalabad | 1 | 2 | 0 | 57 | 56 | 28.50 | | 1 | 2 | 56.1 | 9 | 142 | 4 | 35.50 | | | 3/66 | 2.52 |
| Kensington Oval, Bridgetown, Barbados | 1 | 2 | 0 | 15 | 15 | 15.00 | | | 2 | 29.2 | 6 | 78 | 7 | 11.14 | 1 | | 5/58 | 2.65 |
| M Chinnaswamy Stadium, Bangalore | 1 | 1 | 0 | 0 | 0 | 0.00 | | | | 28 | 9 | 50 | 4 | 12.50 | | | 4/50 | 1.78 |
| MA Chidambaram Stadium, Chepauk, Chennai | 1 | 2 | 0 | 22 | 18 | 11.00 | | | 2 | 40.4 | 3 | 113 | 4 | 28.25 | | | 3/49 | 2.77 |
| Melbourne Cricket Ground | 1 | 2 | 0 | 38 | 25 | 19.00 | | | | 22 | 1 | 77 | 3 | 25.66 | | | 3/77 | 3.50 |
| Multan Cricket Stadium | 1 | 2 | 0 | 56 | 45 | 28.00 | | | | 48 | 9 | 156 | 8 | 19.50 | | | 4/68 | 3.25 |
| Queen's Park Oval, Port of Spain, Trinidad | 1 | 1 | 0 | 23 | 23 | 23.00 | | | 2 | 22 | 4 | 65 | 2 | 32.50 | | | 2/27 | 2.95 |
| Sardar Patel (Gujarat) Stadium, Motera | 1 | 2 | 0 | 4 | 4 | 2.00 | | | | 30 | 11 | 59 | 2 | 29.50 | | | 2/42 | 1.96 |
| Sinhalese Sports Club, Colombo | 1 | 2 | 0 | 107 | 77 | 53.50 | | 1 | | 18 | 0 | 47 | 2 | 23.50 | | | 2/47 | 2.61 |
| SuperSport Park, Centurion | 1 | 2 | 1 | 91 | 77 | 91.00 | | 1 | | 32 | 8 | 90 | 6 | 15.00 | | | 4/44 | 2.81 |
| Vidarbha CA Ground, Nagpur | 1 | 2 | 0 | 43 | 43 | 43.00 | | 1 | 2 | 46 | 12 | 147 | 3 | 49.00 | | | 2/79 | 3.19 |
| W.A.C.A.Ground, Perth | 1 | 2 | 0 | 64 | 51 | 32.00 | | 1 | | 28 | 4 | 112 | 0 | - | | | - | 4.00 |
| Wankhede Stadium, Mumbai | 1 | 2 | 0 | 100 | 50 | 50.00 | | 2 | | 32 | 8 | 82 | 4 | 20.50 | | | 3/14 | 2.56 |
| Riverside Ground, Chester-le-Street | 1 | - | - | - | - | - | - | - | - | 22 | 5 | 72 | 4 | 18.00 | | | 3/58 | 3.27 |
| Sir Vivian Richards Stadium, Antigua | 1 | - | - | - | - | - | - | - | - | - | - | - | - | - | - | - | - | - |

# Test record against each opponent

| | M | Inns | NO | Runs | HS | Avge | 100 | 50 | Ct | Overs | M | Runs | Wkt | Avge | 5 | 10 | Best | Econ |
|---|---|---|---|---|---|---|---|---|---|---|---|---|---|---|---|---|---|---|
| Australia | 15 | 29 | 2 | 906 | 102 | 33.55 | 1 | 6 | 4 | 493.5 | 73 | 1660 | 50 | 33.20 | 2 | - | 5/78 | 3.36 |
| Bangladesh | 2 | 2 | - | - | - | - | - | - | 1 | 36.5 | 5 | 138 | 9 | 15.33 | - | - | 3/44 | 3.74 |
| India | 11 | 18 | 0 | 473 | 70 | 26.27 | - | 6 | 9 | 393 | 93 | 1088 | 29 | 37.51 | - | - | 4/50 | 2.76 |
| New Zealand | 6 | 10 | 0 | 459 | 137 | 45.90 | 1 | 4 | 4 | 197.5 | 44 | 604 | 19 | 31.78 | - | - | 3/49 | 3.05 |
| Pakistan | 3 | 6 | 0 | 125 | 56 | 20.83 | - | 1 | 3 | 140.1 | 21 | 409 | 13 | 31.46 | - | - | 4/68 | 2.91 |
| South Africa | 19 | 32 | 3 | 935 | 142 | 32.24 | 1 | 5 | 8 | 608.1 | 138 | 1796 | 48 | 37.41 | - | - | 4/44 | 2.95 |
| Sri Lanka | 9 | 14 | 2 | 232 | 77 | 19.33 | - | 1 | 8 | 332.5 | 63 | 887 | 27 | 32.85 | 1 | - | 3/42 | 2.66 |
| West Indies | 12 | 18 | 2 | 682 | 167 | 42.62 | 2 | 3 | 15 | 276.1 | 65 | 793 | 31 | 25.58 | 1 | - | 5/58 | 2.87 |
| Zimbabwe | 2 | 3 | 0 | 33 | 16 | 11.00 | - | - | - | 13 | 5 | 35 | 0 | - | - | - | - | 2.69 |

## Test centuries (5)

| | | |
|---|---|---|
| 137 | v New Zealand at Christchurch 2001-02 | |
| 142 | v South Africa at Lord's 2003 | |
| 102* | v West Indies at Antigua 2003-04 | |
| 167 | v West Indies at Edgbaston 2004 | |
| 102 | v Australia at Trent Bridge 2005 | |

## Five wickets in an innings (2)

| | |
|---|---|
| 5/58 | v West Indies at Bridgetown, Barbados 2003-04 |
| 5/78 | v Australia at The Oval 2005 |
| 5/92 | v Australia at Lord's 2009 |

# Wicket breakdown

| | Batting | Bowling |
|---|---|---|
| Bowled | 20 | 39 |
| Caught | 84 | 155 |
| LBW | 13 | 30 |
| Run Out | 1 | - |
| Stumped | 3 | - |
| Hit Wicket | 0 | 2 |
| Not Out | 9 | - |
| Total | 130 | 226 |

# ANDREW FLINTOFF
# IN ONE-DAY INTERNATIONAL
# CRICKET

All records and statistics up to and including
West Indies v England, 3 April 2009

by Victor and Richard V. Isaacs

# ONE-DAY INTERNATIONAL CAREER RECORD

| | M | Inns | NO | Runs | HS | Avge | SR | 100 | 50 | Ct | Overs | M | Runs | Wkt | Avge | SR | 4 | 5 | Best | Econ |
|---|---|---|---|---|---|---|---|---|---|---|---|---|---|---|---|---|---|---|---|---|
| For England | 138 | 119 | 16 | 3293 | 123 | 31.97 | 89.16 | 3 | 18 | 46 | 916 | 66 | 3968 | 168 | 23.61 | 32.71 | 6 | 2 | 5/19 | 4.33 |
| For ICC World XI | 3 | 3 | 0 | 101 | 42 | 33.66 | 79.52 | – | – | 1 | 21.2 | 1 | 153 | 1 | 153.00 | 128.00 | – | – | 1/64 | 7.17 |
| *Total* | 141 | 122 | 16 | 3394 | 123 | 32.01 | 88.84 | 3 | 18 | 47 | 937.2 | 67 | 4121 | 169 | 24.38 | 33.27 | 6 | 2 | 5/19 | 4.39 |

# Series by Series

| | M | Inns | NO | Runs | HS | Avge | SR | 100 | 50 | Ct | Overs | M | Runs | Wkt | Avge | SR | 4 | 5 | Best | Econ |
|---|---|---|---|---|---|---|---|---|---|---|---|---|---|---|---|---|---|---|---|---|
| England in Sharjah 1998-99 | 4 | 4 | 0 | 85 | 50 | 21.25 | | – | 1 | – | 22.2 | 0 | 132 | 5 | 26.40 | – | – | – | 2/3 | 5.91 |
| ICC World Cup in England 1999 | 5 | 2 | 0 | 15 | 15 | 7.50 | | – | – | – | 18 | 0 | 96 | 2 | 48.00 | – | – | – | 1/28 | 5.33 |
| NatWest Series in England (v WI & Zim) 2000 | 6 | 5 | 1 | 70 | 42* | 17.50 | | – | – | 3 | 4 | 0 | 20 | 0 | – | – | – | – | – | 5.00 |
| England in Kenya 2000-01 | 2 | 1 | 0 | 25 | 25 | 25.00 | | – | – | 1 | – | – | – | – | – | – | – | – | – | – |
| England in Pakistan 2000-01 | 3 | 3 | 0 | 111 | 84 | 37.00 | | – | 1 | 1 | – | – | – | – | – | – | – | – | – | – |
| England in Sri Lanka 2000-01 | 3 | 3 | 0 | 36 | 24 | 12.00 | | – | – | 1 | – | – | – | – | – | – | – | – | – | – |
| England in India 2001-02 | 6 | 6 | 0 | 147 | 52 | 24.50 | | – | 1 | 1 | 49.5 | 2 | 217 | 7 | 31.00 | – | – | – | 3/38 | 4.35 |
| England in New Zealand 2001-02 | 5 | 5 | 0 | 60 | 26 | 12.00 | | – | – | 5 | 41.5 | 1 | 183 | 7 | 26.14 | 1 | – | – | 4/17 | 4.37 |
| England in Zimbabwe 2001-02 | 5 | 3 | 1 | 108 | 46 | 54.00 | | – | – | 2 | 30.3 | 1 | 143 | 6 | 23.83 | – | – | – | 2/12 | 4.68 |
| NatWest Series in England (v SL & Ind) 2002 | 7 | 6 | 1 | 190 | 51 | 38.00 | | – | 2 | 3 | 52.1 | 0 | 276 | 9 | 30.66 | 1 | – | – | 3/49 | 5.29 |
| England in Australia 2002-03 | 1 | 1 | 0 | 16 | 16 | 16.00 | | – | – | 1 | 10 | 0 | 56 | 1 | 56.00 | – | – | – | 1/56 | 5.60 |
| ICC World Cup in Ken, SA & Zim 2002-03 | 5 | 5 | 0 | 156 | 64 | 31.20 | | – | 1 | 3 | 48.4 | 9 | 140 | 7 | 20.00 | – | – | – | 2/15 | 2.87 |
| NatWest Challenge in England (v Pak) 2003 | 3 | 3 | 1 | 69 | 39 | 34.50 | | – | – | 1 | 28 | 5 | 91 | 5 | 18.20 | 1 | – | – | 4/32 | 3.25 |
| NatWest Series in England (v SA & Zim) 2003 | 7 | 7 | 2 | 210 | 54 | 42.00 | | – | 2 | 4 | 47.3 | 6 | 181 | 10 | 18.10 | – | – | – | 3/13 | 3.81 |
| England in Bangladesh 2003-04 | 3 | 3 | 3 | 177 | 70* | – | | – | 3 | 1 | 29.4 | 9 | 63 | 7 | 9.00 | 1 | – | – | 4/14 | 2.12 |
| England in Sri Lanka 2003-04 | 1 | 1 | 0 | 3 | 3 | 3.00 | | – | – | – | 3.5 | 0 | 27 | 0 | – | – | – | – | – | 7.04 |
| England in West Indies 2003-04 | 5 | 4 | 0 | 121 | 59 | 30.25 | | – | 1 | 2 | 35 | 3 | 156 | 5 | 31.20 | – | – | – | 2/22 | 4.45 |
| NatWest Series in England (v NZ & WI) 2004 | 3 | 3 | 1 | 250 | 123 | 125.00 | | 2 | 1 | 1 | – | – | – | – | – | – | – | – | – | – |
| NatWest Challenge in England (v Ind) 2004 | 2 | 2 | 1 | 133 | 99 | 133.00 | | – | 1 | 1 | 15.3 | 1 | 59 | 2 | 29.50 | – | – | – | 1/28 | 3.80 |
| ICC Champions Trophy in England 2004 | 4 | 4 | 0 | 129 | 104 | 32.25 | | 1 | – | 1 | 31 | 1 | 126 | 9 | 14.00 | – | – | – | 3/11 | 4.06 |
| NatWest Series in England (v Aus & Bang) 2005 | 7 | 5 | 0 | 110 | 44 | 22.00 | | – | – | 1 | 60 | 6 | 260 | 12 | 21.66 | 1 | – | – | 4/29 | 4.33 |

| Series | M | Inns | NO | Runs | HS | Avge | 100 | 50 | Ct | Overs | M | Runs | Wkt | Avge | 4 | Best | Econ |
|---|---|---|---|---|---|---|---|---|---|---|---|---|---|---|---|---|---|
| NatWest Challenge in England (v Aus) 2005 | 3 | 2 | 0 | 92 | 87 | 46.00 | – | 1 | 1 | 27 | 0 | 132 | 2 | 66.00 | – | 1/44 | 4.88 |
| ICC Super Series ODIs in Australia 2005-06 | 3 | 3 | 0 | 101 | 42 | 33.66 | – | – | 1 | 21.2 | 1 | 153 | 1 | 153.00 | – | 1/64 | 7.17 |
| England in Pakistan 2005/06 | 5 | 5 | 0 | 187 | 72* | 46.75 | – | 1 | 2 | 35.5 | 3 | 180 | 7 | 25.71 | – | 3/73 | 5.02 |
| England in India 2005/06 | 4 | 4 | 0 | 73 | 41 | 18.25 | – | – | 1 | 35 | 1 | 149 | 6 | 24.83 | – | 3/56 | 4.25 |
| ICC Champions Trophy in India 2006/07 | 3 | 3 | 0 | 29 | 25 | 9.66 | – | – | – | 5 | 0 | 27 | 0 | – | – | – | 5.40 |
| England in Australia 2006/07 | 10 | 10 | 2 | 281 | 72* | 35.12 | – | 1 | 3 | 81.1 | 9 | 356 | 12 | 29.66 | 1 | 4/21 | 4.38 |
| ICC World Cup in West Indies 2006/07 | 8 | 7 | 0 | 92 | 42 | 13.14 | – | – | 3 | 69 | 3 | 298 | 14 | 21.28 | 1 | 4/43 | 4.31 |
| NatWest Series in England (v Ind) 2007 | 4 | 2 | 0 | 14 | 9 | 7.00 | – | – | 2 | 35.3 | 3 | 144 | 10 | 14.40 | 1 | 5/56 | 4.05 |
| England in Scotland 2008 | 1 | – | – | – | – | – | – | – | 1 | 8 | 1 | 21 | 3 | 7.00 | – | 3/21 | 2.62 |
| NatWest Series in England (v SA) 2008 | 5 | 3 | 2 | 187 | 78* | 187.00 | – | 1 | 2 | 30.4 | 2 | 129 | 10 | 12.90 | 1 | 3/21 | 4.20 |
| England in India 2008/09 | 5 | 5 | 0 | 114 | 43 | 22.80 | – | – | – | 42 | 0 | 210 | 4 | 52.50 | 1 | 3/31 | 5.00 |
| England in West Indies 2008/09 | 3 | 2 | 0 | 3 | 3 | 1.50 | – | – | 4 | 19 | 0 | 96 | 6 | 16.00 | 1 | 5/19 | 5.05 |

## One-day international record against each opponent

| Opponent | M | Inns | NO | Runs | HS | Avge | 100 | 50 | Ct | Overs | M | Runs | Wkt | Avge | 4 | Best | Econ |
|---|---|---|---|---|---|---|---|---|---|---|---|---|---|---|---|---|---|
| Australia | 21 | 19 | 2 | 519 | 87 | 28.83 | – | 3 | 4 | 167.1 | 9 | 808 | 19 | 42.52 | – | 3/23 | 4.83 |
| Bangladesh | 8 | 6 | 3 | 239 | 70* | 79.66 | – | 3 | 3 | 59.4 | 12 | 206 | 12 | 17.16 | 2 | 4/14 | 3.45 |
| India | 30 | 27 | 1 | 708 | 99 | 27.23 | – | 4 | 10 | 235.2 | 9 | 1069 | 37 | 28.89 | 1 | 5/56 | 4.54 |
| Ireland | 1 | 1 | 0 | 43 | 43 | 43.00 | – | – | 1 | 8.1 | 1 | 43 | 4 | 10.75 | – | 4/43 | 5.26 |
| Kenya | 2 | – | – | – | – | – | – | – | – | 9 | 0 | 35 | 2 | 17.50 | – | 2/35 | 3.88 |
| Namibia | 1 | 1 | 0 | 21 | 21 | 21.00 | – | – | 1 | 10 | 2 | 33 | 2 | 16.50 | – | 2/33 | 3.30 |
| Netherlands | 1 | 1 | 0 | 0 | 0 | 0.00 | – | – | – | 10 | 2 | 29 | 1 | 29.00 | – | 1/29 | 2.90 |
| New Zealand | 11 | 11 | 1 | 277 | 106 | 27.70 | 1 | 1 | 7 | 89.5 | 8 | 361 | 14 | 25.78 | 2 | 4/17 | 4.01 |
| Pakistan | 14 | 14 | 2 | 443 | 84 | 36.91 | – | 3 | 4 | 82.1 | 10 | 373 | 17 | 21.94 | 1 | 4/32 | 4.53 |
| Scotland | 1 | – | – | – | – | – | – | – | – | 8 | 1 | 21 | 3 | 7.00 | – | 3/21 | 2.62 |
| South Africa | 12 | 10 | 3 | 321 | 78* | 45.85 | – | 3 | 4 | 79.2 | 5 | 351 | 19 | 18.47 | 1 | 3/21 | 4.42 |
| Sri Lanka | 10 | 9 | 1 | 222 | 104 | 27.75 | 1 | 1 | – | 43.3 | 0 | 191 | 11 | 17.36 | – | 3/35 | 4.39 |
| West Indies | 15 | 12 | 1 | 313 | 123 | 28.45 | 1 | 1 | 8 | 78.5 | 3 | 376 | 16 | 23.50 | 1 | 5/19 | 4.76 |
| Zimbabwe | 14 | 11 | 3 | 288 | 53 | 36.00 | – | 1 | 4 | 56.2 | 5 | 225 | 12 | 18.75 | – | 3/11 | 3.99 |

## Wicket breakdown

|            | Batting | Bowling |
|------------|---------|---------|
| Bowled     | 20      | 49      |
| Caught     | 71      | 110     |
| LBW        | 9       | 10      |
| Run Out    | 2       | –       |
| Stumped    | 4       | –       |
| Hit Wicket | –       | –       |
| Not Out    | 16      | –       |
| Total      | 122     | 169     |

## One-day international centuries (3)

| 106 | v New Zealand at Bristol 2004     |
|-----|-----------------------------------|
| 123 | v West Indies at Lord's 2004      |
| 104 | v Sri Lanka at Southampton 2004   |

## Four wickets in an innings (8)

| 4/17 | v New Zealand at Auckland 2001-02   |
|------|-------------------------------------|
| 4/32 | v Pakistan at Lord's 2003           |
| 4/14 | v Bangladesh at Chittagong 2003-04  |
| 4/29 | v Bangladesh at Headingley 2005     |
| 4/21 | v New Zealand at Adelaide 2006-07   |
| 4/43 | v Ireland at Providence 2006-07     |
| 5/56 | v India at Bristol 2007             |
| 5/19 | v West Indies at Gros Islet 2008-09 |

# ANDREW FLINTOFF
# IN FIRST-CLASS CRICKET

All records and statistics up to and including
West Indies v England, St John's 2008-09

by Victor and Richard V. Isaacs

# FIRST-CLASS CRICKET CAREER

## Record

Debut: Lancashire v Hampshire at Portsmouth 1995

| M | Inns | NO | Runs | HS | Avge | 100 | 50 | Ct | Overs | M | Runs | Wkt | Avge | SR | 5 | 10 | Best | Econ |
|---|------|----|------|----|------|-----|----|----|-------|---|------|-----|------|----|---|----|------|------|
| 183 | 290 | 23 | 9027 | 167 | 33.80 | 15 | 53 | 185 | 3799.5 | 828 | 11059 | 350 | 31.59 | 65.1 | 4 | - | 5/24 | 2.91 |

## Season by season

| Season | Team | Venue | M | Inns | NO | Runs | HS | Avge | 100 | 50 | Ct | Overs | M | Runs | Wkt | Avge | 5 | 10 | Best |
|--------|------|-------|---|------|----|------|----|------|-----|----|----|-------|---|------|-----|------|---|----|------|
| 1995 | Lancashire | England | 1 | 2 | 0 | 7 | 7 | 3.50 | - | - | 2 | 11 | 0 | 39 | 0 | - | - | - | - |
| 1996 | Lancashire | England | 1 | 1 | 0 | 2 | 2 | 2.00 | - | - | 1 | - | - | - | - | - | - | - | - |
| 1997 | Lancashire | England | 5 | 8 | 0 | 243 | 117 | 30.37 | 1 | 1 | 4 | 10 | 6 | 11 | 1 | 11.00 | - | - | 1/11 |
| 1997/98 | England A | Kenya | 1 | 1 | 1 | 2 | 2* | - | - | - | 1 | - | - | - | - | - | - | - | - |
| 1997/98 | England A | Sri Lanka | 2 | 4 | 2 | 97 | 83 | 48.50 | - | 1 | 4 | - | - | - | - | - | - | - | - |
| 1998 | Lancs/England | England | 17 | 25 | 1 | 608 | 124 | 24.32 | 1 | 3 | 23 | 139 | 30 | 429 | 7 | 61.28 | - | - | 3/51 |
| 1998/99 | England A | Zimbabwe | 3 | 5 | 1 | 247 | 88 | 61.75 | - | 3 | 2 | 47.2 | 17 | 92 | 1 | 92.00 | - | - | 1/25 |
| 1998/99 | England A | South Africa | 2 | 3 | 0 | 295 | 145 | 98.33 | 1 | 2 | 2 | 52 | 17 | 111 | 1 | 111.00 | - | - | 1/19 |
| 1999 | Lancashire | England | 13 | 21 | 2 | 727 | 160 | 38.26 | 2 | 2 | 25 | 145.4 | 30 | 419 | 15 | 27.93 | 1 | - | 5/24 |
| 1999/00 | England | South Africa | 7 | 11 | 2 | 396 | 89* | 44.00 | - | 2 | 6 | 98.3 | 23 | 285 | 12 | 23.75 | - | - | 3/6 |
| 2000 | Lancs/England | England | 13 | 19 | 1 | 631 | 119 | 35.05 | 1 | 4 | 12 | 135.2 | 47 | 290 | 15 | 19.33 | - | - | 4/18 |
| 2000/01 | England XI | Pakistan | 1 | 1 | 0 | 0 | 0 | 0.00 | - | - | 1 | - | - | - | - | - | - | - | - |
| 2001 | Lancashire | England | 14 | 23 | 1 | 686 | 120 | 31.18 | 1 | 2 | 17 | 245.3 | 48 | 736 | 19 | 38.73 | - | - | 3/36 |
| 2001/02 | England | India | 4 | 7 | 0 | 66 | 40 | 9.42 | - | - | 1 | 126 | 42 | 263 | 12 | 21.91 | - | - | 4/50 |
| 2001/02 | England | New Zealand | 5 | 9 | 0 | 260 | 137 | 28.88 | 1 | 1 | 4 | 119 | 27 | 381 | 10 | 38.10 | - | - | 3/49 |
| 2002 | Lancs/England | England | 7 | 10 | 0 | 284 | 137 | 28.40 | 1 | 1 | 8 | 251 | 53 | 768 | 14 | 54.85 | - | - | 2/22 |
| 2002/03 | England | Australia | 2 | 3 | 0 | 19 | 15 | 6.33 | - | - | 2 | 36 | 1 | 174 | 2 | 87.00 | - | - | 2/112 |
| 2003 | Lancs/England | England | 10 | 14 | 1 | 942 | 154 | 72.46 | 3 | 5 | 7 | 232 | 57 | 727 | 15 | 48.46 | - | - | 2/47 |
| 2003/04 | England | Sri Lanka | 4 | 7 | 0 | 190 | 77 | 27.14 | - | 1 | - | 111 | 22 | 262 | 10 | 26.20 | - | - | 3/42 |
| 2003/04 | England | West Indies | 5 | 6 | 1 | 204 | 102* | 40.80 | 1 | - | 9 | 112.2 | 25 | 320 | 11 | 29.09 | 1 | - | 5/58 |
| 2004 | England | England | 7 | 11 | 1 | 603 | 167 | 60.30 | 1 | 6 | 7 | 193.2 | 41 | 588 | 24 | 24.50 | - | - | 3/25 |

| Season | Opponent | Team | M | Inns | NO | Runs | HS | Avge | 100 | 50 | Ct | Overs | M | Runs | Wkt | Avge | 5 | 10 | Best |
|---|---|---|---|---|---|---|---|---|---|---|---|---|---|---|---|---|---|---|---|
| 2004/05 | South Africa | England | 6 | 11 | 1 | 252 | 77 | 25.20 | – | 2 | 3 | 219.2 | 44 | 634 | 26 | 24.38 | – | – | 4/44 |
| 2005 | England | Lancs/England | 11 | 16 | 1 | 586 | 102 | 39.06 | 1 | 5 | 8 | 250.3 | 43 | 852 | 34 | 25.05 | 1 | – | 5/78 |
| 2005/06 | Australia | ICC World XI | 1 | 2 | 0 | 50 | 35 | 25.00 | – | – | – | 34 | 5 | 107 | 7 | 15.28 | – | – | 4/59 |
| 2005/06 | Pakistan | England | 4 | 8 | 0 | 162 | 56 | 20.25 | – | 1 | 5 | 157.3 | 23 | 489 | 16 | 30.56 | – | – | 4/68 |
| 2005/06 | India | England | 4 | 7 | 0 | 267 | 70 | 38.14 | – | 4 | 4 | 128.4 | 26 | 412 | 14 | 29.42 | – | – | 4/96 |
| 2006 | England | Lancs/England | 4 | 7 | 2 | 88 | 37 | 17.60 | – | – | 6 | 151.5 | 27 | 410 | 14 | 29.28 | – | – | 3/52 |
| 2006/07 | Australia | England | 6 | 11 | 1 | 301 | 89 | 30.10 | – | 2 | – | 155 | 21 | 533 | 12 | 44.41 | – | – | 4/99 |
| 2007 | England | Lancashire | 3 | 4 | 0 | 128 | 61 | 32.00 | – | 1 | 4 | 34.5 | 10 | 120 | 5 | 24.00 | – | – | 3/38 |
| 2008 | England | Lancs/England | 8 | 14 | 4 | 245 | 62* | 24.50 | – | 1 | 8 | 263.1 | 72 | 664 | 22 | 30.18 | – | – | 4/21 |
| 2008/09 | India | England | 2 | 3 | 0 | 84 | 62 | 28.00 | – | 1 | 2 | 84 | 14 | 206 | 7 | 29.42 | – | – | 3/49 |
| 2008/09 | West Indies | England | 3 | 4 | 0 | 67 | 43 | 16.75 | – | – | 2 | 62.2 | 19 | 151 | 5 | 30.20 | – | – | 3/47 |
| 2009 | England | Lancs/England | 7 | 12 | 1 | 288 | 74 | 26.18 | – | 2 | 5 | 304.2 | 39 | 586 | 19 | 30.84 | 1 | – | 5/92 |

## First-class record for each team

| | M | Inns | NO | Runs | HS | Avge | 100 | 50 | Ct | Overs | M | Runs | Wkt | Avge | 5 | 10 | Best |
|---|---|---|---|---|---|---|---|---|---|---|---|---|---|---|---|---|---|
| England | 78 | 128 | 9 | 3795 | 167 | 31.89 | 5 | 26 | 52 | 2457.5 | 502 | 7303 | 219 | 33.34 | 3 | – | 5/58 |
| England 'A' | 8 | 13 | 4 | 641 | 145 | 71.22 | 1 | 6 | 9 | 99.2 | 34 | 203 | 2 | 101.50 | – | – | 1/19 |
| England XI | 15 | 23 | 2 | 480 | 89* | 22.85 | – | 2 | 15 | 228.4 | 41 | 743 | 27 | 27.51 | – | – | 3/6 |
| Lancashire | 80 | 123 | 8 | 4042 | 160 | 35.14 | 9 | 19 | 108 | 967 | 240 | 2683 | 92 | 29.16 | 1 | – | 5/24 |
| ICC World XI | 1 | 2 | 0 | 50 | 35 | 25.00 | – | – | – | 34 | 5 | 107 | 7 | 15.28 | – | – | 4/59 |

# First-class record against each team

| | M | Inns | NO | Runs | HS | Avge | 100 | 50 | Ct | Overs | M | Runs | Wkt | Avge | 5 | 10 | Best |
|---|---|---|---|---|---|---|---|---|---|---|---|---|---|---|---|---|---|
| Australia | 15 | 29 | 2 | 906 | 102 | 33.55 | 1 | 6 | 4 | 493.5 | 73 | 1660 | 50 | 33.20 | 2 | – | 5/78 |
| Australia 'A' | 1 | 2 | 0 | 16 | 15 | 8.00 | – | – | – | 10 | 0 | 62 | 0 | – | – | – | – |
| Bangladesh | 2 | 1 | 1 | – | – | – | – | – | – | 36.5 | 5 | 138 | 9 | 15.33 | – | – | 3/44 |
| Cambridge University | 1 | 1 | 1 | 80 | 80* | – | – | 1 | 1 | 7 | 4 | 8 | 0 | – | – | – | – |
| Canterbury | 1 | 1 | 0 | 1 | 1 | 1.00 | – | – | 1 | 19 | 4 | 56 | 1 | 56.00 | – | – | 1/45 |
| Derbyshire | 4 | 6 | 0 | 79 | 31 | 13.16 | – | – | 3 | 4 | 0 | 19 | 0 | – | – | – | – |
| Durham | 6 | 11 | 0 | 100 | 55 | 9.09 | – | 1 | 6 | 90.4 | 32 | 209 | 15 | 13.93 | – | – | 4/21 |
| Durham Univ. Centre of Cricketing Excellence | 1 | 1 | 0 | 120 | 120 | 120.00 | 1 | – | – | 9 | 4 | 23 | 0 | – | – | – | – |
| Essex | 4 | 6 | 0 | 154 | 52 | 25.66 | – | 1 | 7 | 57 | 12 | 127 | 5 | 25.40 | – | – | 3/48 |
| Free State & Griqualand West Combined XI | 1 | 2 | 1 | 102 | 65 | 102.00 | 1 | – | – | – | – | – | – | – | – | – | – |
| Gauteng and Northerns Combined XI | 1 | 2 | 0 | 50 | 26 | 25.00 | – | 1 | 1 | 9.1 | 2 | 23 | 5 | 4.60 | – | – | 3/6 |
| Gauteng XI | 1 | 1 | 0 | 145 | 145 | 145.00 | 1 | – | – | 24 | 8 | 45 | 0 | – | – | – | – |
| Glamorgan | 2 | 3 | 0 | 114 | 68 | 38.00 | – | 1 | 6 | 29 | 4 | 114 | 1 | 114.00 | – | – | 1/79 |
| Gloucestershire | 1 | 1 | 0 | 158 | 158 | 158.00 | 1 | – | – | – | – | – | – | – | – | – | – |
| Hampshire | 9 | 15 | 2 | 470 | 117 | 36.15 | 1 | 3 | 11 | 124.5 | 25 | 364 | 17 | 21.41 | 1 | – | 5/24 |
| India | 11 | 18 | 0 | 473 | 70 | 26.27 | – | 6 | 9 | 393 | 93 | 1088 | 29 | 37.51 | – | – | 4/50 |
| India 'A' | 1 | 2 | 0 | 40 | 40 | 20.00 | – | – | 1 | 34 | 11 | 74 | 6 | 12.33 | – | – | 3/27 |
| Indian Board President's XI | 1 | 2 | 0 | 3 | 2 | 1.50 | – | – | – | 23.4 | 3 | 76 | 3 | 25.33 | – | – | 3/74 |
| Kent | 8 | 13 | 2 | 456 | 154 | 41.45 | 1 | 1 | 10 | 92 | 18 | 238 | 6 | 39.66 | – | – | 2/27 |
| Kenya | 1 | 1 | 1 | 2 | 2* | – | – | – | 1 | – | – | – | – | – | – | – | – |
| KwaZulu-Natal | 1 | 1 | 1 | 89 | 89* | – | – | 1 | 3 | 22.3 | 5 | 72 | 2 | 36.00 | – | – | 2/47 |
| Leicestershire | 6 | 7 | 1 | 375 | 119 | 62.50 | 1 | 3 | 7 | 98 | 24 | 293 | 11 | 26.63 | – | – | 3/36 |
| Middlesex | 3 | 2 | 0 | 121 | 111 | 60.50 | 1 | – | 7 | 13 | 7 | 29 | 1 | 29.00 | – | – | 1/17 |
| New Zealand | 6 | 10 | 0 | 459 | 137 | 45.90 | 1 | 4 | 4 | 197.5 | 44 | 604 | 19 | 31.78 | – | – | 3/49 |
| Northamptonshire | 3 | 6 | 0 | 239 | 124 | 39.83 | 1 | – | 8 | 28 | 7 | 85 | 1 | 85.00 | – | – | 1/58 |
| Nottinghamshire | 2 | 3 | 0 | 129 | 97 | 43.00 | – | 1 | 3 | 14 | 4 | 30 | 1 | 30.00 | – | – | 1/23 |
| Otago | 1 | 2 | 0 | 16 | 16 | 8.00 | – | – | 1 | 7 | 3 | 12 | 0 | – | – | – | – |
| Pakistan | 3 | 6 | 0 | 125 | 56 | 20.83 | – | 1 | 3 | 140.1 | 21 | 409 | 13 | 31.46 | – | – | 4/68 |
| Pakistan 'A' | 1 | 2 | 0 | 37 | 28 | 18.50 | – | – | 2 | 17.2 | 2 | 80 | 3 | 26.66 | – | – | 3/67 |
| Pakistan Cricket Board XI | 1 | 1 | 0 | 0 | 0 | 0.00 | – | – | 1 | – | – | – | – | – | – | – | – |
| Queensland | 1 | 1 | 0 | 3 | 3 | 3.00 | – | – | 2 | 26 | 1 | 112 | 2 | 56.00 | – | – | 2/112 |
| Somerset | 5 | 7 | 1 | 118 | 45 | 19.66 | – | – | 6 | 61.1 | 15 | 175 | 5 | 35.00 | – | – | 2/7 |
| South Africa | 19 | 32 | 3 | 935 | 142 | 32.24 | 1 | 5 | 8 | 608.1 | 138 | 1796 | 48 | 37.41 | – | – | 4/44 |

| | M | I | NO | Runs | HS | Avg | 100 | 50 | Ct | O | M | R | W | Avg | 5w | Best |
|---|---|---|---|---|---|---|---|---|---|---|---|---|---|---|---|---|
| South Africa 'A' | 1 | 2 | 0 | 25 | 21 | 12.50 | – | 1 | – | 18 | 2 | 60 | 3 | 20.00 | – | 3/50 |
| South African Board President's XI | 1 | 2 | 0 | 150 | 80 | 75.00 | – | 2 | – | 28 | 9 | 66 | 1 | 66.00 | – | 1/19 |
| South Australia | 1 | 1 | 0 | 47 | 47 | 47.00 | – | – | – | 18 | 2 | 52 | 1 | 52.00 | – | 1/34 |
| Sri Lanka | 9 | 14 | 2 | 232 | 77 | 19.33 | – | 1 | 8 | 332.5 | 63 | 887 | 27 | 32.85 | – | 3/42 |
| Sri Lanka 'A' | 2 | 4 | 1 | 15 | 11 | 5.00 | – | – | 3 | 9 | 2 | 17 | 0 | – | – | – |
| Sri Lanka Board President's XI | 2 | 3 | 1 | 140 | 83 | 70.00 | – | 1 | 3 | 14 | 2 | 41 | 1 | 41.00 | – | 1/32 |
| Surrey | 7 | 12 | 0 | 398 | 137 | 33.16 | 1 | – | 9 | 143.5 | 34 | 388 | 11 | 35.27 | – | 2/32 |
| Sussex | 3 | 5 | 1 | 179 | 68 | 44.75 | – | 2 | 4 | 46 | 15 | 124 | 0 | – | – | – |
| University of West Indies Vice-Chancellor's XI | 1 | 1 | 0 | 4 | 4 | 4.00 | – | – | 2 | 10 | 4 | 23 | 0 | – | – | – |
| Warwickshire | 2 | 3 | 0 | 122 | 70 | 40.66 | – | 2 | 3 | 6 | 0 | 31 | 0 | – | – | – |
| West Indies | 12 | 18 | 2 | 682 | 167 | 42.62 | 2 | 3 | 15 | 276.1 | 65 | 793 | 31 | 25.58 | 1 | 5/58 |
| Worcestershire | 4 | 6 | 0 | 206 | 83 | 34.33 | – | 2 | 6 | 33.3 | 5 | 122 | 6 | 20.33 | – | 3/27 |
| Yorkshire | 8 | 13 | 0 | 413 | 160 | 31.76 | 1 | 1 | 10 | 101 | 28 | 287 | 12 | 23.91 | – | 3/38 |
| Zimbabwe | 2 | 3 | 0 | 33 | 16 | 11.00 | – | – | – | 13 | 5 | 35 | 0 | – | – | – |
| Zimbabwe 'A' | 2 | 3 | 1 | 170 | 88 | 85.00 | – | 2 | 1 | 40.2 | 17 | 75 | 1 | 75.00 | – | 1/25 |
| Zimbabwe Cricket Union President's XI | 1 | 2 | 0 | 77 | 61 | 38.50 | – | 1 | 1 | 7 | 0 | 17 | 0 | – | – | – |

## Wicket breakdown

|  | Batting | Bowling |
|---|---|---|
| Bowled | 50 | 59 |
| Caught keeper | 45 | 90 |
| Caught fielder | 135 | 159 |
| LBW | 31 | 40 |
| Run Out | 1 | – |
| Stumped | 4 | – |
| Hit Wicket | – | 2 |
| Not Out | 23 | – |
| Total | 290 | 350 |

## First-class centuries (15)

| | |
|---|---|
| 117 | Lancashire v Hampshire at Southampton 1997 |
| 124 | Lancashire v Northamptonshire at Northampton 1998 |
| 145 | England 'A' v Gauteng at Johannesburg 1998-99 |
| 158 | Lancashire v Gloucestershire at Bristol 1999 |
| 160 | Lancashire v Yorkshire at Old Trafford 1999 |
| 119 | Lancashire v Leicestershire at Old Trafford 2000 |
| 120 | Lancashire v Durham UE at Durham University 2001 |
| 137 | England v New Zealand at Christchurch 2001-02 |
| 137 | Lancashire v Surrey at The Oval 2002 |
| 111 | Lancashire v Middlesex at Lord's 2003 |
| 154 | Lancashire v Kent at Canterbury 2003 |
| 142 | England v South Africa at Lord's 2003 |
| 102* | England v West Indies at St John's 2003-04 |
| 167 | England v West Indies at Edgbaston 2004 |
| 102 | England v Australia at Trent Bridge 2005 |

## Five wickets in an innings (3)

| | |
|---|---|
| 5/24 | Lancashire v Hampshire at Southampton 1999 |
| 5/58 | England v West Indies at Bridgetown 2004 |
| 5/78 | England v Australia at The Oval 2005 |
| 5/92 | England v Australia at Lord's 2009 |

# ANDREW FLINTOFF
# TEST CAREER RECORD
# (2005–2009)

All records and statistics from Andrew Flintoff's 53rd
Test, up to and including Fifth Test v Australia at
The Oval 2009

53.  ICC World XI v Australia at Sydney 14-17 October 2005 – lost by 210 runs
     Toss: Australia
     Australia 345 (M.L.Hayden 111) & 199; ICC World XI 190 & 144
     (S.C.G.MacGill 5-43)

     | | | | |
     |---|---|---|---|
     | 1st innings | c B.Lee b S.C.G.MacGill | 35 | 18-3-59-4 |
     | 2nd innings | c sub (B.J.Hodge) b S.C.G.MacGill | 15 | 16-2-48-3 |

     Match highlights:
     *Reached 150 Test wickets when he dismissed S.R.Watson in the Australia second innings.*

54.  v Pakistan at Multan 12-16 November 2005 – lost by 22 runs
     Toss: Pakistan
     Pakistan 274 & 341 (Salman Butt 122); England 418 (M.E.Trescothick
     193) & 175

     | | | | |
     |---|---|---|---|
     | 1st innings | c Shoaib Malik b Shoaib Akhtar | 45 | 23-6-68-4 |
     | 2nd innings | c Younus Khan b Danish Kaneria | 11 | 25-3-88-4 |

55.  v Pakistan at Faisalabad 20-24 November 2005 – Match drawn
     Toss: Pakistan
     Pakistan 462 (Inzamam-ul-Haq 109) & 268-9dec (Inzamam-ul-Haq 100*);
     England 446 (I.R.Bell 115, K.P.Pietersen 100) & 164-6

     | | | | |
     |---|---|---|---|
     | 1st innings | b Shoaib Akhtar | 1 | 29-2-76-1 |
     | 2nd innings | c sub (Hasan Raza) b Shoaib Akhtar | 56 | 27.1-2-66-3 |

56.  v Pakistan at Lahore 29 November-3 December 2005 – lost by an innings
     and 100 runs
     Toss: England
     England 288 & 248 (Shoaib Akhtar 5-71); Pakistan 636-8dec (Mohammad
     Yousuf 223, Kamran Akmal 154)

     | | | | |
     |---|---|---|---|
     | 1st innings | c Shoaib Akhtar b Naved-ul-Hasan | 12 | 36-8-111-1 |
     | 2nd innings | b Danish Kaneria | 0 | |

57.  v India at Nagpur 1-5 March 2006 – match drawn
     Toss: England
     England 393 (P.D.Collingwood 134*) & 297-3 dec (A.N.Cook 104*); India
     323 (M.J.Hoggard 6-57) & 260-6 (W.Jaffer 100)

     | | | | |
     |---|---|---|---|
     | 1st innings | lbw b A.Kumble | 43 | 29-10-68-1 |
     | 2nd innings | did not bat | | 17-2-79-2 |

     Match highlights:
     *England captain.*

58.  v India at Mohali 9-13 March 2006 – lost by 9 wickets
     Toss: England
     England 300 (A.Kumble 5-76) & 181; India 338 & 144-1

     | | | | |
     |---|---|---|---|
     | 1st innings | c and b M.M.Patel | 70 | 22-3-96-4 |
     | 2nd innings | c M.M.Patel b P.P.Chawla | 51 | 5-0-11-0 |

     Match highlights:
     *England captain.*

59. v India at Mumbai 18-22 March 2006 – won by 212 runs
Toss: India
England 400 (A.J.Strauss 128) & 191; India 279 & 100 (S.D.Udal 4-14)
1st innings    c S.R.Tendulkar b A.Kumble       50       21-4-68-1
2nd innings   st M.S.Dhoni b A.Kumble           50       11-4-14-3

Match highlights:
*England captain. Passed 3,000 Test runs when he reached 20 in England's first innings. Became the 147th batsman in Test history to record four scores of 50 or more.*

60. v Sri Lanka at Lord's 11-15 May 2006 – match drawn
Toss: England
England 551-6 dec (K.P.Pietersen 158, M.E.Trescothick 106); Sri Lanka 192 & 537-9 following on (D.P.M.D.Jayawardene 119)
1st innings    not out                          33       17.3-2-55-2
2nd innings                                              51-11-131-2

Match highlights:
*England captain.*

61. v Sri Lanka at Edgbaston 25-28 May 2006 – won by 6 wickets
Toss: Sri Lanka
Sri Lanka 141 & 231 (M.G.Vandort 105); England 295 (K.P.Pietersen 142, M.Muralitharan 6-86) & 81-4
1st innings    b S.L.Malinga                     9       13.2-4-28-2
2nd innings   not out                            4       19-3-50-2

Match highlights:
*England captain.*

62. v Sri Lanka at Trent Bridge 2-5 June 2006 – lost by 134 runs
Toss: Sri Lanka
Sri Lanka 231 & 322 (M.S.Panesar 5-78); England 229 & 190 (M.Muralitharan 8-70)
1st innings    c D.P.M.D.Jayawardene b S.T.Jayasuriya  1   15-2-52-3
2nd innings   c T.M.Dilshan b M.Muralitharan          0   13-1-38-1

Match highlights:
*England captain.*

63. v Australia at Brisbane 23-27 November 2006 – lost by 277 runs
Toss: Australia
Australia 602-9 dec (R.T.Ponting 192) & 202-1 dec (J.L.Langer 100*); England 157 (G.D.McGrath 6-50) & 370
1st innings    c A.C.Gilchrist b B.Lee           0       30-4-99-4
2nd innings   c J.L.Langer b S.K.Warne          16        5-2-11-0

Match highlights:
*England captain.*

64. v Australia at Adelaide 1-5 December 2006 – lost by 6 wickets
Toss: England
England 551-6 dec (P.D.Collingwood 206, K.P.Pietersen 158) & 129;
Australia 513 (R.T.Ponting 142, M.J.Clarke 124, M.J.Hoggard 7-109) &
168-4

| | | | |
|---|---|---|---|
| 1st innings | not out | 38 | 26-5-82-1 |
| 2nd innings | c A.C.Gilchrist b B.Lee | 2 | 9-0-44-2 |

Match highlights:
*England captain.*

65. v Australia at Perth 14-18 December 2006 – lost by 206 runs
Toss: Australia
Australia 244 (M.S.Panesar 5-92) & 527-5 dec (M.J.Clarke 135*,
M.E.K.Hussey 103, A.C.Gilchrist 102*); England 215 & 350 (A.N.Cook
116)

| | | | |
|---|---|---|---|
| 1st innings | c S.K.Warne b A.Symonds | 13 | 9-2-36-0 |
| 2nd innings | b S.K.Warne | 51 | 19-2-76-0 |

Match highlights:
*England captain.*

66. v Australia at Melbourne 26-28 December 2006 – lost by an innings and
99 runs
Toss: England
England 159 (S.K.Warne 5-39) & 161; Australia 419 (A.Symonds 156,
M.L.Hayden 153)

| | | | |
|---|---|---|---|
| 1st innings | c S.K.Warne b S.R.Clark | 13 | 22-1-77-3 |
| 2nd innings | lbw b S.R.Clark | 25 | |

Match highlights:
*England captain.*

67. v Australia at Sydney 2-5 January 2007 – lost by 10 wickets
Toss: England
England 291 & 147; Australia 393 & 46-0

| | | | |
|---|---|---|---|
| 1st innings | c A.C.Gilchrist b S.R.Clark | 89 | 17-2-56-1 |
| 2nd innings | st A.C.Gilchrist b S.K.Warne | 7 | |

Match highlights:
*England captain. England lost the series 5-0, just the second time in England
Test history.*

68. v South Africa at Headingley 18-21 July 2008 – lost by 10 wickets
Toss: South Africa
England 203 & 327; South Africa 522 (A.G.Prince 149, A.B.de Villiers 174)
& 9-0

| | | | |
|---|---|---|---|
| 1st innings | c M.V.Boucher b D.W.Steyn | 17 | 40-12-77-1 |
| 2nd innings | c M.V.Boucher b D.W.Steyn | 38 | |

69.  v South Africa at Edgbaston 30 July-2 August 2008 – lost by 5 wickets
Toss: England
England 231 & 363 (P.D.Collingwood 135); South Africa 314 & 283-5
(G.C.Smith 154*)

| 1st innings | not out | 36 | 30-8-89-4 |
| 2nd innings | c H.M.Amla b P.L.Harris | 2 | 20-5-72-2 |

Match highlights:
*Reached 200 Test wickets when he dismissed N.D.McKenzie in South Africa
first innings.*

70.  v South Africa at The Oval 7-11 August 2008 – won by 6 wickets
Toss: South Africa
South Africa 194 & 318; England 316 (K.P.Pietersen 100, M.Ntini 5-94) &
198-4

| 1st innings | c M.V.Boucher b J.H.Kallis | 9 | 15-2-37-1 |
| 2nd innings | not out | 11 | 18-4-53-1 |

71.  v India at Chennai 11-15 December 2008 – lost by 6 wickets
Toss: England
England 316 (A.J.Strauss 123) & 311-9dec (A.J.Strauss 108,
P.D.Collingwood 108); India 241 & 387-4 (S.R.Tendulkar 103*)

| 1st innings | c G.Gambhir b A.Mishra | 18 | 18.4-2-49-3 |
| 2nd innings | c M.S.Dhoni b I.Sharma | 4 | 22-1-64-1 |

Match highlights:
*Passed 3,500 Test runs when he reached 6 in the first innings.*

72.  v India at Mohali 19-23 December 2008 – match drawn
Toss: India
India 453 (G.Gambhir 179, R.Dravid 136) & 251-7dec; England 302
(K.P.Pietersen 144) & 64-1

| 1st innings | c G.Gambhir b A.Mishra | 62 | 30.2-10-54-3 |
| 2nd innings | did not bat | | 13-1-39-0 |

73.  v West Indies at Kingston 4-7 February 2009 – lost by an innings and 23
runs
Toss: England
England 318 & 51 (J.E.Taylor 5-11); West Indies 392 (C.H.Gayle 104,
R.R.Sarwan 107, S.C.J.Broad 5-85)

| 1st innings | c B.P.Nash b D.B-L.Powell | 43 | 33-11-72-2 |
| 2nd innings | b F.H.Edwards | 24 | |

74.  v West Indies at North Sound 13 February 2009 – match drawn
Toss: West Indies
England 7-0; West Indies did not bat

| 1st innings | | did not bat |

Match highlights:
*Match was abandoned after just 10 balls due to the dangerously sandy outfield.*

75. v West Indies at St John's 15-19 February 2009 – match drawn
    Toss: West Indies
    England 566-9dec (A.J.Strauss 169, P.D.Collingwood 113) & 221-8dec;
    West Indies 285 (G.P.Swann 5-57) & 370-9 (R.R.Sarwan 106)
    1st innings   b J.E.Taylor                      0        14.2-3-47-3
    2nd innings   c R.O.Hinds b S.J.Benn            0        15-5-32-0

    Match highlights:
    *Recorded his third 'pair' in Test cricket.*

76. v Australia at Cardiff 8-12 July 2009 – match drawn
    Toss: England
    England 435 & 252-9; Australia 674-6dec (S.M.Katich 122, R.T.Ponting
    150, M.J.North 125*, B.J.Haddin 121)
    1st innings   b P.M.Siddle                      37       35-3-128-1
    2nd innings   c R.T.Ponting b M.G.Johnson       26

77. v Australia at Lord's 16-20 July 2009 – won by 115 runs
    Toss: England
    England 425 (A.J.Strauss 161) & 311-6dec; Australia 215 & 406 (M.J.Clarke
    136, A.Flintoff 5-92)
    1st innings   c R.T.Ponting b B.W.Hilfenhaus    4        12-4-27-1
    2nd innings   not out                           30       27-4-92-5

    Match highlights:
    *Recorded his third five-wicket haul in Test cricket.*

78. v Australia at Edgbaston 30 July-3 August 2009 – match drawn
    Toss: Australia
    Australia 263 (J.M.Anderson 5-80) & 375-5 (M.J.Clarke 103*); England 376
    1st innings   c M.J.Clarke b N.M.Hauritz        74       15-2-58-0
    2nd innings                                              15-0-35-0

79. v Australia at The Oval 20-24 August 2009 – won by 197 runs
    Toss: England
    England
    1st innings   c B.J.Haddin b M.G.Johnson        7
    2nd innings   c Siddle b North                  22

# THE ASHES 2005 AND 2006/07 SCORECARDS

Compiled by Victor Isaacs

## THE ASHES 2005
## First Test, Lord's, 21–24 July

Australia won by 239 runs

Australia won the toss
Umpires: Aleem Dar and RE Koertzen
Man of the Match: GD McGrath

Close of play:
Day 1: Australia 190, England 92/7 (Pietersen 28*)
Day 2: Australia 190 & 279/7 (Katich 10*), England 155
Day 3: Australia 190 & 384, England 155 & 156/5 (Pietersen 42*, GO Jones 6*)

| Australia 1st innings | | | Runs | Mins | Balls | 4s | 6s |
|---|---|---|---|---|---|---|---|
| JL Langer | c Harmison | b Flintoff | 40 | 77 | 44 | 5 | 0 |
| ML Hayden | | b Hoggard | 12 | 38 | 25 | 2 | 0 |
| *RT Ponting | c Strauss | b Harmison | 9 | 38 | 18 | 1 | 0 |
| DR Martyn | c GO Jones | b SP Jones | 2 | 13 | 4 | 0 | 0 |
| MJ Clarke | lbw | b SP Jones | 11 | 35 | 22 | 2 | 0 |
| SM Katich | c GO Jones | b Harmison | 27 | 107 | 67 | 5 | 0 |
| +AC Gilchrist | c GO Jones | b Flintoff | 26 | 30 | 19 | 6 | 0 |
| SK Warne | | b Harmison | 28 | 40 | 29 | 5 | 0 |
| B Lee | c GO Jones | b Harmison | 3 | 13 | 8 | 0 | 0 |
| JN Gillespie | lbw | b Harmison | 1 | 19 | 11 | 0 | 0 |
| GD McGrath | not out | | 10 | 9 | 6 | 2 | 0 |
| Extras | (b 5, lb 4, w 1, nb 11) | | 21 | | | | |
| Total | (all out, 40.2 overs) | | 190 | | | | |

FoW: 1-35, 2-55, 3-66, 4-66, 5-87, 6-126, 7-175, 8-178, 9-178, 10-190

| Bowling | O | M | R | W | |
|---|---|---|---|---|---|
| Harmison | 11.2 | 0 | 43 | 5 | |
| Hoggard | 8 | 0 | 40 | 1 | (2nb) |
| Flintoff | 11 | 2 | 50 | 2 | (9nb) |
| SP Jones | 10 | 0 | 48 | 2 | (1w) |

| England 1st innings | | | Runs | Mins | Balls | 4s | 6s |
|---|---|---|---|---|---|---|---|
| ME Trescothick | c Langer | b McGrath | 4 | 24 | 17 | 1 | 0 |
| AJ Strauss | c Warne | b McGrath | 2 | 28 | 21 | 0 | 0 |
| *MP Vaughan | | b McGrath | 3 | 29 | 20 | 0 | 0 |
| IR Bell | | b McGrath | 6 | 34 | 25 | 1 | 0 |
| KP Pietersen | c Martyn | b Warne | 57 | 148 | 89 | 8 | 2 |
| A Flintoff | | b McGrath | 0 | 8 | 4 | 0 | 0 |
| +GO Jones | c Gilchrist | b Lee | 30 | 85 | 56 | 6 | 0 |
| AF Giles | c Gilchrist | b Lee | 11 | 14 | 13 | 2 | 0 |
| MJ Hoggard | c Hayden | b Warne | 0 | 18 | 16 | 0 | 0 |
| SJ Harmison | c Martyn | b Lee | 11 | 35 | 19 | 1 | 0 |
| SP Jones | not out | | 20 | 21 | 14 | 3 | 0 |
| Extras | (b 1, lb 5, nb 5) | | 11 | | | | |
| Total | (all out, 48.1 overs) | | 155 | | | | |

FoW: 1-10, 2-11, 3-18, 4-19, 5-21, 6-79, 7-92, 8-101, 9-122, 10-155

| Bowling | O | M | R | W | |
|---|---|---|---|---|---|
| McGrath | 18 | 5 | 53 | 5 | |
| Lee | 15.1 | 5 | 47 | 3 | (4nb) |
| Gillespie | 8 | 1 | 30 | 0 | (1nb) |
| Warne | 7 | 2 | 19 | 2 | |

| Australia 2nd innings | | Runs | Mins | Balls | 4s | 6s |
|---|---|---|---|---|---|---|
| JL Langer | run out (Pietersen) | 6 | 24 | 15 | 1 | 0 |
| ML Hayden | b Flintoff | 34 | 65 | 54 | 5 | 0 |
| *RT Ponting | c sub (JC Hildreth) b Hoggard | 42 | 100 | 65 | 3 | 0 |
| DR Martyn | lbw b Harmison | 65 | 215 | 138 | 8 | 0 |
| MJ Clarke | b Hoggard | 91 | 151 | 106 | 15 | 0 |
| SM Katich | c SP Jones b Harmison | 67 | 177 | 113 | 8 | 0 |
| +AC Gilchrist | b Flintoff | 10 | 26 | 14 | 1 | 0 |
| SK Warne | c Giles b Harmison | 2 | 13 | 7 | 0 | 0 |
| B Lee | run out (Giles) | 8 | 16 | 16 | 1 | 0 |
| JN Gillespie | b SP Jones | 13 | 72 | 52 | 3 | 0 |
| GD McGrath | not out | 20 | 44 | 32 | 3 | 0 |
| Extras | (b 10, lb 8, nb 8) | 26 | | | | |
| Total | (all out, 100.4 overs) | 384 | | | | |

FoW: 1-18, 2-54, 3-100, 4-255, 5-255, 6-274, 7-279, 8-289, 9-341, 10-384

| Bowling | O | M | R | W | |
|---|---|---|---|---|---|
| Harmison | 27.4 | 6 | 54 | 3 | |
| Hoggard | 16 | 1 | 56 | 2 | (2nb) |
| Flintoff | 27 | 4 | 123 | 2 | (5nb) |
| SP Jones | 18 | 1 | 69 | 1 | (1nb) |
| Giles | 11 | 1 | 56 | 0 | |
| Bell | 1 | 0 | 8 | 0 | |

| England 2nd innings | | | Runs | Mins | Balls | 4s | 6s |
|---|---|---|---|---|---|---|---|
| ME Trescothick | c Hayden | b Warne | 44 | 128 | 103 | 8 | 0 |
| AJ Strauss | | c & b Lee | 37 | 115 | 67 | 6 | 0 |
| *MP Vaughan | b Lee | | 4 | 47 | 26 | 1 | 0 |
| IR Bell | lbw | b Warne | 8 | 18 | 15 | 0 | 0 |
| KP Pietersen | not out | | 64 | 120 | 79 | 6 | 2 |
| A Flintoff | c Gilchrist | b Warne | 3 | 14 | 11 | 0 | 0 |
| +GO Jones | c Gillespie | b McGrath | 6 | 51 | 27 | 1 | 0 |
| AF Giles | c Hayden | b McGrath | 0 | 2 | 2 | 0 | 0 |
| MJ Hoggard | lbw | b McGrath | 0 | 18 | 15 | 0 | 0 |
| SJ Harmison | lbw | b Warne | 0 | 3 | 1 | 0 | 0 |
| SP Jones | c Warne | b McGrath | 0 | 12 | 6 | 0 | 0 |
| Extras | (b 6, lb 5, nb 3) | | 14 | | | | |
| Total | (all out, 58.1 overs) | | 180 | | | | |

FoW: 1-80, 2-96, 3-104, 4-112, 5-119, 6-158, 7-158, 8-164, 9-167, 10-180

| Bowling | O | M | R | W | |
|---|---|---|---|---|---|
| McGrath | 17.1 | 2 | 29 | 4 | |
| Lee | 15 | 3 | 58 | 2 | (1nb) |
| Gillespie | 6 | 0 | 18 | 0 | (2nb) |
| Warne | 20 | 2 | 64 | 4 | |

# THE ASHES 2005
## Second Test, Edgbaston, 4–7 August

England won by 2 runs

Australia won the toss
Umpires: BF Bowden and RE Koertzen
Man of the Match: A Flintoff

Close of play:
Day 1: England 407
Day 2: England 407 & 25/1 (Trescothick 19*, Hoggard 0*), Australia 308
Day 3: England 407 & 182, Australia 308 & 175/8 (Warne 20*)

| England 1st innings | | | Runs | Mins | Balls | 4s | 6s |
|---|---|---|---|---|---|---|---|
| ME Trescothick | c Gilchrist | b Kasprowicz | 90 | 143 | 102 | 15 | 2 |
| AJ Strauss | | b Warne | 48 | 113 | 76 | 10 | 0 |
| *MP Vaughan | c Lee | b Gillespie | 24 | 54 | 41 | 3 | 0 |
| IR Bell | c Gilchrist | b Kasprowicz | 6 | 2 | 3 | 1 | 0 |
| KP Pietersen | c Katich | b Lee | 71 | 152 | 76 | 10 | 1 |
| A Flintoff | c Gilchrist | b Gillespie | 68 | 74 | 62 | 6 | 5 |
| +GO Jones | c Gilchrist | b Kasprowicz | 1 | 14 | 15 | 0 | 0 |
| AF Giles | lbw | b Warne | 23 | 34 | 30 | 4 | 0 |
| MJ Hoggard | lbw | b Warne | 16 | 62 | 49 | 2 | 0 |
| SJ Harmison | | b Warne | 17 | 16 | 11 | 2 | 1 |
| SP Jones | not out | | 19 | 39 | 24 | 1 | 1 |
| Extras | (lb 9, w 1, nb 14) | | 24 | | | | |
| Total | (all out, 79.2 overs) | | 407 | | | | |

FoW: 1-112, 2-164, 3-170, 4-187, 5-290, 6-293, 7-342, 8-348, 9-375, 10-407

| Bowling | O | M | R | W | |
|---|---|---|---|---|---|
| Lee | 17 | 1 | 111 | 1 | (3nb, 1w) |
| Gillespie | 22 | 3 | 91 | 2 | (3nb) |
| Kasprowicz | 15 | 3 | 80 | 3 | (8nb) |
| Warne | 25.2 | 4 | 116 | 4 | |

| Australia 1st innings | | | Runs | Mins | Balls | 4s | 6s |
|---|---|---|---|---|---|---|---|
| JL Langer | lbw | b SP Jones | 82 | 276 | 154 | 7 | 0 |
| ML Hayden | c Strauss | b Hoggard | 0 | 5 | 1 | 0 | 0 |
| *RT Ponting | c Vaughan | b Giles | 61 | 87 | 76 | 12 | 0 |
| DR Martyn | run out (Vaughan) | | 20 | 23 | 18 | 4 | 0 |
| MJ Clarke | c GO Jones | b Giles | 40 | 85 | 68 | 7 | 0 |
| SM Katich | c GO Jones | b Flintoff | 4 | 22 | 18 | 1 | 0 |
| +AC Gilchrist | not out | | 49 | 120 | 69 | 4 | 0 |
| SK Warne | | b Giles | 8 | 14 | 14 | 2 | 0 |
| B Lee | c Flintoff | b SP Jones | 6 | 14 | 10 | 1 | 0 |
| JN Gillespie | lbw | b Flintoff | 7 | 36 | 37 | 1 | 0 |
| MS Kasprowicz | lbw | b Flintoff | 0 | 1 | 1 | 0 | 0 |
| Extras | (b 13, lb 7, w 1, nb 10) | | 31 | | | | |
| Total | (all out, 76 overs) | | 308 | | | | |

FoW: 1-0, 2-88, 3-118, 4-194, 5-208, 6-262, 7-273, 8-282, 9-308, 10-308

| Bowling | O | M | R | W | |
|---|---|---|---|---|---|
| Harmison | 11 | 1 | 48 | 0 | (2nb) |
| Hoggard | 8 | 0 | 41 | 1 | (4nb) |
| SP Jones | 16 | 2 | 69 | 2 | (1nb, 1w) |
| Flintoff | 15 | 1 | 52 | 3 | (3nb) |
| Giles | 26 | 2 | 78 | 3 | |

| England 2nd innings | | | Runs | Mins | Balls | 4s | 6s |
|---|---|---|---|---|---|---|---|
| ME Trescothick | c Gilchrist | b Lee | 21 | 51 | 38 | 4 | 0 |
| AJ Strauss | | b Warne | 6 | 28 | 12 | 1 | 0 |
| MJ Hoggard | c Hayden | b Lee | 1 | 35 | 27 | 0 | 0 |
| *MP Vaughan | | b Lee | 1 | 2 | 2 | 0 | 0 |
| IR Bell | c Gilchrist | b Warne | 21 | 69 | 43 | 2 | 0 |
| KP Pietersen | c Gilchrist | b Warne | 20 | 50 | 35 | 0 | 2 |
| A Flintoff | | b Warne | 73 | 133 | 86 | 6 | 4 |
| +GO Jones | c Ponting | b Lee | 9 | 33 | 19 | 1 | 0 |
| AF Giles | c Hayden | b Warne | 8 | 44 | 36 | 0 | 0 |
| SJ Harmison | c Ponting | b Warne | 0 | 2 | 1 | 0 | 0 |
| SP Jones | not out | | 12 | 42 | 23 | 3 | 0 |
| Extras | (lb 1, nb 9) | | 10 | | | | |
| Total | (all out, 52.1 overs) | | 182 | | | | |

FoW: 1-25, 2-27, 3-29, 4-31, 5-72, 6-75, 7-101, 8-131, 9-131, 10-182

| Bowling | O | M | R | W | |
|---|---|---|---|---|---|
| Lee | 18 | 1 | 82 | 4 | (5nb) |
| Gillespie | 8 | 0 | 24 | 0 | (1nb) |
| Kasprowicz | 3 | 0 | 29 | 0 | (3nb) |
| Warne | 23.1 | 7 | 46 | 6 | |

| Australia 2nd innings | | | Runs | Mins | Balls | 4s | 6s |
|---|---|---|---|---|---|---|---|
| JL Langer | | b Flintoff | 28 | 54 | 47 | 4 | 0 |
| ML Hayden | c Trescothick | b SP Jones | 31 | 106 | 64 | 4 | 0 |
| *RT Ponting | c GO Jones | b Flintoff | 0 | 4 | 5 | 0 | 0 |
| DR Martyn | c Bell | b Hoggard | 28 | 64 | 36 | 5 | 0 |
| MJ Clarke | | b Harmison | 30 | 101 | 57 | 4 | 0 |
| SM Katich | c Trescothick | b Giles | 16 | 27 | 21 | 3 | 0 |
| +AC Gilchrist | c Flintoff | b Giles | 1 | 8 | 4 | 0 | 0 |
| JN Gillespie | lbw | b Flintoff | 0 | 4 | 2 | 0 | 0 |
| SK Warne | hit wicket | b Flintoff | 42 | 79 | 59 | 4 | 2 |
| B Lee | not out | | 43 | 99 | 75 | 5 | 0 |
| MS Kasprowicz | c GO Jones | b Harmison | 20 | 60 | 31 | 3 | 0 |
| Extras | (b 13, lb 8, w 1, nb 18) | | 40 | | | | |
| Total | (all out, 64.3 overs) | | 279 | | | | |

FoW: 1-47, 2-48, 3-82, 4-107, 5-134, 6-136, 7-137, 8-175, 9-220, 10-279

| Bowling | O | M | R | W | |
|---|---|---|---|---|---|
| Harmison | 17.3 | 3 | 62 | 2 | (1nb, 1w) |
| Hoggard | 5 | 0 | 26 | 1 | |
| Giles | 15 | 3 | 68 | 2 | |
| Flintoff | 22 | 3 | 79 | 4 | (13nb) |
| SP Jones | 5 | 1 | 23 | 1 | |

# THE ASHES 2005
## Third Test, Old Trafford, 11–15 August

Match drawn

England won the toss
Umpires: BF Bowden and SA Bucknor
Man of the Match: RT Ponting

Close of play:
Day 1: England 341/5 (Bell 59*)
Day 2: England 444, Australia 214/7 (Warne 45*, Gillespie 4*)
Day 3: England 444, Australia 264/7 (Warne 78*, Gillespie 7*)
Day 4: England 444 & 280-6dec; Australia 302 & 24/0 (Langer 14*, Hayden 5*)

| England 1st innings | | | Runs | Mins | Balls | 4s | 6s |
|---|---|---|---|---|---|---|---|
| ME Trescothick | c Gilchrist | b Warne | 63 | 196 | 117 | 9 | 0 |
| AJ Strauss | | b Lee | 6 | 43 | 28 | 0 | 0 |
| *MP Vaughan | c McGrath | b Katich | 166 | 281 | 215 | 20 | 1 |
| IR Bell | c Gilchrist | b Lee | 59 | 205 | 155 | 8 | 0 |
| KP Pietersen | c sub (BJ Hodge) | b Lee | 21 | 50 | 28 | 1 | 0 |
| MJ Hoggard | | b Lee | 4 | 13 | 10 | 1 | 0 |
| A Flintoff | c Langer | b Warne | 46 | 93 | 67 | 7 | 0 |
| +GO Jones | | b Gillespie | 42 | 86 | 51 | 6 | 0 |
| AF Giles | c Hayden | b Warne | 0 | 11 | 6 | 0 | 0 |
| SJ Harmison | not out | | 10 | 13 | 11 | 1 | 0 |
| SP Jones | | b Warne | 0 | 7 | 4 | 0 | 0 |
| Extras | (b 4, lb 5, w 3, nb 15) | | 27 | | | | |
| Total | (all out, 113.2 overs) | | 444 | | | | |

FoW: 1-26, 2-163, 3-290, 4-333, 5-341, 6-346, 7-433, 8-434, 9-438, 10-444

| Bowling | O | M | R | W | |
|---|---|---|---|---|---|
| McGrath | 25 | 6 | 86 | 0 | (4nb) |
| Lee | 27 | 6 | 100 | 4 | (5nb, 2w) |
| Gillespie | 19 | 2 | 114 | 1 | (2nb, 1w) |
| Warne | 33.2 | 5 | 99 | 4 | (2nb) |
| Katich | 9 | 1 | 36 | 1 | |

| Australia 1st innings | | | Runs | Mins | Balls | 4s | 6s |
|---|---|---|---|---|---|---|---|
| JL Langer | c Bell | b Giles | 31 | 76 | 50 | 4 | 0 |
| ML Hayden | lbw | b Giles | 34 | 112 | 71 | 5 | 0 |
| *RT Ponting | c Bell | b SP Jones | 7 | 20 | 12 | 1 | 0 |
| DR Martyn | | b Giles | 20 | 71 | 41 | 2 | 0 |
| SM Katich | | b Flintoff | 17 | 39 | 28 | 1 | 0 |
| +AC Gilchrist | c GO Jones | b SP Jones | 30 | 74 | 49 | 4 | 0 |
| SK Warne | c Giles | b SP Jones | 90 | 183 | 122 | 11 | 1 |
| MJ Clarke | c Flintoff | b SP Jones | 7 | 19 | 18 | 0 | 0 |
| JN Gillespie | lbw | b SP Jones | 26 | 144 | 111 | 1 | 1 |
| B Lee | c Trescothick | b SP Jones | 1 | 17 | 16 | 0 | 0 |
| GD McGrath | not out | | 1 | 20 | 4 | 0 | 0 |
| Extras | (b 8, lb 7, w 8, nb 15) | | 38 | | | | |
| Total | (all out, 84.5 overs) | | 302 | | | | |

FoW: 1-58, 2-73, 3-86, 4-119, 5-133, 6-186, 7-201, 8-287, 9-293, 10-302

| Bowling | O | M | R | W | |
|---|---|---|---|---|---|
| Harmison | 10 | 0 | 47 | 0 | (3nb) |
| Hoggard | 6 | 2 | 22 | 0 | |
| Flintoff | 20 | 1 | 65 | 1 | (8nb) |
| SP Jones | 17.5 | 6 | 53 | 6 | (1nb, 2w) |
| Giles | 31 | 4 | 100 | 3 | (1w) |

| England 2nd innings | | | Runs | Mins | Balls | 4s | 6s |
|---|---|---|---|---|---|---|---|
| ME Trescothick | | b McGrath | 41 | 71 | 56 | 6 | 0 |
| AJ Strauss | c Martyn | b McGrath | 106 | 246 | 158 | 9 | 2 |
| *MP Vaughan | c sub (BJ Hodge) | b Lee | 14 | 45 | 37 | 2 | 0 |
| IR Bell | c Katich | b McGrath | 65 | 165 | 103 | 4 | 1 |
| KP Pietersen | lbw | b McGrath | 0 | 3 | 1 | 0 | 0 |
| A Flintoff | | b McGrath | 4 | 20 | 18 | 0 | 0 |
| +GO Jones | not out | | 27 | 15 | 12 | 2 | 2 |
| AF Giles | not out | | 0 | 4 | 0 | 0 | 0 |
| Extras | (b 5, lb 3, w 1, nb 14) | | 23 | | | | |
| Total | (6 wickets dec, 61.5 overs) | | 280 | | | | |

DNB: MJ Hoggard, SJ Harmison, SP Jones.

FoW: 1-64, 2-97, 3-224, 4-225, 5-248, 6-264

| Bowling | O | M | R | W | |
|---|---|---|---|---|---|
| McGrath | 20.5 | 1 | 115 | 5 | (6nb, 1w) |
| Lee | 12 | 0 | 60 | 1 | (4nb) |
| Warne | 25 | 3 | 74 | 0 | |
| Gillespie | 4 | 0 | 23 | 0 | (4nb) |

| Australia 2nd innings | | | Runs | Mins | Balls | 4s | 6s |
|---|---|---|---|---|---|---|---|
| JL Langer | c GO Jones | b Hoggard | 14 | 42 | 41 | 3 | 0 |
| ML Hayden | | b Flintoff | 36 | 123 | 91 | 5 | 1 |
| *RT Ponting | c GO Jones | b Harmison | 156 | 411 | 275 | 16 | 1 |
| DR Martyn | lbw | b Harmison | 19 | 53 | 36 | 3 | 0 |
| SM Katich | c Giles | b Flintoff | 12 | 30 | 23 | 2 | 0 |
| +AC Gilchrist | c Bell | b Flintoff | 4 | 36 | 30 | 0 | 0 |
| MJ Clarke | | b SP Jones | 39 | 73 | 63 | 7 | 0 |
| JN Gillespie | lbw | b Hoggard | 0 | 8 | 5 | 0 | 0 |
| SK Warne | c GO Jones | b Flintoff | 34 | 99 | 69 | 5 | 0 |
| B Lee | not out | | 18 | 44 | 25 | 4 | 0 |
| GD McGrath | not out | | 5 | 17 | 9 | 1 | 0 |
| Extras | (b 5, lb 8, w 1, nb 20) | | 34 | | | | |
| Total | (9 wickets, 108 overs) | | 371 | | | | |

FoW: 1-25, 2-96, 3-129, 4-165, 5-182, 6-263, 7-264, 8-340, 9-354

| Bowling | O | M | R | W | |
|---|---|---|---|---|---|
| Harmison | 22 | 4 | 67 | 2 | (4nb, 1w) |
| Hoggard | 13 | 0 | 49 | 2 | (6nb) |
| Giles | 26 | 4 | 93 | 0 | |
| Vaughan | 5 | 0 | 21 | 0 | |
| Flintoff | 25 | 6 | 71 | 4 | (9nb) |
| SP Jones | 17 | 3 | 57 | 1 | |

# THE ASHES 2005
## Fourth Test, Trent Bridge, 25–28 August

England won by 3 wickets

England won the toss
Umpires: Aleem Dar and SA Bucknor
Man of the Match: A Flintoff

Close of play:
Day 1: England 229/4 (Pietersen 33*, Flintoff 8*)
Day 2: England 477, Australia 99/5 (Katich 20*)
Day 3: England 477, Australia 218 & 222/4 (Clarke 39*, Katich 24*)

| England 1st innings | | | Runs | Mins | Balls | 4s | 6s |
|---|---|---|---|---|---|---|---|
| ME Trescothick | | b Tait | 65 | 138 | 111 | 8 | 1 |
| AJ Strauss | c Hayden | b Warne | 35 | 99 | 64 | 4 | 0 |
| *MP Vaughan | c Gilchrist | b Ponting | 58 | 138 | 99 | 9 | 0 |
| IR Bell | c Gilchrist | b Tait | 3 | 12 | 5 | 0 | 0 |
| KP Pietersen | c Gilchrist | b Lee | 45 | 131 | 108 | 6 | 0 |
| A Flintoff | lbw | b Tait | 102 | 201 | 132 | 14 | 1 |
| +GO Jones | | c & b Kasprowicz | 85 | 205 | 149 | 8 | 0 |
| AF Giles | lbw | b Warne | 15 | 45 | 35 | 3 | 0 |
| MJ Hoggard | c Gilchrist | b Warne | 10 | 46 | 28 | 1 | 0 |
| SJ Harmison | st Gilchrist | b Warne | 2 | 9 | 6 | 0 | 0 |
| SP Jones | not out | | 15 | 32 | 27 | 3 | 0 |
| Extras | (b 1, lb 15, w 1, nb 25) | | 42 | | | | |
| Total | (all out, 123.1 overs) | | 477 | | | | |

FoW: 1-105, 2-137, 3-146, 4-213, 5-241, 6-418, 7-450, 8-450, 9-454, 10-477

| Bowling | O | M | R | W | |
|---|---|---|---|---|---|
| Lee | 32 | 2 | 131 | 1 | (8nb) |
| Kasprowicz | 32 | 3 | 122 | 1 | (13nb) |
| Tait | 24 | 4 | 97 | 3 | (4nb) |
| Warne | 29.1 | 4 | 102 | 4 | |
| Ponting | 6 | 2 | 9 | 1 | (1w) |

| Australia 1st innings | | | Runs | Mins | Balls | 4s | 6s |
|---|---|---|---|---|---|---|---|
| JL Langer | c Bell | b Hoggard | 27 | 95 | 59 | 5 | 0 |
| ML Hayden | lbw | b Hoggard | 7 | 41 | 27 | 1 | 0 |
| *RT Ponting | lbw | b SP Jones | 1 | 6 | 6 | 0 | 0 |
| DR Martyn | lbw | b Hoggard | 1 | 4 | 3 | 0 | 0 |
| MJ Clarke | lbw | b Harmison | 36 | 93 | 53 | 5 | 0 |
| SM Katich | c Strauss | b SP Jones | 45 | 91 | 66 | 7 | 0 |
| +AC Gilchrist | c Strauss | b Flintoff | 27 | 58 | 36 | 3 | 1 |
| SK Warne | c Bell | b SP Jones | 0 | 2 | 1 | 0 | 0 |
| B Lee | c Bell | b SP Jones | 47 | 51 | 44 | 5 | 3 |
| MS Kasprowicz | | b SP Jones | 5 | 8 | 7 | 1 | 0 |
| SW Tait | not out | | 3 | 27 | 9 | 0 | 0 |
| Extras | (lb 2, w 1, nb 16) | | 19 | | | | |
| Total | (all out, 49.1 overs) | | 218 | | | | |

FoW: 1-20, 2-21, 3-22, 4-58, 5-99, 6-157, 7-157, 8-163, 9-175, 10-218

| Bowling | O | M | R | W | |
|---|---|---|---|---|---|
| Harmison | 9 | 1 | 48 | 1 | (3nb) |
| Hoggard | 15 | 3 | 70 | 3 | (4nb) |
| SP Jones | 14.1 | 4 | 44 | 5 | (1nb) |
| Flintoff | 11 | 1 | 54 | 1 | (8nb, 1w) |

## Australia 2nd innings (following on)

| | | | Runs | Mins | Balls | 4s | 6s |
|---|---|---|---|---|---|---|---|
| JL Langer | c Bell | b Giles | 61 | 149 | 112 | 8 | 0 |
| ML Hayden | c Giles | b Flintoff | 26 | 57 | 41 | 4 | 0 |
| *RT Ponting | run out (sub [GJ Pratt]) | | 48 | 137 | 89 | 3 | 1 |
| DR Martyn | c GO Jones | b Flintoff | 13 | 56 | 30 | 1 | 0 |
| MJ Clarke | c GO Jones | b Hoggard | 56 | 209 | 170 | 6 | 0 |
| SM Katich | lbw | b Harmison | 59 | 262 | 183 | 4 | 0 |
| +AC Gilchrist | lbw | b Hoggard | 11 | 20 | 11 | 2 | 0 |
| SK Warne | st GO Jones | b Giles | 45 | 68 | 42 | 5 | 2 |
| B Lee | not out | | 26 | 77 | 39 | 3 | 0 |
| MS Kasprowicz | c GO Jones | b Harmison | 19 | 30 | 26 | 1 | 0 |
| SW Tait | | b Harmison | 4 | 20 | 16 | 1 | 0 |
| Extras | (b 1, lb 4, nb 14) | | 19 | | | | |
| Total | (all out, 124 overs) | | 387 | | | | |

FoW: 1-50, 2-129, 3-155, 4-161, 5-261, 6-277, 7-314, 8-342, 9-373, 10-387

| Bowling | O | M | R | W | |
|---|---|---|---|---|---|
| Hoggard | 27 | 7 | 72 | 2 | (1nb) |
| SP Jones | 4 | 0 | 15 | 0 | |
| Harmison | 30 | 5 | 93 | 3 | (1nb) |
| Flintoff | 29 | 4 | 83 | 2 | (9nb) |
| Giles | 28 | 3 | 107 | 2 | |
| Bell | 6 | 2 | 12 | 0 | (3nb) |

## England 2nd innings

| | | | Runs | Mins | Balls | 4s | 6s |
|---|---|---|---|---|---|---|---|
| ME Trescothick | c Ponting | b Warne | 27 | 24 | 22 | 4 | 0 |
| AJ Strauss | c Clarke | b Warne | 23 | 68 | 37 | 3 | 0 |
| *MP Vaughan | c Hayden | b Warne | 0 | 8 | 6 | 0 | 0 |
| IR Bell | c Kasprowicz | b Lee | 3 | 38 | 20 | 0 | 0 |
| KP Pietersen | c Gilchrist | b Lee | 23 | 51 | 34 | 3 | 0 |
| A Flintoff | | b Lee | 26 | 63 | 34 | 3 | 0 |
| +GO Jones | c Kasprowicz | b Warne | 3 | 25 | 13 | 0 | 0 |
| AF Giles | not out | | 7 | 30 | 17 | 0 | 0 |
| MJ Hoggard | not out | | 8 | 20 | 13 | 1 | 0 |
| Extras | (lb 4, nb 5) | | 9 | | | | |
| Total | (7 wickets, 31.5 overs) | | 129 | | | | |

DNB: SJ Harmison, SP Jones.

FoW: 1-32, 2-36, 3-57, 4-57, 5-103, 6-111, 7-116

| Bowling | O | M | R | W | |
|---|---|---|---|---|---|
| Lee | 12 | 0 | 51 | 3 | (5nb) |
| Kasprowicz | 2 | 0 | 19 | 0 | |
| Warne | 13.5 | 2 | 31 | 4 | |
| Tait | 4 | 0 | 24 | 0 | |

# THE ASHES 2005
## Fifth Test, The Oval, 8–12 September

England won by 3 wickets

England won the toss
Umpires: BF Bowden and RE Koertzen
Man of the Match: KP Pietersen
Men of the Series: A Flintoff and SK Warne

Close of play:
Day 1: England 319/7 (Jones 21*, Giles 5*, 88 ov)
Day 2: England 373, Australia 112/0 (Langer 75*, Hayden 32*, 33 ov)
Day 3: England 373, Australia 277/2 (Hayden 110*, Martyn 9*, 78.4 ov)
Day 4: England 373 & 34/1 (Trescothick 14*, Vaughan 19*), Australia 367

| England 1st innings | | | Runs | Mins | Balls | 4s | 6s |
|---|---|---|---|---|---|---|---|
| ME Trescothick | c Hayden | b Warne | 43 | 77 | 65 | 8 | 0 |
| AJ Strauss | c Katich | b Warne | 129 | 351 | 210 | 17 | 0 |
| *MP Vaughan | c Clarke | b Warne | 11 | 26 | 25 | 2 | 0 |
| IR Bell | lbw | b Warne | 0 | 9 | 7 | 0 | 0 |
| KP Pietersen | | b Warne | 14 | 30 | 25 | 2 | 0 |
| A Flintoff | c Warne | b McGrath | 72 | 162 | 115 | 12 | 1 |
| PD Collingwood | lbw | b Tait | 7 | 26 | 26 | 1 | 0 |
| +GO Jones | | b Lee | 25 | 60 | 41 | 5 | 0 |
| AF Giles | lbw | b Warne | 32 | 120 | 70 | 1 | 0 |
| MJ Hoggard | c Martyn | b McGrath | 2 | 47 | 36 | 0 | 0 |
| SJ Harmison | not out | | 20 | 25 | 20 | 4 | 0 |
| Extras | (b 4, lb 6, w 1, nb 7) | | 18 | | | | |
| Total | (all out, 105.3 overs) | | 373 | | | | |

FoW: 1-82, 2-102, 3-104, 4-131, 5-274, 6-289, 7-297, 8-325, 9-345, 10-373

| Bowling | O | M | R | W | |
|---|---|---|---|---|---|
| McGrath | 27 | 5 | 72 | 2 | (1w) |
| Lee | 23 | 3 | 94 | 1 | (3nb) |
| Tait | 15 | 1 | 61 | 1 | (3nb) |
| Warne | 37.3 | 5 | 122 | 6 | |
| Katich | 3 | 0 | 14 | 0 | |

| Australia 1st innings | | | Runs | Mins | Balls | 4s | 6s |
|---|---|---|---|---|---|---|---|
| JL Langer | | b Harmison | 105 | 233 | 146 | 11 | 2 |
| ML Hayden | lbw | b Flintoff | 138 | 416 | 303 | 18 | 0 |
| *RT Ponting | c Strauss | b Flintoff | 35 | 81 | 56 | 3 | 0 |
| DR Martyn | c Collingwood | b Flintoff | 10 | 36 | 29 | 1 | 0 |
| MJ Clarke | lbw | b Hoggard | 25 | 119 | 59 | 2 | 0 |
| SM Katich | lbw | b Flintoff | 1 | 12 | 11 | 0 | 0 |
| +AC Gilchrist | lbw | b Hoggard | 23 | 32 | 20 | 4 | 0 |
| SK Warne | c Vaughan | b Flintoff | 0 | 18 | 10 | 0 | 0 |
| B Lee | c Giles | b Hoggard | 6 | 22 | 10 | 0 | 0 |
| GD McGrath | c Strauss | b Hoggard | 0 | 6 | 6 | 0 | 0 |
| SW Tait | not out | | 1 | 7 | 2 | 0 | 0 |
| Extras | (b 4, lb 8, w 2, nb 9) | | 23 | | | | |
| Total | (all out, 107.1 overs) | | 367 | | | | |

FoW: 1-185, 2-264, 3-281, 4-323, 5-329, 6-356, 7-359, 8-363, 9-363, 10-367

| Bowling | O | M | R | W | |
|---|---|---|---|---|---|
| Harmison | 22 | 2 | 87 | 1 | (2nb, 2w) |
| Hoggard | 24.1 | 2 | 97 | 4 | (1nb) |
| Flintoff | 34 | 10 | 78 | 5 | (6nb) |
| Giles | 23 | 1 | 76 | 0 | |
| Collingwood | 4 | 0 | 17 | 0 | |

| **England 2nd innings** | | | Runs | Mins | Balls | 4s | 6s |
|---|---|---|---|---|---|---|---|
| ME Trescothick | lbw | b Warne | 33 | 150 | 84 | 1 | 0 |
| AJ Strauss | c Katich | b Warne | 1 | 16 | 7 | 0 | 0 |
| *MP Vaughan | c Gilchrist | b McGrath | 45 | 80 | 65 | 6 | 0 |
| IR Bell | c Warne | b McGrath | 0 | 2 | 1 | 0 | 0 |
| KP Pietersen | | b McGrath | 158 | 285 | 187 | 15 | 7 |
| A Flintoff | | c & b Warne | 8 | 20 | 13 | 1 | 0 |
| PD Collingwood | c Ponting | b Warne | 10 | 72 | 51 | 1 | 0 |
| +GO Jones | | b Tait | 1 | 24 | 12 | 0 | 0 |
| AF Giles | | b Warne | 59 | 159 | 97 | 7 | 0 |
| MJ Hoggard | not out | | 4 | 45 | 35 | 0 | 0 |
| SJ Harmison | c Hayden | b Warne | 0 | 2 | 2 | 0 | 0 |
| Extras | (b 4, w 7, nb 5) | | 16 | | | | |
| Total | (all out, 91.3 overs) | | 335 | | | | |

FoW: 1-2, 2-67, 3-67, 4-109, 5-126, 6-186, 7-199, 8-308, 9-335, 10-335

| Bowling | O | M | R | W | |
|---|---|---|---|---|---|
| McGrath | 26 | 3 | 85 | 3 | (1nb) |
| Lee | 20 | 4 | 88 | 0 | (4nb, 1w) |
| Warne | 38.3 | 3 | 124 | 6 | (1w) |
| Clarke | 2 | 0 | 6 | 0 | |
| Tait | 5 | 0 | 28 | 1 | (1w) |

| **Australia 2nd innings** | | Runs | Mins | Balls | 4s | 6s |
|---|---|---|---|---|---|---|
| JL Langer | not out | 0 | 3 | 4 | 0 | 0 |
| ML Hayden | not out | 0 | 3 | 0 | 0 | 0 |
| Extras | (lb 4) | 4 | | | | |
| Total | (0 wickets, 0.4 overs) | 4 | | | | |

DNB: *RT Ponting, DR Martyn, MJ Clarke, SM Katich, +AC Gilchrist, SK Warne, B Lee, GD McGrath, SW Tait.

| Bowling | O | M | R | W |
|---|---|---|---|---|
| Harmison | 0.4 | 0 | 0 | 0 |

# THE ASHES 2006–07
## First Test, Brisbane, 23–27 November

Australia won by 277 runs

Australia won the toss
Umpires: BF Bowden and SA Bucknor
Man of the Match: RT Ponting

Close of play:
Day 1: Australia 346/3 (Ponting 137*, Hussey 63*)
Day 2: Australia 602/9d, England 53/3 (Bell 13*, Pietersen 6*)
Day 3: Australia 602/9d & 181/1 (Langer 88*, Ponting 51*); England 157
Day 4: Australia 602/9d & 202/1d, England 157 & 293/5 (Pietersen 92*, Jones 12*)

| Australia 1st innings | | | Runs | Mins | Balls | 4s | 6s |
|---|---|---|---|---|---|---|---|
| JL Langer | c Pietersen | b Flintoff | 82 | 136 | 98 | 13 | 0 |
| ML Hayden | c Collingwood | b Flintoff | 21 | 88 | 47 | 2 | 0 |
| *RT Ponting | lbw | b Hoggard | 196 | 464 | 319 | 24 | 0 |
| DR Martyn | c Collingwood | b Giles | 29 | 79 | 62 | 2 | 0 |
| MEK Hussey | | b Flintoff | 86 | 257 | 187 | 8 | 0 |
| MJ Clarke | c Strauss | b Anderson | 56 | 153 | 94 | 5 | 1 |
| +AC Gilchrist | lbw | b Hoggard | 0 | 3 | 3 | 0 | 0 |
| SK Warne | c Jones | b Harmison | 17 | 42 | 26 | 1 | 0 |
| B Lee | not out | | 43 | 90 | 61 | 6 | 0 |
| SR Clark | | b Flintoff | 39 | 34 | 23 | 3 | 2 |
| GD McGrath | not out | | 8 | 26 | 17 | 0 | 0 |
| Extras | (b 2, lb 8, w 8, nb 7) | | 25 | | | | |
| Total | (9 wickets dec, 155 overs) | | 602 | | | | |

FoW: 1-79, 2-141, 3-198, 4-407, 5-467, 6-467, 7-500, 8-528, 9-578

| Bowling | O | M | R | W | |
|---|---|---|---|---|---|
| Harmison | 30 | 4 | 123 | 1 | (1nb, 6w) |
| Hoggard | 31 | 5 | 98 | 2 | (1nb) |
| Anderson | 29 | 6 | 141 | 1 | (1w) |
| Flintoff | 30 | 4 | 99 | 4 | (3nb, 1w) |
| Giles | 25 | 2 | 91 | 1 | |
| Bell | 1 | 0 | 12 | 0 | (2nb) |
| Pietersen | 9 | 1 | 28 | 0 | |

| England 1st innings | | | Runs | Mins | Balls | 4s | 6s |
|---|---|---|---|---|---|---|---|
| AJ Strauss | c Hussey | b McGrath | 12 | 25 | 21 | 2 | 0 |
| AN Cook | c Warne | b McGrath | 11 | 27 | 15 | 1 | 0 |
| IR Bell | c Ponting | b Clark | 50 | 228 | 162 | 5 | 0 |
| PD Collingwood | c Gilchrist | b Clark | 5 | 24 | 13 | 1 | 0 |
| KP Pietersen | lbw | b McGrath | 16 | 72 | 44 | 1 | 0 |
| *A Flintoff | c Gilchrist | b Lee | 0 | 4 | 3 | 0 | 0 |
| +GO Jones | lbw | b McGrath | 19 | 90 | 57 | 2 | 0 |
| AF Giles | c Hayden | b McGrath | 24 | 61 | 39 | 4 | 0 |
| MJ Hoggard | c Gilchrist | b Clark | 0 | 12 | 6 | 0 | 0 |
| SJ Harmison | c Gilchrist | b McGrath | 0 | 5 | 5 | 0 | 0 |
| JM Anderson | not out | | 2 | 9 | 8 | 0 | 0 |

| Extras | (b 2, lb 8, w 2, nb 6) | 18 |
| Total | (all out, 61.1 overs) | 157 |

FoW: 1-28, 2-28, 3-42, 4-78, 5-79, 6-126, 7-149, 8-153, 9-154, 10-157

| Bowling | O | M | R | W | |
|---|---|---|---|---|---|
| Lee | 15 | 3 | 51 | 1 | (5nb, 2w) |
| McGrath | 23.1 | 8 | 50 | 6 | (1nb) |
| Clark | 14 | 5 | 21 | 3 | |
| Warne | 9 | 0 | 25 | 0 | |

**Australia 2nd innings**

| | | Runs | Mins | Balls | 4s | 6s |
|---|---|---|---|---|---|---|
| JL Langer | not out | 100 | 199 | 146 | 9 | 0 |
| ML Hayden | run out (Anderson/Jones) | 37 | 67 | 41 | 6 | 0 |
| *RT Ponting | not out | 60 | 131 | 85 | 4 | 0 |
| Extras | (lb 4, nb 1) | 5 | | | | |
| Total | (1 wicket dec, 45.1 overs) | 202 | | | | |

DNB: DR Martyn, MEK Hussey, MJ Clarke, +AC Gilchrist, SK Warne, B Lee, SR Clark, GD McGrath.

FoW: 1-68

| Bowling | O | M | R | W | |
|---|---|---|---|---|---|
| Hoggard | 11 | 2 | 43 | 0 | |
| Anderson | 9 | 1 | 54 | 0 | |
| Flintoff | 5 | 2 | 11 | 0 | (1nb) |
| Harmison | 12.1 | 1 | 54 | 0 | |
| Giles | 5 | 0 | 22 | 0 | |
| Pietersen | 3 | 0 | 14 | 0 | |

**England 2nd innings**

| | | | Runs | Mins | Balls | 4s | 6s |
|---|---|---|---|---|---|---|---|
| AJ Strauss | c sub (RA Broad) | b Clark | 11 | 51 | 31 | 1 | 0 |
| AN Cook | c Hussey | b Warne | 43 | 128 | 94 | 4 | 0 |
| IR Bell | lbw | b Warne | 0 | 11 | 4 | 0 | 0 |
| PD Collingwood | st Gilchrist | b Warne | 96 | 216 | 155 | 13 | 2 |
| KP Pietersen | c Martyn | b Lee | 92 | 227 | 155 | 14 | 0 |
| *A Flintoff | c Langer | b Warne | 16 | 37 | 26 | 4 | 0 |
| +GO Jones | | b McGrath | 33 | 68 | 48 | 5 | 0 |
| AF Giles | c Warne | b Clark | 23 | 55 | 38 | 3 | 0 |
| MJ Hoggard | c Warne | b Clark | 8 | 49 | 35 | 1 | 0 |
| SJ Harmison | c McGrath | b Clark | 13 | 31 | 18 | 2 | 0 |
| JM Anderson | not out | | 4 | 7 | 8 | 1 | 0 |
| Extras | (b 8, lb 10, w 2, nb 11) | | 31 | | | | |
| Total | (all out, 100.1 overs) | | 370 | | | | |

FoW: 1-29, 2-36, 3-91, 4-244, 5-271, 6-293, 7-326, 8-346, 9-361, 10-370

| Bowling | O | M | R | W | |
|---|---|---|---|---|---|
| Lee | 22 | 1 | 98 | 1 | (7nb, 1w) |
| McGrath | 19 | 3 | 53 | 1 | (3nb) |
| Clark | 24.1 | 6 | 72 | 4 | |
| Warne | 34 | 7 | 124 | 4 | (1nb, 1w) |
| Hussey | 1 | 0 | 5 | 0 | |

# THE ASHES 2006–07
## Second Test, Adelaide, 1–5 December

Australia won by 6 wickets

England won the toss
Umpires: SA Bucknor and RE Koertzen
Man of the Match: RT Ponting

Close of play:
Day 1: England 266/3 (Collingwood 98*, Pietersen 60*)
Day 2: England 551/6d, Australia 28/1 (Hayden 12*, Ponting 11*)
Day 3: England 551/6d, Australia 312/5 (Clarke 30*, Gilchrist 13*)
Day 4: England 551/6d & 59/1 (Strauss 31*, Bell 18*), Australia 513

| England 1st innings | | | Runs | Mins | Balls | 4s | 6s |
|---|---|---|---|---|---|---|---|
| AJ Strauss | c Martyn | b Clark | 14 | 63 | 44 | 0 | 0 |
| AN Cook | c Gilchrist | b Clark | 27 | 90 | 57 | 2 | 0 |
| IR Bell | | c & b Lee | 60 | 189 | 148 | 6 | 0 |
| PD Collingwood | c Gilchrist | b Clark | 206 | 515 | 392 | 16 | 0 |
| KP Pietersen | run out (Ponting) | | 158 | 377 | 257 | 15 | 1 |
| *A Flintoff | not out | | 38 | 101 | 67 | 2 | 1 |
| +GO Jones | c Martyn | b Warne | 1 | 10 | 7 | 0 | 0 |
| AF Giles | not out | | 27 | 63 | 44 | 4 | 0 |
| Extras | (lb 10, w 2, nb 8) | | 20 | | | | |
| Total | (6 wickets dec, 168 overs) | | 551 | | | | |

DNB: MJ Hoggard, SJ Harmison, JM Anderson.

FoW: 1-32, 2-45, 3-158, 4-468, 5-489, 6-491

| Bowling | O | M | R | W | |
|---|---|---|---|---|---|
| Lee | 34 | 1 | 139 | 1 | (8nb, 1w) |
| McGrath | 30 | 5 | 107 | 0 | |
| Clark | 34 | 6 | 75 | 3 | |
| Warne | 53 | 9 | 167 | 1 | (1w) |
| Clarke | 17 | 2 | 53 | 0 | |

| Australia 1st innings | | | Runs | Mins | Balls | 4s | 6s |
|---|---|---|---|---|---|---|---|
| JL Langer | c Pietersen | b Flintoff | 4 | 9 | 8 | 1 | 0 |
| ML Hayden | c Jones | b Hoggard | 12 | 57 | 30 | 1 | 0 |
| *RT Ponting | c Jones | b Hoggard | 142 | 353 | 245 | 12 | 0 |
| DR Martyn | c Bell | b Hoggard | 11 | 42 | 33 | 1 | 0 |
| MEK Hussey | | b Hoggard | 91 | 298 | 212 | 7 | 1 |
| MJ Clarke | c Giles | b Hoggard | 124 | 318 | 224 | 10 | 0 |
| +AC Gilchrist | c Bell | b Giles | 64 | 111 | 79 | 8 | 0 |
| SK Warne | lbw | b Hoggard | 43 | 157 | 108 | 4 | 0 |
| B Lee | not out | | 7 | 47 | 33 | 0 | 0 |
| SR Clark | | b Hoggard | 0 | 9 | 7 | 0 | 0 |
| GD McGrath | c Jones | b Anderson | 1 | 25 | 21 | 0 | 0 |
| Extras | (b 4, lb 2, w 1, nb 7) | | 14 | | | | |
| Total | (all out, 165.3 overs) | | 513 | | | | |

FoW: 1-8, 2-35, 3-65, 4-257, 5-286, 6-384, 7-502, 8-505, 9-507, 10-513

| Bowling | O | M | R | W | |
|---|---|---|---|---|---|
| Hoggard | 42 | 6 | 109 | 7 | |
| Flintoff | 26 | 5 | 82 | 1 | (5nb) |
| Harmison | 25 | 5 | 96 | 0 | (2nb, 1w) |
| Anderson | 21.3 | 3 | 85 | 1 | |
| Giles | 42 | 7 | 103 | 1 | |
| Pietersen | 9 | 0 | 32 | 0 | |

| England 2nd innings | | | Runs | Mins | Balls | 4s | 6s |
|---|---|---|---|---|---|---|---|
| AJ Strauss | c Hussey | b Warne | 34 | 125 | 79 | 3 | 0 |
| AN Cook | c Gilchrist | b Clark | 9 | 48 | 35 | 1 | 0 |
| IR Bell | run out (Clarke/Warne) | | 26 | 85 | 73 | 2 | 0 |
| PD Collingwood | not out | | 22 | 198 | 119 | 2 | 0 |
| KP Pietersen | | b Warne | 2 | 8 | 5 | 0 | 0 |
| *A Flintoff | c Gilchrist | b Lee | 2 | 25 | 24 | 0 | 0 |
| +GO Jones | c Hayden | b Lee | 10 | 41 | 24 | 1 | 0 |
| AF Giles | c Hayden | b Warne | 0 | 14 | 8 | 0 | 0 |
| MJ Hoggard | | b Warne | 4 | 27 | 24 | 0 | 0 |
| SJ Harmison | lbw | b McGrath | 8 | 25 | 21 | 0 | 0 |
| JM Anderson | lbw | b McGrath | 1 | 41 | 28 | 0 | 0 |
| Extras | (b 3, lb 5, w 1, nb 2) | | 11 | | | | |
| Total | (all out, 73 overs) | | 129 | | | | |

FoW: 1-31, 2-69, 3-70, 4-73, 5-77, 6-94, 7-97, 8-105, 9-119, 10-129

| Bowling | O | M | R | W | |
|---|---|---|---|---|---|
| Lee | 18 | 3 | 35 | 2 | (2nb) |
| McGrath | 10 | 6 | 15 | 2 | (1w) |
| Warne | 32 | 12 | 49 | 4 | |
| Clark | 13 | 4 | 22 | 1 | |

| Australia 2nd innings | | | Runs | Mins | Balls | 4s | 6s |
|---|---|---|---|---|---|---|---|
| JL Langer | c Bell | b Hoggard | 7 | 12 | 8 | 1 | 0 |
| ML Hayden | c Collingwood | b Flintoff | 18 | 31 | 17 | 2 | 0 |
| *RT Ponting | c Strauss | b Giles | 49 | 95 | 65 | 5 | 0 |
| MEK Hussey | not out | | 61 | 129 | 66 | 5 | 0 |
| DR Martyn | c Strauss | b Flintoff | 5 | 4 | 4 | 1 | 0 |
| MJ Clarke | not out | | 21 | 47 | 39 | 0 | 0 |
| Extras | (b 2, lb 2, w 1, nb 2) | | 7 | | | | |
| Total | (4 wickets, 32.5 overs) | | 168 | | | | |

DNB: +AC Gilchrist, SK Warne, B Lee, SR Clark, GD McGrath.

FoW: 1-14, 2-33, 3-116, 4-121

| Bowling | O | M | R | W | |
|---|---|---|---|---|---|
| Hoggard | 4 | 0 | 29 | 1 | |
| Flintoff | 9 | 0 | 44 | 2 | (2nb) |
| Giles | 10 | 0 | 46 | 1 | |
| Harmison | 4 | 0 | 15 | 0 | (1w) |
| Anderson | 3.5 | 0 | 23 | 0 | |
| Pietersen | 2 | 0 | 7 | 0 | |

## THE ASHES 2006–07
## Third Test, Perth, 14–18 December

Australia won by 206 runs

Australia won the toss
Umpires: Aleem Dar and RE Koertzen
Man of the Match: MEK Hussey

Close of play:
Day 1: Australia 244, England 51/2 (Strauss 24*, Collingwood 10*)
Day 2: Australia 244 & 119/1 (Hayden 57*, Ponting 57*), England 215
Day 3: Australia 244 & 527/5d, England 215 & 19/1 (Cook 7*, Bell 9*)
Day 4: Australia 244 & 527/5d, England 215 & 265/5 (Pietersen 37*, Flintoff 2*)

| Australia 1st innings | | | Runs | Mins | Balls | 4s | 6s |
|---|---|---|---|---|---|---|---|
| JL Langer | | b Panesar | 37 | 116 | 68 | 6 | 0 |
| ML Hayden | c Jones | b Hoggard | 24 | 48 | 33 | 3 | 0 |
| *RT Ponting | lbw | b Harmison | 2 | 19 | 11 | 0 | 0 |
| MEK Hussey | not out | | 74 | 244 | 162 | 10 | 0 |
| MJ Clarke | | c & b Harmison | 37 | 62 | 67 | 4 | 0 |
| A Symonds | c Jones | b Panesar | 26 | 39 | 30 | 2 | 2 |
| +AC Gilchrist | c Bell | b Panesar | 0 | 7 | 4 | 0 | 0 |
| SK Warne | c Jones | b Panesar | 25 | 32 | 22 | 3 | 0 |
| B Lee | lbw | b Panesar | 10 | 32 | 25 | 2 | 0 |
| SR Clark | | b Harmison | 3 | 13 | 5 | 0 | 0 |
| GD McGrath | c Cook | b Harmison | 1 | 4 | 2 | 0 | 0 |
| Extras | (w 1, nb 4) | | 5 | | | | |
| Total | (all out, 71 overs) | | 244 | | | | |

FoW: 1-47, 2-54, 3-69, 4-121, 5-172, 6-172, 7-214, 8-234, 9-242, 10-244

| Bowling | O | M | R | W | |
|---|---|---|---|---|---|
| Hoggard | 12 | 2 | 40 | 1 | |
| Flintoff | 9 | 2 | 36 | 0 | (3nb) |
| Harmison | 19 | 4 | 48 | 4 | (1w) |
| Panesar | 24 | 4 | 92 | 5 | |
| Mahmood | 7 | 2 | 28 | 0 | |

| England 1st innings | | | Runs | Mins | Balls | 4s | 6s |
|---|---|---|---|---|---|---|---|
| AJ Strauss | c Gilchrist | b Clark | 42 | 101 | 71 | 6 | 0 |
| AN Cook | c Langer | b McGrath | 15 | 26 | 15 | 2 | 0 |
| IR Bell | c Gilchrist | b Lee | 0 | 5 | 2 | 0 | 0 |
| PD Collingwood | c Hayden | b McGrath | 11 | 45 | 33 | 1 | 0 |
| KP Pietersen | c Symonds | b Lee | 70 | 180 | 123 | 8 | 1 |
| *A Flintoff | c Warne | b Symonds | 13 | 46 | 31 | 2 | 0 |
| +GO Jones | c Langer | b Symonds | 0 | 11 | 4 | 0 | 0 |
| SI Mahmood | c Gilchrist | b Clark | 10 | 24 | 18 | 1 | 0 |
| MJ Hoggard | c Hayden | b Warne | 4 | 47 | 39 | 0 | 0 |
| SJ Harmison | c Lee | b Clark | 23 | 56 | 33 | 3 | 0 |
| MS Panesar | not out | | 16 | 41 | 26 | 3 | 0 |
| Extras | (w 1, nb 10) | | 11 | | | | |
| Total | (all out, 64.1 overs) | | 215 | | | | |

FoW: 1-36, 2-37, 3-55, 4-82, 5-107, 6-114, 7-128, 8-155, 9-175, 10-215

| Bowling | O | M | R | W | |
|---|---|---|---|---|---|
| Lee | 18 | 1 | 69 | 2 | (6nb) |
| McGrath | 18 | 5 | 48 | 2 | (4nb) |
| Clark | 15.1 | 3 | 49 | 3 | (1w) |
| Warne | 9 | 0 | 41 | 1 | |
| Symonds | 4 | 1 | 8 | 2 | |

| **Australia 2nd innings** | | | Runs | Mins | Balls | 4s | 6s |
|---|---|---|---|---|---|---|---|
| JL Langer | | b Hoggard | 0 | 1 | 1 | 0 | 0 |
| ML Hayden | c Collingwood | b Panesar | 92 | 252 | 159 | 12 | 0 |
| *RT Ponting | c Jones | b Harmison | 75 | 194 | 128 | 9 | 0 |
| MEK Hussey | c Jones | b Panesar | 103 | 224 | 156 | 12 | 0 |
| MJ Clarke | not out | | 135 | 251 | 164 | 17 | 1 |
| A Symonds | c Collingwood | b Panesar | 2 | 9 | 6 | 0 | 0 |
| +AC Gilchrist | not out | | 102 | 103 | 59 | 12 | 4 |
| Extras | (lb 15, w 2, nb 1) | | 18 | | | | |
| Total | (5 wickets dec, 112 overs) | | 527 | | | | |

DNB: SK Warne, B Lee, SR Clark, GD McGrath.

FoW: 1-0, 2-144, 3-206, 4-357, 5-365

| Bowling | O | M | R | W | |
|---|---|---|---|---|---|
| Hoggard | 20 | 4 | 85 | 1 | |
| Flintoff | 19 | 2 | 76 | 0 | |
| Harmison | 24 | 3 | 116 | 1 | |
| Panesar | 34 | 3 | 145 | 3 | |
| Mahmood | 10 | 0 | 59 | 0 | (1nb, 2w) |
| Pietersen | 5 | 1 | 31 | 0 | |

| **England 2nd innings** | | | Runs | Mins | Balls | 4s | 6s |
|---|---|---|---|---|---|---|---|
| AJ Strauss | lbw | b Lee | 0 | 2 | 4 | 0 | 0 |
| AN Cook | c Gilchrist | b McGrath | 116 | 389 | 290 | 9 | 0 |
| IR Bell | c Langer | b Warne | 87 | 234 | 163 | 8 | 2 |
| PD Collingwood | c Gilchrist | b Clark | 5 | 45 | 36 | 0 | 0 |
| KP Pietersen | not out | | 60 | 243 | 150 | 6 | 0 |
| MJ Hoggard | | b McGrath | 0 | 2 | 2 | 0 | 0 |
| *A Flintoff | | b Warne | 51 | 96 | 67 | 8 | 1 |
| +GO Jones | run out (Ponting) | | 0 | 11 | 7 | 0 | 0 |
| SI Mahmood | lbw | b Clark | 4 | 14 | 10 | 0 | 0 |
| SJ Harmison | lbw | b Warne | 0 | 3 | 1 | 0 | 0 |
| MS Panesar | | b Warne | 1 | 8 | 9 | 0 | 0 |
| Extras | (b 7, lb 8, w 6, nb 5) | | 26 | | | | |
| Total | (all out, 122.2 overs) | | 350 | | | | |

FoW: 1-0, 2-170, 3-185, 4-261, 5-261, 6-336, 7-336, 8-345, 9-346, 10-350

| Bowling | O | M | R | W | |
|---|---|---|---|---|---|
| Lee | 22 | 3 | 75 | 1 | (1nb) |
| McGrath | 27 | 9 | 61 | 2 | (4nb, 1w) |
| Clark | 25 | 7 | 56 | 2 | |
| Warne | 39.2 | 6 | 115 | 4 | |
| Symonds | 9 | 1 | 28 | 0 | (1w) |

# THE ASHES 2006–07
## Fourth Test, Melbourne, 26–28 December

Australia won by an innings and 99 runs

England won the toss
Umpires: Aleem Dar and RE Koertzen
Man of the Match: SK Warne

Close of play:
Day 1: England 159, Australia 48/2 (Hayden 17*, Ponting 0*)
Day 2: England 159, Australia 372/7 (Symonds 154*, Warne 4*)

| England 1st innings | | | Runs | Mins | Balls | 4s | 6s |
|---|---|---|---|---|---|---|---|
| AJ Strauss | | b Warne | 50 | 206 | 132 | 1 | 0 |
| AN Cook | c Gilchrist | b Lee | 11 | 49 | 37 | 1 | 0 |
| IR Bell | lbw | b Clark | 7 | 46 | 30 | 0 | 0 |
| PD Collingwood | c Ponting | b Lee | 28 | 115 | 82 | 4 | 0 |
| KP Pietersen | c Symonds | b Warne | 21 | 104 | 70 | 0 | 0 |
| *A Flintoff | c Warne | b Clark | 13 | 36 | 31 | 1 | 0 |
| +CMW Read | c Ponting | b Warne | 3 | 28 | 17 | 0 | 0 |
| SI Mahmood | c Gilchrist | b McGrath | 0 | 11 | 9 | 0 | 0 |
| SJ Harmison | c Clarke | b Warne | 7 | 11 | 12 | 1 | 0 |
| MS Panesar | c Symonds | b Warne | 4 | 27 | 19 | 0 | 0 |
| MJ Hoggard | not out | | 9 | 15 | 10 | 1 | 0 |
| Extras | (b 2, lb 1, nb 3) | | 6 | | | | |
| Total | (all out, 74.2 overs) | | 159 | | | | |

FoW: 1-23, 2-44, 3-101, 4-101, 5-122, 6-135, 7-136, 8-145, 9-146, 10-159

| Bowling | O | M | R | W | |
|---|---|---|---|---|---|
| Lee | 13 | 4 | 36 | 2 | (2nb) |
| McGrath | 20 | 8 | 37 | 1 | (1nb) |
| Clark | 17 | 6 | 27 | 2 | |
| Symonds | 7 | 2 | 17 | 0 | |
| Warne | 17.2 | 4 | 39 | 5 | |

| Australia 1st innings | | | Runs | Mins | Balls | 4s | 6s |
|---|---|---|---|---|---|---|---|
| JL Langer | c Read | b Flintoff | 27 | 45 | 29 | 3 | 0 |
| ML Hayden | c Read | b Mahmood | 153 | 418 | 265 | 13 | 2 |
| B Lee | c Read | b Flintoff | 0 | 2 | 1 | 0 | 0 |
| *RT Ponting | c Cook | b Flintoff | 7 | 37 | 28 | 0 | 0 |
| MEK Hussey | | b Hoggard | 6 | 37 | 20 | 0 | 0 |
| MJ Clarke | c Read | b Harmison | 5 | 6 | 5 | 0 | 0 |
| A Symonds | c Read | b Harmison | 156 | 327 | 220 | 15 | 1 |
| +AC Gilchrist | c Collingwood | b Mahmood | 1 | 10 | 8 | 0 | 0 |
| SK Warne | not out | | 40 | 75 | 54 | 6 | 0 |
| SR Clark | c Read | b Mahmood | 8 | 34 | 24 | 0 | 0 |
| GD McGrath | c Bell | b Mahmood | 0 | 9 | 6 | 0 | 0 |
| Extras | (lb 6, w 1, nb 9) | | 16 | | | | |
| Total | (all out, 108.3 overs) | | 419 | | | | |

FoW: 1-44, 2-44, 3-62, 4-79, 5-84, 6-363, 7-365, 8-383, 9-417, 10-419

| Bowling | O | M | R | W | |
|---|---|---|---|---|---|
| Hoggard | 21 | 6 | 82 | 1 | (1nb) |
| Flintoff | 22 | 1 | 77 | 3 | (8nb) |
| Harmison | 28 | 6 | 69 | 2 | |
| Mahmood | 21.3 | 1 | 100 | 4 | (1w) |
| Panesar | 12 | 1 | 52 | 0 | |
| Collingwood | 3 | 0 | 20 | 0 | |
| Pietersen | 1 | 0 | 13 | 0 | |

## England 2nd innings

| | | | Runs | Mins | Balls | 4s | 6s |
|---|---|---|---|---|---|---|---|
| AJ Strauss | c Gilchrist | b Lee | 31 | 173 | 107 | 2 | 0 |
| AN Cook | | b Clark | 20 | 64 | 46 | 1 | 0 |
| IR Bell | lbw | b McGrath | 2 | 21 | 11 | 0 | 0 |
| KP Pietersen | | b Clark | 1 | 7 | 8 | 0 | 0 |
| PD Collingwood | c Langer | b Lee | 16 | 52 | 38 | 0 | 0 |
| *A Flintoff | lbw | b Clark | 25 | 60 | 45 | 2 | 0 |
| +CMW Read | not out | | 26 | 127 | 77 | 1 | 0 |
| SI Mahmood | lbw | b Warne | 0 | 3 | 2 | 0 | 0 |
| SJ Harmison | lbw | b Warne | 4 | 44 | 26 | 0 | 0 |
| MS Panesar | c Clarke | b Lee | 14 | 20 | 19 | 2 | 0 |
| MJ Hoggard | | b Lee | 5 | 21 | 20 | 0 | 0 |
| Extras | (lb 12, w 1, nb 4) | | 17 | | | | |
| Total | (all out, 65.5 overs) | | 161 | | | | |

FoW: 1-41, 2-48, 3-49, 4-75, 5-90, 6-108, 7-109, 8-127, 9-146, 10-161

| Bowling | O | M | R | W | |
|---|---|---|---|---|---|
| Lee | 18.5 | 6 | 47 | 4 | (3nb) |
| McGrath | 12 | 2 | 26 | 1 | (1w) |
| Clark | 16 | 6 | 30 | 3 | (1nb) |
| Warne | 19 | 3 | 46 | 2 | |

# THE ASHES 2006–07
## Fifth Test, Sydney, 2–5 January

Australia won by 10 wickets

England won the toss
Umpires: Aleem Dar and BF Bowden
Man of the Match: SR Clark
Man of the Series: RT Ponting

Close of play:
Day 1: England 234/4 (Collingwood 25*, Flintoff 42*, 80 ov)
Day 2: England 291, Australia 188/4 (Hussey 37*, Symonds 22*, 55 ov)
Day 3: England 291 & 114/5 (Pietersen 29*, Panesar 0*, 43 ov), Australia 393

| England 1st innings | | | *Runs* | *Mins* | *Balls* | *4s* | *6s* |
|---|---|---|---|---|---|---|---|
| AJ Strauss | c Gilchrist | b Lee | 29 | 64 | 52 | 3 | 0 |
| AN Cook | c Gilchrist | b Clark | 20 | 88 | 47 | 2 | 0 |
| IR Bell | | b McGrath | 71 | 194 | 153 | 8 | 0 |
| KP Pietersen | c Hussey | b McGrath | 41 | 162 | 104 | 1 | 0 |
| PD Collingwood | c Gilchrist | b McGrath | 27 | 119 | 73 | 4 | 0 |
| *A Flintoff | c Gilchrist | b Clark | 89 | 195 | 142 | 11 | 1 |
| +CMW Read | c Gilchrist | b Lee | 2 | 13 | 9 | 0 | 0 |
| SI Mahmood | c Hayden | b Lee | 0 | 2 | 1 | 0 | 0 |
| SJ Harmison | lbw | b Clark | 2 | 51 | 24 | 0 | 0 |
| MS Panesar | lbw | b Warne | 0 | 20 | 14 | 0 | 0 |
| JM Anderson | not out | | 0 | 6 | 5 | 0 | 0 |
| Extras | (lb 5, w 3, nb 2) | | 10 | | | | |
| Total | (all out, 103.4 overs) | | 291 | | | | |

FoW: 1-45, 2-58, 3-166, 4-167, 5-245, 6-258, 7-258, 8-282, 9-291, 10-291

| *Bowling* | *O* | *M* | *R* | *W* | |
|---|---|---|---|---|---|
| McGrath | 29 | 8 | 67 | 3 | (2nb) |
| Lee | 22 | 5 | 75 | 3 | (1w) |
| Clark | 24 | 6 | 62 | 3 | (2w) |
| Warne | 22.4 | 1 | 69 | 1 | |
| Symonds | 6 | 2 | 13 | 0 | |

| Australia 1st innings | | | *Runs* | *Mins* | *Balls* | *4s* | *6s* |
|---|---|---|---|---|---|---|---|
| JL Langer | c Read | b Anderson | 26 | 41 | 27 | 4 | 0 |
| ML Hayden | c Collingwood | b Harmison | 33 | 113 | 77 | 5 | 0 |
| *RT Ponting | run out (Anderson) | | 45 | 96 | 72 | 6 | 0 |
| MEK Hussey | c Read | b Anderson | 37 | 120 | 100 | 3 | 1 |
| MJ Clarke | c Read | b Harmison | 11 | 39 | 24 | 1 | 0 |
| A Symonds | | b Panesar | 48 | 138 | 95 | 6 | 0 |
| +AC Gilchrist | c Read | b Anderson | 62 | 118 | 72 | 8 | 0 |
| SK Warne | st Read | b Panesar | 71 | 114 | 65 | 9 | 2 |
| B Lee | c Read | b Flintoff | 5 | 14 | 10 | 1 | 0 |
| SR Clark | c Pietersen | b Mahmood | 35 | 55 | 41 | 1 | 0 |
| GD McGrath | not out | | 0 | 6 | 3 | 0 | 0 |
| Extras | (lb 10, w 4, nb 6) | | 20 | | | | |
| Total | (all out, 96.3 overs) | | 393 | | | | |

FoW: 1-34, 2-100, 3-118, 4-155, 5-190, 6-260, 7-318, 8-325, 9-393, 10-393

| Bowling | O | M | R | W | |
|---|---|---|---|---|---|
| Flintoff | 17 | 2 | 56 | 1 | (3nb, 1w) |
| Anderson | 26 | 8 | 98 | 3 | (1w) |
| Harmison | 23 | 5 | 80 | 2 | (1nb, 2w) |
| Mahmood | 11 | 1 | 59 | 1 | (2nb) |
| Panesar | 19.3 | 0 | 90 | 2 | |

| England 2nd innings | | | Runs | Mins | Balls | 4s | 6s |
|---|---|---|---|---|---|---|---|
| AJ Strauss | lbw | b Clark | 24 | 68 | 45 | 3 | 0 |
| AN Cook | c Gilchrist | b Lee | 4 | 11 | 8 | 1 | 0 |
| IR Bell | c Gilchrist | b Lee | 28 | 85 | 51 | 5 | 0 |
| KP Pietersen | c Gilchrist | b McGrath | 29 | 139 | 95 | 3 | 0 |
| PD Collingwood | c Hayden | b Clark | 17 | 67 | 36 | 3 | 0 |
| *A Flintoff | st Gilchrist | b Warne | 7 | 31 | 21 | 1 | 0 |
| MS Panesar | run out (Symonds) | | 0 | 27 | 19 | 0 | 0 |
| +CMW Read | c Ponting | b Lee | 4 | 26 | 17 | 1 | 0 |
| SI Mahmood | | b McGrath | 4 | 13 | 11 | 1 | 0 |
| SJ Harmison | not out | | 16 | 42 | 26 | 2 | 0 |
| JM Anderson | c Hussey | b McGrath | 5 | 37 | 22 | 1 | 0 |
| Extras | (b 2, lb 3, w 1, nb 3) | | 9 | | | | |
| Total | (all out, 58 overs) | | 147 | | | | |

FoW: 1-5, 2-55, 3-64, 4-98, 5-113, 6-114, 7-114, 8-122, 9-123, 10-147

| Bowling | O | M | R | W | |
|---|---|---|---|---|---|
| Lee | 14 | 5 | 39 | 3 | (1nb, 1w) |
| McGrath | 21 | 11 | 38 | 3 | (1nb) |
| Clark | 12 | 4 | 29 | 2 | (1nb) |
| Warne | 6 | 1 | 23 | 1 | |
| Symonds | 5 | 2 | 13 | 0 | |

| Australia 2nd innings | | Runs | Mins | Balls | 4s | 6s |
|---|---|---|---|---|---|---|
| JL Langer | not out | 20 | 44 | 43 | 2 | 0 |
| ML Hayden | not out | 23 | 44 | 22 | 2 | 1 |
| Extras | (lb 3) | 3 | | | | |
| Total | (0 wickets, 10.5 overs) | 46 | | | | |

DNB: *RT Ponting, MEK Hussey, MJ Clarke, A Symonds, +AC Gilchrist, SK Warne, B Lee, SR Clark, GD McGrath.

| Bowling | O | M | R | W |
|---|---|---|---|---|
| Anderson | 4 | 0 | 12 | 0 |
| Harmison | 5 | 1 | 13 | 0 |
| Mahmood | 1.5 | 0 | 18 | 0 |

# INDEX